English
Syntax

English Syntax

Marjolyn Stevenson

NORTHEAST LOUISIANA UNIVERSITY

Little, Brown and Company

BOSTON   TORONTO

Library of Congress Cataloging-in-Publication Data

Stevenson, Marjolyn.
  English syntax.

  Includes index.
  1. English language — Syntax. 2. English language —
Grammar — 1950–   . 3. English language — Text-books
for foreign speakers. I. Title.
PE1375.S74   1987   428.2'4   86–27852
ISBN 0–316–81423–7

Copyright © 1987 by Marjolyn Stevenson

Library of Congress Catalog Card No. 86–27852

ISBN 0-316-81423-7

9 8 7 6 5 4 3 2 1

MV

Published simultaneously in Canada
by Little, Brown & Company (Canada) Limited

Printed in the United States of America

Acknowledgments

CHAPTER ONE

Seeing the Earth from Space by Irving and Ruth Adler. John Day Books. Copyright 1957 and 1959. Reprinted by permission of the author.

"Wordless Workshop." Page 102, *Popular Science,* January 1985. Reprinted from *Popular Science* with permission © 1985, Times Mirror Magazines, Inc. Reprinted also with permission from Roy Doty.

"The Kind Father's Will." From *More Fun with Puzzles* by Joseph Leeming (J. B. Lippincott). Copyright © 1947 by Joseph Leeming. Reprinted by permission of Harper & Row, Publishers, Inc., and McIntosh and Otis, Inc.

"The Cathode Ray Oscilloscope." From *Electronics* by Robert Irving. Copyright © 1961 by Robert Irving. Reprinted by permission of Alfred A. Knopf, Inc. and John K. Payne Literary Agency, Inc.

Exercises 16, 18, 19, and 20. Reprinted from *Salted Peanuts* by E. C. McKenzie by permission of the publisher, Baker Book House. Copyright 1972.

(Continued on page 377)

Preface

English Syntax is designed to be used as the main textbook in an advanced-level ESL structure-writing course or as a supplementary text in an advanced writing class.

The textbook is designed to improve writing skills — at the sentence, paragraph, and essay level — through understanding of syntax and extensive practice in writing. In the textbook we explain what structures mean and encourage students to use structures that focus ideas in their writing. We believe that understanding what structures mean will also improve students' listening, reading, and speaking skills.

The grammar is focused on problem areas in composition, built up gradually, and presented in clear, concise language with examples in diagrams.

Organization and unity are implicitly taught through the specific instructions with each paragraph and essay assignment.

To appeal to those studying in technical and business disciplines, we have based most of the exercises on short articles, anecdotes, and advertisements with current, interesting, and controversial topics, such as using airbags in cars, or nuclear power.

The material is organized into ten chapters. To show that the grammar of the English language is a system and that all the material discussed in the textbook is related, the first two chapters provide an overview of all the material to be discussed, and form a foundation for the text.

Chapter 1 has an overview of the English sentence. After learning that an English sentence consists of a few basic parts — subject, verb phrase, and completer — and that these parts almost always occur in this order, students are introduced to the types of structures such as clauses, verbals, and phrases that may function as such parts. Having learned to analyze sentences, they are taught to recognize the types of sentences — simple, compound, and complex — which they will learn to form later.

In Chapter 2, we study the four verb forms and their uses. The finite form is emphasized because it is essential in mastering rules for agreement, forming the verb phrase, and learning to form questions, clauses, and phrases. With the help of a diagram for ordering auxiliary verbs, students learn that the verb phrase can express differences in tense, aspect, voice, and mood. After they learn to recognize the verb forms and use them with helping verbs, we attempt to show how three of the four verb forms also function outside the verb phrase.

Note: Although the ability to analyze sentences is useful and helps students understand how the material throughout the text is related, sentence analysis is not necessary for understanding the later chapters. If time is limited or if a skills approach is preferred to a cognitive approach, the course can start with Chapter 3.

Except for the first two chapters, each chapter presents a group of structures related in function and meaning. Chapter 3 presents the formation of the compound sentence. After discussing the punctuation and reduction rules for each type of compound sentence, we explain in detail the meaning relationships that the coordinate conjunctions and conjunctive adverbs express.

Starting with Chapter 4, we alternate verb chapters with sentence chapters to present materials that facilitate understanding of the following sentence chapter. For example, Chapter 4 presents the English verb tense and aspect system and emphasizes the differences in meaning expressed by the use of the progressive, perfect, and subjunctive forms to prepare for the adverbial clause chapter, which shows that several types of subordinate conjunctions require use of a specific tense.

In Chapter 5, we discuss the formation of adverbial clauses and the verbal phrases and prepositional phrases that are derived from them, emphasizing the meanings of the subordinate conjunctions and giving in-depth explanations for phrases. A summary diagram of sentence connectors at the end of the chapter shows how similar meaning relationships such as addition, cause, and concession may be expressed with coordinate conjunctions, conjunctive adverbs, subordinate conjunctions, or verbal and prepositional phrases.

Chapter 6 explains the forms and uses of the passive voice to prepare for the chapter on adjectivals because passive forms often occur in adjective phrases. A diagram in this chapter summarizes verb structures in the simple, progressive, active, and passive forms.

In Chapter 7, a detailed discussion of the full adjective clause prepares students for the many derivatives of adjective clauses.

In Chapter 8, we discuss mood and the meanings expressed by the modal auxiliaries, summarized with a diagram, to prepare for noun clauses, which may require a subjunctive mood. Also, noun clauses that contain a subjunctive mood or a modal auxiliary are often reduced to *to*-infinitive constructions, which are discussed in both Chapters 9 and 10.

After discussing the formation of noun clauses and the formation of *to*-infinitive phrases, gerund phrases, and other types of noun phrases made from verbs, we emphasize in Chapter 9 the use of articles and other modifiers within verbal phrases.

Chapter 10 gives an overview of the many patterns the direct object may have. We group verbs related in meaning to show what kinds of verbs are followed by *to*-infinitive phrases and what kinds by gerund phrases or participial phrases. At the end of the chapter, a diagram gives an overview of how each verb form can be used in nominal, adjectival, and adverbial phrases, and can express differences in meaning depending on both the form and position of the phrase.

Each chapter is divided into four sections. The Preview/Review section at the beginning of each chapter helps students understand how the structures they have previously learned are related to the structures they will learn in that chapter. In addition to expanding information previously learned, this spiraling approach provides for a generous amount of review.

In the Grammar and Meaning section, rules are explained with the help of examples in diagrams. Each grammar explanation is followed by exercises, which first help students recognize and identify the structures discussed and then encourage them to use these structures creatively. In addition to sentence-combination and sentence-completion exercises, other exercises require students to create sentences based on a real-world situation or to correct a passage without punctuation marks. Short writing assignments then allow students to integrate the newly learned grammatical structures into their writing.

We briefly review the trouble points that advanced ESL students usually have in their own writing in the Solving Problems section. This review is followed by an editing exercise that forces students to give systematic attention to specific types of errors. A sentence-completion exercise based on a reading passage requires students to practice alternative expression of an idea.

The Assignment for Writing concludes each chapter. To simulate academic writing, which often covers subjects that students have already studied, they are first asked to read an advertisement or reading passage that provides visual clues, vocabulary, and information. The questions that follow are designed to create a flow of information from students to teacher and from students to students, making them think analytically and generate ideas. The actual writing assignment, which stresses organization and unity, requires students to incorporate the newly learned information into their writing. A proofreading guide encourages them to delay looking for errors in grammar and punctuation until final drafts to force them to concentrate on content and organization in initial drafts. In the section titled Writing Workshop in the Appendix we give suggestions for revision, group reading, and peer editing.

Although the text is designed to be taught in the order in which it is presented, the materials are not so integrated that the chapters cannot be reordered. Also, depending on the level and the needs of the class, the instructor may choose to emphasize or drop different chapters, sections, and exercises. No matter how the text is taught, we hope it provides a challenging, useful, and enjoyable learning experience for students.

Acknowledgments

I am grateful to the many people who have helped me as I wrote *English Syntax*. My friends Bessie Cummings, Peggy Hintz, and Barbara Bailey helped with the typing and proofreading of early drafts. Discussions with my colleagues Karen Lewis, Lea Olsan, Yves Verret, and Sharon Doucet helped shape the organization and presentation of the materials. My colleagues Dev Hathaway, Cindy Chinelly, and Fae Dremock read later drafts and gave suggestions for improving the text discussion and writing assignments. Over the years many students, especially Yavuz Ergin and Kwanjai Jintamalit, identified weaknesses in the explanations. I am also grateful to David K. Jeffrey, head of the English Department at Northeast Louisiana University, for the encouragement and support he gave me during the long process of writing.

I wish to thank the many reviewers who gave invaluable suggestions for improving the text: Jon Amastae of the University of Texas, Mary Barr of Columbia University, Patricia Byrd of Georgia State University, Keith Groff of Idaho State University, Margo Jang of Northern Kentucky University, John B. Jensen of Florida International University, Elliott Judd of the University of Illinois, Robert Kantor of Ohio State University, John Roberts of the University of Miami, Lori Roberts of Wayne State University, and Julia Villasenor of the International Institute of Akron.

At Little, Brown and Company many people have helped improve the text. I especially want to thank Pamela Sharpe of Language Training Consultants and Joe Opiela, English Editor, for their expertise and encouragement, as well as Janice Friedman, who did a marvelous job of transforming the manuscript.

Finally, for their support and patience, I want to thank my parents, Paul and Loes Verspoor; my parents-in-law, Carl and Floy Stevenson; my children, Claire, Audrey, and Michael Stevenson; and especially my husband, Carl Stevenson.

Contents

3   The Compound Sentence   83

4   Tense and Aspect   114

5   The Adverbial Clause   156

6   The Passive Voice   199

7 _____ **The Adjective Clause** _____ **224**

8 _____ **Mood** _____ **255**

9 _____ Noun Clauses and Reduced Noun Clauses _____ 290

10 _____ Direct Object Patterns and Related Structures _____ 323

English
Syntax

1

The English Sentence

Before you start reading this chapter, you might want to skim the book. How many chapters are there? How is each chapter organized? Is there an appendix? How will you use the index? As you can see from the Contents, the first two chapters discuss the English sentence and verb system in general. Later chapters discuss their separate parts. What do you think is the purpose of Chapters 1 and 2?

Preview

Read the following passages and compare them. Then answer the questions that follow.

These three passages, labeled A, B, and C, each have the same information. Every sentence in Passage A is numbered. When you get to Passage B and Passage C, you will notice that some sentences have more than one number. That is because they include the information from more than one sentence. In Passage B, for example, the first sentence includes the information of sentences 1, 2, and 3 of Passage A.

A. (1) Every month we say something. (2) There is a new moon in the sky. (3) It really isn't a new moon at all. (4) It is only the old moon. (5) It's hiding its face again in its own shadow. (6) But now there are moons in the sky. (7) They are really new. (8) They are man-made moons. (9) They are designed by scientists. (10) They are built in laboratories. (11) They are hurled into space from the ground. (12) They are tiny when they are compared to the old moon. (13) They are much closer to earth than the old moon. (14) But the old moon is a satellite of the earth. (15) And each new moon is a satellite of the earth. (16) Both revolve around the earth in orbits of their own.

B. (1, 2, 3) Every month we say that there is a new moon in the sky, but it really isn't a new moon at all. (4, 5) It is only the old moon, but it's hiding its face again in its own shadow. (6, 7) But now there are moons in the sky, and they are really new. (8, 9, 10) They are man-made moons, which are designed by scientists, and which are built in laboratories. (11) They are hurled into space from the ground. (12, 13) They are tiny when they are compared to the old moon, and they are much closer to earth than the old moon. (14, 15) But both the old moon and each new moon are satellites of the earth. (16) Both revolve around the earth in orbits of their own.

C. (1, 2, 3) Every month we say that there is a new moon in the sky, although it really isn't a new moon at all. (4, 5) It is only the old moon, hiding its face again in its own shadow. (6, 7) But now there are really new moons in the sky. (8, 9, 10, 11) They are man-made moons, designed by scientists, built in laboratories, and hurled into space from the ground. (12, 13) They are tiny when compared to the old moon, and much closer to earth. (14, 15, 16) But both the old moon and each new moon are satellites of the earth revolving around the earth in orbits of their own.

To answer the questions that follow, write each answer on the line after the question.

Questions

1. Which passage uses the most sentences? _____

2. Which passage uses the most connecting words, such as *and* and *but?* _____

3. Which passage uses the fewest sentences? _____

4. List some words that connect sentences. _____

_____

5. List some ways to make sentences more compact. _____

_____

6. Which passage is the easiest to understand? _____

7. Which passage is the best-written one? _____

Most people will probably agree that passage C is the best-written because most of its sentences express several thoughts that are joined logically with connecting words, and needless repetition has been avoided by deleting repeated sentence parts.

Now that you have a little experience with sentence connections, see if you can do the following exercise.

Exercise 1   Locate the beginnings and ends of the sentences in the following passage. Put a period at the end of each sentence and a capital letter at the beginning of each new sentence. Which sentences express more than one thought?

There are also new planets in the sky they were launched from the earth in the direction of the moon, but they sped past the moon and began to circle around the sun the first man-made moon was launched by scientists of the Soviet Union on October 4, 1957 on that day the whole world began using a new word, *sputnik,* the Russian word for *satellite* one month later a second sputnik was in the sky carrying the first space traveler, a small dog called Laika in 1958, six more earth satellites were successfully placed in orbit five of them were fired into space by the United States and one by the Soviet Union in February and April, 1959, the United States launched two more satellites, and there were many more to follow by the end of 1959 only six of the first ten man-made moons were still revolving around the earth the other four had already fallen back to the earth, burning up as they fell

Exercise 2   The following sentences are derived from the sentences in Exercise 1. What changes have been made in the short simple sentences to create the longer complex sentences? You will be able to tell if you locate each sentence in Exercise 1 that has the same information as each of the following sentences. Underline words in these sentences that were not needed in Exercise 1.

1. On that day, the whole world began doing something.

   The world used a new word.

   This word was *sputnik.*

   Sputnik is the Russian word for *satellite.*

2. One month later a second sputnik was in the sky.

   It was carrying the first space traveler.

   The first space traveler was a small dog.

   This dog was called Laika.

3. In 1958 five satellites were fired into space by the United States.

   In 1958 one of them was fired into space by the Soviet Union.

4. In February and April, 1959, the United States launched two more satellites.

There were many more to follow.

5. Four of the first ten satellites fell back to the earth.

They burned up as they fell.

The work you have been doing is called making complex sentences out of simple sentences. It is complex sentences that make writing compact and interesting. This grammar text is based on the theory that a complex sentence is basically two or more simple sentences combined according to specific rules. To understand the formation of a complex sentence, therefore, you must understand the basic structure of a short simple sentence. In the remainder of this chapter, you will learn the basic structure of English sentences, and later on in this text you will see how sentences are joined with connecting words or by changing them.

Note: The following section contains many grammatical terms. You need to be familiar with them so that you can understand the sentence combination rules later in this text. Most of the terms will be explained carefully below.

Grammar and Meaning

The Components of a Sentence

The following diagram, which gives you an overview of the three basic structures of English sentences, describes almost every sentence in the English language. Each sentence part is named in the diagram. The lines and symbols tell how each sentence part may be used. You may want to look back at this diagram when each part is discussed and explained separately below. *Note:* There is a key to the symbols after the diagram.

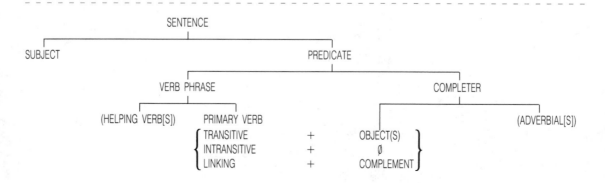

Parentheses ( ) indicate that something is optional; in other words, it may or may not be used.

Braces { } indicate that you must choose one.

The zero symbol Ø indicates that no word should be used.

- -

Every sentence consists of a subject and predicate. As you see from the diagram above, the predicate contains a verb part and a completer part, the form of which depends on the type of verb used in the verb part. In the following section, we will study each of these components separately.

Subject and Predicate

To understand what a subject and a predicate are, study the diagram below.

- -

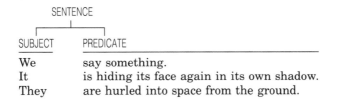

SENTENCE

SUBJECT	PREDICATE
We	say something.
It	is hiding its face again in its own shadow.
They	are hurled into space from the ground.

- -

Almost every sentence consists of two major parts, the subject and the predicate. The *subject* tells us what the topic is (it tells us *who* or *what* is or does something), and the *predicate* tells us what the subject is or does.

Exercise 3   Analyze the sentences below by putting a slash (/) between the subject and the predicate.

EXAMPLE:

The new moon / is really the old moon hiding its face again in its own shadow.

1. Another word for *moon* is *satellite*.

2. A man-made moon is much smaller than the real moon.

3. Both the real moon and a man-made moon revolve around the earth.

4. A man-made moon is much closer to the earth.

5. A little dog called Laika was the first space traveler in the world.

Verb Phrase

To understand the verb phrase and completer, study the diagram below.

```
SUBJECT         PREDICATE
                ┌──────┴──────┐
             VERB PHRASE    COMPLETER        _____
We           say            something.
It           is hiding      its face in its own shadow.
They         are            really  new.
John         is singing.
```

A predicate usually consists of two parts, the verb phrase and completer. The verb phrase explains what the action or state is of the subject. It is usually (but not always) followed by a completer.

Exercise 4   Now that you know what a completer is, complete each of the following sentences with a meaningful completer.

1. Every month, the old moon hides _____

   _____ .

2. Compared to the old moon, man-made moons _____

   _____ .

3. On October 4, 1957, scientists of the Soviet Union launched _____

   _____ .

4. A small dog, called Laika, was _____

   _____ .

5. In 1958 scientists placed _____ .

Auxiliary Verbs and Primary Verbs

To understand auxiliary verbs and primary verbs, study the diagram below.

SUBJECT	VERB PHRASE		COMPLETER
	(AUXILIARY VERB[S])	PRIMARY VERB	
It	is	hiding	its face in its own shadow.
They		are	man-made moons.
Scientists		build	them in laboratories.
They	are	hurled	into space from the ground.
It		revolves	around the world in an orbit of its own.
We	have	studied	the universe.
We	might	fly	to Mars.
He	might have	left	already.

MEANINGLESS: They are into space from the ground.

MEANINGLESS: We have the universe.

INCOMPLETE: They man-made moons.

The diagram above showed you that verb phrases are not all alike. A verb phrase sometimes has only one word, such as *are, build,* and *revolve,* and sometimes two or more words, such as *is hiding, have studied,* and *might have left.* Words like *hide, are, build,* and *hurl* tell what the action or the state of the subject is. They are called *primary* verbs. A sentence would be meaningless or incomplete if it had no primary verb or if the primary verb was not understood from the context.

The words in the verb phrase before the primary verb are *auxiliary verbs.* They are to show the *aspect, voice, mood,* and so on, of the verb phrase. These grammatical terms and the uses of the auxiliary verbs will be explained in Chapter 2, but the list below will help you recognize them.

Auxiliary verbs

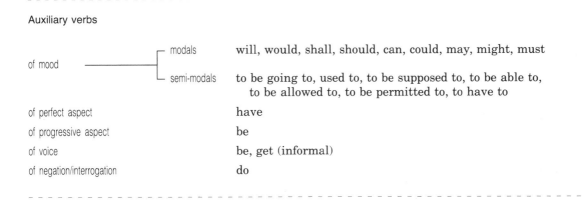

of mood	modals	will, would, shall, should, can, could, may, might, must
	semi-modals	to be going to, used to, to be supposed to, to be able to, to be allowed to, to be permitted to, to have to
of perfect aspect		have
of progressive aspect		be
of voice		be, get (informal)
of negation/interrogation		do

Wordless Workshop

By ROY DOTY

$50 to John Y. Yoon of Harvard University for this idea. Send yours (with Social Security No.) to Wordless, POPULAR SCIENCE, 380 Madison Ave., New York, N.Y. 10017. Only purchased ideas are acknowledged.

Exercise 5 In the following passage, identify the italicized verbs as auxiliary verbs or primary verbs, by putting an *A* or *P* above each.

Many years ago, contact lenses *were invented*. However, the first contact lenses often *hurt* because they *did* not *let* much oxygen through to the cornea, which *could swell up* without oxygen. Now engineers *have created* a new plastic lens that *can soak up* water like a sponge. The water *lets* the oxygen through to the cornea. Now contact lens wearers *can leave* their plastic disks on their eyes for a long time.

Exercise 6 Look at the "Wordless Workshop" on page 8. What's happening here? For each picture write two sentences on a separate sheet of paper. In each sentence find the primary verb(s) and underline them. (If you write longer, complex sentences, you will have more than one primary verb.)

EXAMPLE:
Picture 1:
a. Johnnie and his father <u>are</u> at a telephone store.
b. Johnnie and his father are going to <u>buy</u> a new telephone.

Exercise 7 Pretend that you are John Y. Yoon of Harvard University. On a separate piece of paper, write a letter to "Wordless Workshop" to explain your idea. You may use the telephone idea, but an original idea would be even better. Describe the idea in a few paragraphs. You may include a simple drawing. Be very specific in your descriptions so that all the details are clear.

Subject-Verb Agreement

You have just learned that there is a difference in meaning between auxiliary verbs and primary verbs. Another very important distinction to make is one of form. Read the sentences in the following diagram. The subject of each sentence is underlined for you. An arrow has been drawn from subject to verb.

- -

Plural subject

Many years ago <u>contact lenses</u> *were* invented.

Now <u>engineers</u> *have* created a new plastic lens.

<u>Hard contact lenses</u> sometimes *hurt*.

Singular subject

Many years ago <u>the contact lens</u> *was* invented.

Now <u>a company</u> *has* created a new softer lens.

<u>A hard contact lens</u> sometimes *hurts*.

Present tense

Contact wearers *are* leaving their plastic
disks on their eyes for a long time.

Past tense

Contact wearers *were* leaving their plastic
disks on their eyes for a long time.

Compare the sentences in the diagram above under "Plural subject"
with the sentences under "Singular subject." As you can see, the first verb
in the verb phrase changed when the subject of the sentence changed from
a plural subject to a singular subject. (Using the right verb for each
subject is called *subject-verb agreement.*) The verb also changed when the
tense changed from present to past. It did not matter whether the first
verb was a helping verb or a primary verb. Notice that the other verbs in
the verb phrase remained the same (*leaving, created,* and *invented*). The
meaning of the verb did not really change; only the form of the verb
changed. The form of the verb that must agree with the subject and that
changes when the tense is changed is called the *finite* verb. It is always
the first verb in the verb phrase.

Note: We will study the formation of the finite verb in Chapter 2.

Exercise 8   In the following passage, each finite verb is written in italics. Find the
subject that agrees with it and underline that subject. Then draw an
arrow from each subject to its verb. The first one is done for you.

There *was* once a kind father who *had* two sons in college, and, as

kind fathers often *do,* he *bought* each of them a car. Everything *was* all

right while both *were* away at college, but, when they *came* home for

summer vacation, all the peace *was* gone at the old homestead.

These boys *had* the speed bug, and many days *were* spent racing each

other to see whose car *was* faster. Both parents *were* driven to distrac-

tion because they *feared* that the boys *would* break their necks or worse.

Finally, the father *had* a good idea. He *wrote* his will, and in it he *stated*

that most of his fortune *was* to go to the son whose car *was* the last one

to come in during a ten-mile race that *was* to be held the next day. "That

will teach them to drive slowly," he *told* his long-suffering wife.

When each of the cars *was* lined up for the race, the signal to go *was*

given, and away they *went.* If you *think* that they *drove* at a snail's

pace, you *are* wrong. On the contrary, the sons *drove* off in the greatest

burst of speed ever.

Each son *wanted* to inherit the fortune. Why *did* each still try to beat the other? *Note:* The answer to this riddle can be found under Transitive Verbs and Objects.

Exercise 9

Here is some more work about the boys who had the speed bug. Answer the following questions in complete sentences. First make sure that your answers are meaningful. Then circle the finite verbs in your sentences.

EXAMPLE:
Why (were) the parents driven to distraction?
They were worried about their sons.

1. Why was all the peace gone when the two sons came home during the summer? _____ .

2. Why were the parents worried? _____

_____ .

3. What is a will? _____ .

4. Was the father rich? _____ How do you know? _____

_____ .

5. Was the slowest car or the slowest person going to win the race?

_____ .

6. How did the sons drive when the signal to go was given? _____

_____ .

7. What mistake did the father make when he wrote his will? _____

_____ .

Completers

Early in this chapter you learned that sentences have subjects and predicates. You discovered that the predicate of every sentence contains a verb part and a completer part. You have studied subjects and verb phrases. Now you will study the last part of the sentence, the *completer*. The type of completer that is needed depends on the type of primary verb. There are three types of primary verbs: *transitive, intransitive,* and *linking*.

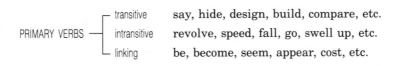

PRIMARY VERBS
- transitive   say, hide, design, build, compare, etc.
- intransitive   revolve, speed, fall, go, swell up, etc.
- linking   be, become, seem, appear, cost, etc.

Each type of primary verb and its completer is presented to you separately.

Transitive Verbs and Objects

SUBJECT	VERB PHRASE	COMPLETER	
	TRANSITIVE VERB + DIRECT OBJECT		(ADVERBIAL[S])
Scientists of the Soviet Union	launched	the first man-made moon	on October 4, 1957.
The whole world	learned	a new word	on that day.
The Russians	used	the word *Sputnik*	for *satellite.*
The second Sputnik	carried	a small dog called Laika.	

If you study the diagram carefully, you will know that something must follow a transitive verb.

A transitive verb is a verb that must be followed by a *direct object* to complete the meaning of the verb. The verb usually expresses some kind of physical or mental action that is transmitted from the subject to the object. That's why it's called transitive.

To find out what part of the sentence is the direct object, you can ask a *what* or *whom* question.

EXAMPLE:

The boys drove each other's car.
What *did the boys drive?* (*each other's car* is the direct object.)

These boys had the speed bug.
What *did the boys have?* (*the speed bug* is the direct object.)

The parents feared that the boys would break their necks or worse.
What *did the parents fear?* (*that the boys would break their necks or worse* is the direct object.)

The sons wanted to inherit the fortune.
What *did the boys want?* (*to inherit the fortune* is the direct object.)

The boys raced each other every day.
Whom *did the boys race?* (*each other* is the direct object.)

As you can see from the examples, the direct object may have different forms. The formation and use of these different forms will be discussed in Chapters 9 and 10.

In reading these examples you have practiced asking *what* or *whom* questions to find the direct object of each transitive verb. Now you will be able to do this by yourself in the following exercise.

Exercise 10   In the following passage, transitive verbs are written in italics. Underline the direct objects that complete their meaning. Two of them in the first sentence are already done for you.

Sonic Booms

In today's jet age, there are not many people who have not yet been startled by what apparently is a nearby explosion on a quiet afternoon as fighter planes *break* the so-called sound-barrier and *produce* a wave of compressed air that *strikes* the earth with audible and sometimes destructive effects. If there was any question about the energy of sound waves, this peculiarity of the jet age should *dismiss* it.

What actually happens is that supersonic aircraft *set up* a bow wave much like that *preceding* the prow of a boat moving through the water. In the case of aircraft, however, the wave spreads out in all directions in the atmosphere. When this wave of compression *reaches* the earth, the energy it contains is made audible as the earth and objects *resist* the progress of the wave. In a way, the boom felt by those nearby when the wave *encounters* the land is much like a water wave breaking on the beach. The destructive effects of sonic booms have *brought* dozens of complaints from citizens to the Air Force. There also have been attempts to *recover* the cost of replacing shattered windows. So far the most prolonged sonic boom on record has come from the Air Force bomber that streaked at supersonic speed from the east coast to the west and back again nonstop, *leaving* below it a trail of shattered window glass that stretched from New York to Los Angeles.

There are also some transitive verbs that can have two objects: *a direct object* and an *indirect object*. Study the following diagram. Notice especially the position of each sentence part.

SUBJECT	TRANSITIVE VERB	INDIRECT OBJECT WITHOUT PREPOSITION	DIRECT OBJECT
He	bought	each of them	a car.
He	told	his wife	something.
That	will teach	them	a lesson.
He	gave	them	the signal to go.

Now study another diagram showing direct and indirect objects. What has happened to the position of each sentence part? Can you figure out why?

SUBJECT	TRANSITIVE VERB	DIRECT OBJECT	INDIRECT OBJECT WITH PREPOSITION (the preposition is in italics)
He	bought	a car	*for* each of his sons.
He	told	something	*to* his wife.
That	will teach	a lesson	*to* the boys.
He	gave	the signal to go	*to* the sons.
He	explained	the rules	*to* his sons.

An indirect object is usually a person *to* whom something is given or *for* whom something is done. Notice that the indirect object may come before the direct object (without preposition) or after the direct object (with preposition). It's the presence of the preposition that has made the difference in where each sentence part occurs.

Note: In Chapter 10 you will find a list of transitive verbs that take indirect objects, with their possible patterns.

Exercise 11   Analyze the following sentences. Separate the sentence components with slashes. Put an *s* over the subject, a *v* over the verb phrase, a *d* over the direct object, and an *i* over the indirect object, if there is one. The phrases telling where, when, how long, and why are adverbials. Place an *a* over them.

EXAMPLE:

Last week/Michael/showed/us/how to prepare a healthy snack.
 a   s   v   i   d

1. Last week Michael taught us how to make fruit leather.

2. He told us to buy overripe and bruised fruit on sale.

3. We bought peaches, apricots, and strawberries for him.

4. He showed us how to cut up the fruit.

5. Then he put it through a food mill.

6. He put the fruit in a large pot.

7. He asked me to add one tablespoon of honey per pound of fruit.

8. He heated the mixture.

9. He stirred it until it boiled.

10. Then he cooked the mixture for three minutes.

11. He showed us how to prepare the paper plates to dry the fruit.

12. He gave us plastic wrap to cover the plates.

13. After stretching the plastic around the plate, we taped it to the back.

14. He told us the plastic had to be tight and flat.

15. We spread a thin layer of fruit on each plate.

16. We placed the plates, covered with cheesecloth, in a shadow box to dry in the sun.

17. We brought the plates inside at night.

18. He explained to us that it would take about two days for the fruit to dry.

19. After three days, Michael brought the dried fruit leather to us.

20. We had prepared ourselves a real treat!

Intransitive Verbs and Adverbials

There are some verbs that do not transmit action and do not require objects. They are called *intransitive* verbs. To learn about them, study the following diagram.

SUBJECT	(AUXILIARY VERB[S])	INTRANSITIVE VERB	Ø	(ADVERBIAL[S])
A bomb	has	exploded.		
Something		happened		yesterday.
The sound wave		spreads out		in all directions.
The prow of a boat	is	moving		through the water.
The water wave		breaks		on the beach.

An intransitive verb is a verb that does not require an object to complete its meaning. It usually expresses a motion and is often followed by an *adverbial*. Adverbials express *when, where, why, under what condition, how, to what degree,* and so on, something takes place. Like direct objects, adverbials may have different forms. These will be discussed in detail in Chapter 5.

Exercise 12

Answer the following questions in complete sentences. First make sure that your answer is meaningful. Then underline any adverbial in your sentence.

EXAMPLE:
How does a wave of compressed air strike the earth?
A wave of compressed air strikes the earth <u>with audible and sometimes destructive effects.</u>

1. *In what age* do we live now? _____

_____ .

2. *When* may we hear a nearby explosion on a quiet afternoon? _____

_____ .

3. *Where* does the prow of a ship usually move? _____

_____ .

4. *How* does a sound wave spread out? _____

_____ .

5. *Where* does a water wave break? _____

_____ .

6. *Where* has the most prolonged sonic boom come from? _____

_____ .

7. *How fast* did the Air Force bomber fly? _____

_____ .

8. *Where* did that bomber fly? _____

_____ .

9. *Where* was a trail of shattered window glass? _____

_____ .

10. *Why,* do you think, will we hear more and more sonic booms in the future? _____ .

Linking Verbs and Complements

Besides the kinds of verbs you have just read about, there are other verbs, called *linking* verbs.

Subject	Linking verb	Complement	The complement is a:
I	am	a student.	noun
He	remained	silent.	adjective
He	became	a lawyer.	noun
John	seems	tired.	adjective
Strawberries	taste	delicious.	adjective
The music	sounds	loud.	adjective
The fur coat	feels	soft.	adjective
The stereo	costs	one hundred dollars.	noun
He	weighs	220 pounds.	noun

A linking verb is a verb that must be followed by a *complement* to complete its meaning. As the name suggests, the main function of a linking verb is to link the subject to the complement. The linking verb by itself does not have much meaning, but the linking verb and the complement together describe the state of the subject.

The complement to a linking verb may be a noun or an adjective. The main linking verb is *be*. Some other linking verbs are *become, remain, seem, look, appear, feel, sound, taste, cost, weigh, total,* and *equal.* A linking verb conveys about the same meaning as the mathematical symbol for equals. Example: *He is a teacher* could be symbolized as *He = a teacher.*

Note: Besides being used as a linking verb, *be* may be used as an intransitive verb. Study the sentences in the diagram. What function do the italicized words and phrases have in the sentences?

Be as an intransitive verb

He is *in the classroom.*
He is *from Venezuela.*
There are also new planets *in the sky.*
There were many more satellites to follow.
There was once a kind father.

When the verb *be* is followed by an adverbial of place, it is an intransitive verb. The intransitive verb *be* also occurs very often with a *there* construction. Example: *There are six people in this room.* In a *there* sentence, the subject usually follows the finite verb.

Exercise 13 In a short passage, describe your first impressions of America (or another place with which you were unfamiliar). Try to use at least five of the following linking verbs in your passage: *be, become, remain, seem, look, appear, feel, sound, taste, cost, weigh, total,* and *equal.* Write your description on a separate piece of paper.

EXAMPLE:

The people looked *friendly. I* felt *shy.*

Now examine the floor plan below.

Floor Plan of an Airport's
Passenger Waiting Area

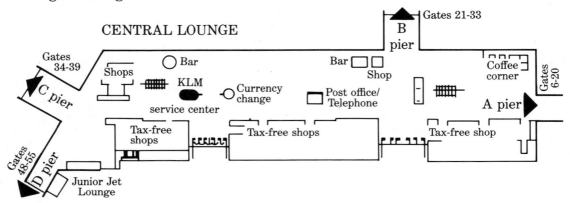

Exercise 14 Using the names of the facilities for passengers at the airport, complete the following sentences in your own words.

1. There is _____ .

2. There are _____ .

3. The waiting area seems _____ .

4. There is _____ .

5. The airport's passenger area looks _____

_____ .

6. In the middle, _____ .

7. On the left, _____ .

8. Next to _____ .

9. In the corner opposite the _____ , there is _____

_____ .

10. Adjacent to _____ .

Note: Some verbs can be used as more than one kind of primary verb depending on the sentences in which they are used. For example, when you look up *read* in the dictionary, you will see it defined as both *vt* (verb, transitive) and *vi* (verb, intransitive).

In the diagram below, you see that *read* can be used as either a transitive or an intransitive verb, and the verb *taste* can be used as either a transitive or a linking verb.

Examples:

John is reading a book.	transitive verb + object
John is reading in the library.	intransitive verb + adverbial
John tasted the soup.	transitive verb + object
The soup tasted delicious.	linking verb + complement

In this diagram, the direct object tells us *what* John was reading and the adverbial tells us *where* he was reading. The direct object of taste tells us *what* John tasted and the complement tells us *how* the soup tasted.

Now you are ready to classify and use intransitive, transitive, and linking verbs.

Exercise 15   First, identify each one of the following verbs as (I) intransitive, (T) transitive, or (L) linking. (Some verbs may be more than one kind.) Then fill in each blank with one of these verbs:

help _____	want _____	drop _____	work _____
produce _____	cause _____	be _____	contain _____
move _____	fire _____	call _____	appear _____

If you need to, change the form of the verb. *Note:* Some verbs have to be changed to *-ing* forms.

There _____ a very useful instrument that _____ us to "see" the changes in an electrical current. We _____ it a *cathode ray oscilloscope*. It _____ a tube that is almost like a television picture tube. An electron gun _____ a beam of electrons at the phosphor screen on the face of the tube. A deflection yoke _____ the beam to move back and forth at a fixed rate. If only this yoke were working, the beam would _____ a horizontal line in the center of the screen. But there is another yoke _____ to make the beam _____ up and down at the same time, so the line has bumps or waves in it. The current whose changes we _____ to see is used to control the up and down motion of the beam. When the voltage of this current rises, the beam swings away from its center position. When the voltage _____, the beam swings back toward the center. Therefore the bumps that _____ on the screen match the rise and fall of the voltage.

Sentence Analysis

At the beginning of this chapter you learned that this grammar text is based on the theory that longer, complex sentences are basically two or more short simple sentences combined according to specific rules. You will have a brief introduction to the way these rules work. In order to understand these rules, it is important that you understand the differences between *sentences, clauses,* and *phrases.* (Study the following diagram.)

The Sentence

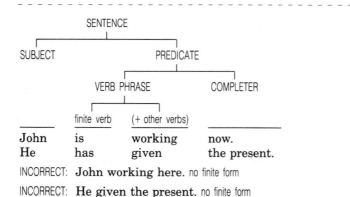

From the diagram above, it is clear that a sentence is a group of words that has a subject and a predicate, the first verb of which has a finite form. In other words, if a group of words has no finite verb, it is not a sentence.

Clauses

When two or more sentences are combined to form one new sentence, the original short sentences often have to be changed somewhat, and they are no longer sentences by themselves but parts of the new sentence. These parts are called *clauses.* The diagram below displays the clauses of a complex sentence.

COMPLEX SENTENCE

one main clause   subordinate clause(s)

Every month we say   that there is a new moon in the sky,   although it isn't a new moon at all.

INCORRECT: Although it isn't a new moon at all. (no main clause)

A sentence must have one main clause and may have one or more subordinate clauses. As you can see in the diagram, a group of words is not a sentence if it does not have a main clause.

The main clause may be a little different from a complete sentence, but it is not preceded by a connecting word. On the other hand, a subordinate clause usually consists of a *connecting word* and a sentence. Therefore the main difference between a main clause and a subordinate clause is that the latter usually has a connecting word.

Note: Sometimes the connecting word *that* is understood. For example, in the sentence *He said he was tired,* the connecting word *that* can be inserted: *He said that he was tired.*

Functions of Subordinate Clauses

What is the function of a subordinate clause in a sentence? It becomes a part of the new sentence and expresses a fuller meaning. Earlier in this chapter you learned about the components of a sentence: subjects, objects, complements, and adverbials. When a sentence becomes a subordinate clause, it becomes one of these components. The diagram below shows how subordinate clauses work. Subordinate clauses are italicized.

SUBJECT	VERB PHRASE	OBJECT/COMPLEMENT	ADVERBIAL
We	say	*that there is a new moon in the sky*	*although it isn't a new moon at all.*
What actually happens	is	*that supersonic aircraft set up a bow wave.*	
The bomber	left	a trail *that stretched from New York to Los Angeles.*	

There is one part of a sentence we have not discussed very much yet: the *adjectival.* An adjectival is a word or group of words that describes a noun. In the simple sentences that you have seen so far, the adjective was used as complement. (Example: *It is destructive.*) Adjectivals may also describe other nouns in a sentence, however. For example, in Exercise 8 you read a sentence about the bomber that flew at supersonic speed: *The bomber left a trail of shattered windows below it that stretched from New York to Los Angeles.* In this sentence, the noun *trail* is modified by several adjectivals.

The last part, *that stretched from New York to Los Angeles,* is an adjective clause. You know it is an adjective because it describes the noun *trail,* and you know it is a clause because it has a connecting word *that* followed by a sentence-like structure.

Notice that the whole structure from *a trail...to Los Angeles* is the direct object of the sentence. The adjectivals are part of the complete direct object.

The next two exercises will give you practice in finding main clauses and subordinate clauses in sentences.

Exercise 16   Identify each sentence part in italics as MC (a main clause) or SC (a subordinate clause).

1. _____ Thomas A. Edison did not make the first electric lightbulb *as it is popularly believed.*

2. _____ Cherrapunji, India, *which has an average annual rainfall of 427 inches,* is the wettest place on earth.

3. _____ *A state of intoxication is a condition* in which there is recognizable disturbance of intellect, movement, and coordination.

4. _____ The largest fish *anyone has ever caught* was a white shark that weighed 2,176 pounds.

5. _____ *If marshmallows packed in tin cans were taken to a height above seven thousand feet,* the lessened air pressure would cause the cans to explode.

6. _____ Only five percent of the people of the United States say *they dream in color.*

7. _____ Naturalists are inclined to believe *no animals are voiceless.*

8. _____ *It has not been proven* that fish bite more readily in certain kinds of weather than in others.

Exercise 17   Complete each of the following sentences.

1. _____ that he is coming.

2. _____ where he works.

3. _____ who came here yesterday

_____ .

4. _____ because he was sick.

5. _____ when you want to.

6. _____ what you said.

7. _____ whom you met _____

_____ .

8. Although I like to study grammar, _____

_____ .

Phrases

At the beginning of this chapter, you saw that sometimes sentences are combined without a connecting word. Example: *It is only the old moon hiding its face again in its own shadow.*

Hiding its face again in its own shadow is not a clause but a *phrase.* It is not a clause because it has no connecting word, subject, or finite verb.

A phrase is a group of words that together function as a component of the sentence, for example as subject, object, adjectival, or adverbial. The main difference between a clause and a phrase is that a phrase has no finite verb.

Exercise 18   Identify the following sentence parts in italics as C (a clause) or Ph (a phrase).

1. _____ At least some sugar is found in practically every food, *including meat.*

2. _____ There are thirty-two teeth *in a full set of adult teeth.*

3. _____ Ink *used in printing* has about the same consistency as molasses.

4. _____ Water does not boil *when dry ice is dropped into it.*

5. _____ *While invading China in 1215 A.D.,* Genghis Khan, Mongol conqueror, introduced the use of gunpowder.

6. _____ Although frost does not cause the chemical process *that produces the brilliant colors in autumn leaves,* it often hastens the coloring process.

7. _____ The opossum, *though slow and stupid,* often feigns death when caught.

8. _____ A single pail of water can produce enough fog to cover 105 square miles *to a depth of fifty feet.*

Sentence Types

As you read earlier, sentences may contain subordinate clauses and/or phrases. The different sentence types may be classified according to the type of clauses they have. They are called (a) *simple,* (b) *compound,* and (c) *complex.* The components of a simple sentence are diagrammed for you below.

The Simple Sentence

Simple sentence

one main clause
one finite verb

John *works* here.
The boy working here *is* my friend.
I *went* to the store to buy some bread.
Having had an accident, she *drove* more carefully.

A sentence that consists of just one main clause is called a simple sentence. It has only one finite verb, even though it may have phrases that contain other verb forms.

The Compound Sentence

A *compound* sentence, however, is different. It has two main clauses. The main clauses in a compound sentence may be put together in more than one way, as you will see in the diagram below.

Main clause	Coordinate conjunction Correlative conjunction	Main clause
John works in the city,	*but*	he lives in the country.
Not only does John work in the city,	*but*	he *also* lives in the city.

Main clause	Semi-colon Semi-colon and adverb	Main clause
John works in the city	;	he lives in the country.
John works in the city	; *however,*	he lives in the country.

In Chapter 3 you will examine the compound sentence. It consists of two main clauses connected by either a coordinate conjunction or a correlative conjunction, or separated by a semi-colon, which may be followed by a conjunctive adverb.

The Complex Sentence

You need to be able to recognize a complex sentence. The diagram below shows you what a complex sentence is.

	main clause	subordinate clause(s)	
noun clause	I know	*that John works there.*	
adverbial clause	I know John	*because he works there.*	
adjective clause	John,	*who works there,*	is my friend.

A sentence that consists of a main clause and one or more subordinate clauses is called a complex sentence. It has more than one finite verb, and there is usually a connecting word preceding the subordinate clause.

Now that you can recognize the three types of sentences (simple, compound, and complex), you will be able to do the next exercise.

Exercise 19   Identify the following sentences as (A) simple, (B) compound, or (C) complex.

1. _____ Unidentical twins are called fraternal twins.

2. _____ It is estimated that the world's average rainfall is sixteen million tons per second.

3. _____ Napoleon Bonaparte originated the idea of placing odd and even numbers on the houses on different sides of the street.

4. _____ The armistice ending the Korean war was signed July 27, 1953.

5. _____ The silkworm is not a worm; on the contrary, it is a caterpillar.

6. _____ The law of gravitation was discovered in 1687.

7. _____ At least ten different species of salmon are known to exist.

8. _____ Pure radium resembles common table salt.

9. _____ The bones of fish are softened by heat, not by oil, as it is popularly believed.

10. _____ Air that is thirty to forty feet above the ground is usually from five to ten degrees warmer than the air that is just above the ground.

Word Order

When people communicate, they have to know *who* or *what* is doing *what where.* In some languages we know what the subject, object, adverbial, and so on, are by looking at the beginning or the ending of the words. In English, though, there are usually no special beginnings or endings to show that a word is a subject, object, adjectival, or adverbial. In English, we usually recognize the function of a sentence part by its position. The word order rules of an English sentence are therefore very strict.

Usually, the parts of the sentence are ordered in the manner that you have seen so far: subject, then verb phrase, then object/complement, then adverbial(s). The object or complement usually comes directly after the verb phrase, and the subject usually precedes the verb phrase.

Word order in English sentences is mapped out for you in the following diagram.

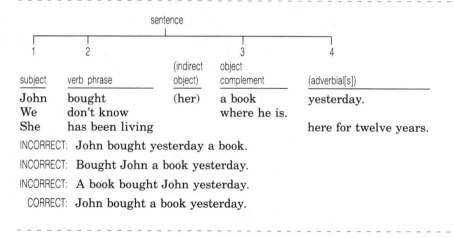

There are only a few exceptions to the pattern shown in this diagram: The subject and finite verb may switch places in certain cases and adverbials may be found in different positions in a sentence. First you will learn about the first of these exceptions.

Inversion of Subject and Finite Verb

In almost every sentence, the subject comes immediately before the finite verb. However, there are four specific cases in which the finite verb precedes the subject. Putting the finite verb before the subject is called *inversion* of subject and verb. Inversion is used in these four cases:

1. in questions,
2. after *so* and *there,* after negative adverbs or other negative expressions,

3. in a sentence beginning with a complement or an object, and
4. in a reduced *if*-clause.

Word Order in Questions

First you will learn to use inversion of subject and verb in questions. The diagram below shows you how word order in a statement differs from word order in a question.

	s	fv		s	fv	
STATEMENT:	*John*	*is*	working in the yard now.	*John*	*bought*	a book yesterday.

	(Wh-word)	fv	s		(Wh-word)	fv	s	
QUESTION:		*Is*	*John* working in the yard now?			*Did*	*John* buy a book yesterday?
	Where	*is*	*John* working now?		When	*did*	*John* buy a book?
	What	*is*	*John* doing now?		What	*did*	*John* buy yesterday?

	Wh-word Subject	fv		Wh-word Subject	fv	
QUESTION:	*Who*	*is*	working in the yard now?	*Who*	*bought*	a book yesterday?

Key

s = subject

fv = finite verb

Wh-word = a word that tells who, what, where, when

You will see from this diagram that in a question the finite verb comes before the subject. A question may begin with the finite verb or with a *Wh*-word. If the *Wh*-word is the subject of the sentence, there is no inversion of subject and finite verb.

Notice that the finite verb must be a helping verb or a form of the linking verb *be*. Example: *Is he poor?* A form of the helping verb *do* must be used if there is no other helping verb in the sentence. Example: *He bought a book. Did he buy a book?*

Use what you have learned about inversion to do the following exercise.

Exercise 20   Change each statement to a question starting with the words after it.

EXAMPLE:

The Eastman Kodak was first marketed April 24, 1888.

(Was...; When...; What...)

Was the Eastman Kodak first marketed April 24, 1888?

When was the Eastman Kodak first marketed?

What was first marketed April 24, 1888?

1. A thermometer registers colder if it has first been thrust into hot water.

   Does _____?

   When _____?

   What _____?

2. The greatest depth of the ocean yet found is 6.7 miles.

   Is _____?

   How many miles _____?

3. Australia is the largest wool-producing country in the world.

   Is _____?

   What country _____?

4. Fingernails grow faster than toenails.

   Do _____?

   What _____?

5. The common housefly is probably the most dangerous insect in America.

   Is _____?

   What _____?

6. The common housefly spreads at least twenty dangerous diseases.

   What _____?

   Does _____?

Word Order after *So, There,* and Negative Words

Now study a diagram that will explain how sentence inversion works on the second of the four cases: after *so* and *there,* and after negative adverbs or other negative expressions.

- -

Inversion after a negative word

I have never seen such a bad movie before.
Never have I seen such a bad movie before.

We rarely go to the movies.
Rarely do we go to the movies.

Immediately after he arrived, he began to complain.
No sooner had he arrived than he began to complain.

Inversion after an *only if/when* clause

I will help you if you study.
Only if you study will I help you.
Only when you study will I help you.
Not until you study will I help you.

Inversion after *so* and *there*

Many people are there.
There are many people.

My friend liked the movie, and I did, too.
My friend liked the movie, and *so did I.*

No inversion if only the subject is negative

Neither my friend nor I liked the movie.

- -

From this diagram you learned that the subject and finite verb are inverted when a sentence starts with a negative adverb that modifies the whole sentence. (The helping verb *do* is needed if there is no other helping verb in the sentence.)

However, if the negative word is not at the beginning of the sentence, or when the negative word comes at the beginning of the sentence but modifies only the subject, the word order is not inverted.

Notice that after an *only if/when* clause the subject and finite verb in the main clause are inverted.

The following exercise will give you practice in rewriting sentences when a negative word is moved to the beginning.

Exercise 21   Start each statement with the word or phrase given after the sentence.

1. We had hardly arrived in the park when it started to rain. Hardly

   _____ .

2. I have never seen such a beautiful sight. Never _____

   _____ .

3. I liked the new apartment, and my roommate did, too. I liked the

   new apartment, and so _____ .

4. She may leave only if she is finished with her work. Only if _____

   _____ .

5. He had scarcely washed his car when it started to rain. Scarcely

   _____ .

6. I have seldom seen such a good movie. Seldom _____

_____ .

7. He had barely entered the room when she left. Barely _____

_____ .

8. We rarely leave this city. Rarely _____

_____ .

Word Order after a Complement or Direct Object

The third case of inversion occurs when word order changes after a complement or a direct object.

Those who help the poor are happy.
Happy are those who help the poor.

The man screamed, 'Help!'
'Help!' screamed the man.

In formal English the sentence may begin with a complement or object for sentence variety or emphasis. Notice that the subject follows the verb when the complement or object is at the beginning of the sentence.

Word Order in Reduced *If*-Clauses

The last of the four cases in which inversion of subject and verb is required in English is the case of the reduced *if*-clause.

In Chapter 8 you will learn about the subjunctive mood and the use of *if* clauses. For now it is enough for you to know that certain *if* clauses may be reduced, as in the diagram below.

If I had had more time, I would have helped you.
Had I had more time, I would have helped you.

If you should see him, please ask him to call me.
Should you see him, please ask him to call me.

An *if* clause containing the verb *should* or a past perfect tense (*had* + past participle) may be reduced by deleting the conjunction *if* and inverting the subject and the finite verb.

Below is a brief exercise giving you practice in inverting by means of a reduced *if*-clause.

Exercise 22   Reduce the following _if_ clauses. Write the new sentence after the one that is given.

1. If you should go to the store, please buy me a loaf of bread. _____

   _____ .

2. If he had not worked so hard, he would not have gotten sick. _____

   _____ .

3. If the train should be late, we would miss our plane. _____

   _____ .

4. If we had not left early, we would not have arrived on time. _____

   _____ .

5. If he had done as he had been told, he would not be in such trouble

   now. _____ .

6. If we should go to New York, we would see the Statue of Liberty.

   _____ .

As you just learned, the normal word order is subject–verb–object/ complement and this order is reversed in only a few cases. Now we will study the position of the remaining sentence part: the adverbial.

Ordering of Adverbials

Adverbials are different from subjects, verb phrases, objects, and complements. First of all, there may be several adverbials in one sentence or clause, whereas there may be only one of each of the other sentence parts. Also, adverbials may be moved around within the sentence or clause, but the other sentence parts may not.

In the diagram below you can see what happens when there are two or more adverbials in a sentence.

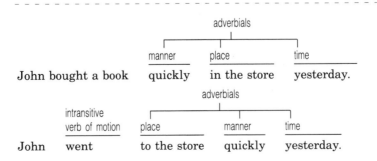

```
                        two time adverbials
                              |
                  ┌───────────────────────┐
              more general              more specific
              _____              _____
I will see you  tomorrow afternoon      at five o'clock.
```

- -

If there are several adverbs in the sentence, the general rule is that an adverbial of *manner* comes before an adverbial of *place,* which in turn comes before an adverbial of *time.* (It might be helpful to note that the letters M(anner)—P(lace)—T(ime) are ordered alphabetically.)

However, if the primary verb is an intransitive verb denoting motion, the adverbial of place usually precedes the adverbial of manner and time.

When there are two adverbials of the same kind, the general rule is that the more general one precedes the more specific one.

The exercise below gives you an opportunity to place adverbial phrases correctly in sentences.

Exercise 23 Read the passage, then fill in the blanks with one of the following adverbial phrases. Notice that more than one answer may fit grammatically, but find the phrase that makes the most sense. Use each phrase only once.

very comfortably	out of its eyes
very easily	in its hump
swiftly and gracefully	in the desert
every day	in the sand
for hours at a time	conveniently

The dromedary can live _____ _____ . Its

wide feet don't sink _____ _____ . It can

gallop _____ _____ . It can store fat _____

_____ _____ , and so it doesn't need to eat _____

_____ . Long eyelashes keep sand _____ .

Adverbials of Frequency

Adverbials of *frequency (always, frequently, often, sometimes, rarely, seldom, never,* and so on) occur right before, right after, or in the middle of the verb phrase.

Study the next diagram. It shows you where, in relation to the verb phrase, adverbials occur. It compares the placement of adverbials in standard sentences, in questions, and in statements with negative words.

subject	adverb of frequency	verb phrase primary verb	rest of completer
She	*always/usually/never*	studies	in the library.
He	*often/seldom/sometimes*	visits	his friends.

QUESTION: Does she *always* study in the library?
NEGATIVE: She does not *always* study in the library.

subject	linking verb	adverb of frequency	rest of completer
He	is	*always/rarely/seldom*	late.
They	are	*usually/never/often*	here.

QUESTION: Is he *always* late?
NEGATIVE: He isn't *always* late.

subject	auxiliary verb(s)	adverb of frequency	primary verb	rest of completer
He	has	*always/never/seldom*	studied	there.
They	may	*occasionally/never*	have done	that.
They	may have	*always*	done	that.

QUESTION: Has he *always* studied there?
NEGATIVE: He hasn't *always* studied there.

The diagram above shows that adverbials of frequency come before the primary verb (but after a linking verb), and if there are any auxiliary verbs the adverbial comes after the first or second one.

The adverbials *often, frequently, occasionally, usually* and *sometimes* are also found at the end of a sentence.

EXAMPLE:
He visits his friends often/frequently/occasionally/usually/sometimes.

On the other hand, the adverbials *always, seldom, rarely,* and *never* are usually close to the verb phrase.

INCORRECT: He visits his friends always.
CORRECT: He always visits his friends.

Exercise 24   Insert into the sentence the adverbial of frequency given.

1. John drinks tea. (usually)

2. Mary has preferred to drink coffee. (always)

3. We can't eat out. (= in a restaurant) (often)

4. She may have eaten at home. (rarely)

5. Do they eat in the cafeteria? (usually)

6. Has she studied in the library? (ever)

7. Are they late? (often)

8. The baby is bathed in the morning. (frequently)

For sentence variation, for coherence, or for emphasis, adverbials may be moved to the beginning of a sentence. The following diagram gives you examples of adverbials at beginnings of sentences.

	adverbial	remainder of sentence
	Examples:	
CLAUSE	Because he had to buy a book,	John went to the store yesterday.
PHRASE	To buy a book,	John went to the store yesterday.
PHRASE	Yesterday, early in the afternoon,	John went to the store.
WORD	Yesterday,	John went to the store.
WORD	Yesterday	John went to the store.

An adverbial at the beginning of the sentence is usually set off from the remainder of the sentence with a comma. However, if the adverbial is very short, a comma is unnecessary.

Exercise 25   With a circle, line, and arrow, move one of the italicized adverbials to the beginning of the sentence if possible, and add a comma if necessary.

Note: An adverbial of manner is usually not put at the beginning of the sentence.

1. The Atlas earth satellite was launched *with a payload of 150 pounds   on December 18, 1958.*

2. Atlas began to serve *as the first relay station in space   in the world on that day.*

3. President Eisenhower's Christmas message to the world was broadcast *to it   before the rocket left the ground.*

4. The satellite recorded the message on tape and rebroadcast it *when ordered to do so by a radio signal   when the satellite was in orbit.*

Solving Problems

At the end of each chapter, you will find a section called Solving Problems. It summarizes, reviews, and sometimes expands upon the main points of that chapter, particularly those that you should keep in mind when you are proofreading something that you have written. (These are also the points often tested in the grammar section on the Test of English as a Foreign Language (TOEFL).) If you don't understand the explanation in this section, go back to the explanation and detail earlier in the chapter.

No Finite Verb

INCORRECT: The boy working here.
CORRECT: The boy is working here.

INCORRECT: Portugal situated on a peninsula.
CORRECT: Portugal is situated on a peninsula.

INCORRECT: He is unable to attend class because he sick.
CORRECT: He is unable to attend class because he is sick.

No Subject

Every finite verb in a sentence must have a subject. A subject has to be a noun or a noun-like structure. A group of words preceded by a preposition (that is, *in, on, at, during, by,* and so on) is usually an adverbial or an adjective phrase.

INCORRECT: In Taiwan is densely populated.
CORRECT: Taiwan is densely populated.
CORRECT: It is densely populated in Taiwan.

INCORRECT: The girl works here is my friend.
CORRECT: The girl who works here is my friend.
CORRECT: The girl working here is my friend.

INCORRECT: By working hard helped him to pass the course.
CORRECT: Working hard helped him to pass the course.

Lack of Subject-Verb Agreement

A subject may have many different forms. It may be a single word, like *Taiwan,* but very often it consists of several words. If it is a clause or a phrase with an *-ing* form or a *to* infinitive, the finite verb is singular. However, if the subject is a noun phrase, the finite verb must agree with the *head noun* or *pronoun.* Pronouns such as *who, what,* and those ending in *one* or *body* are always singular.

INCORRECT: The number of students have increased.
CORRECT: The number of students has increased.

INCORRECT: The lines on the man's face shows he is worried.
CORRECT: The lines on the man's face show he is worried.

INCORRECT: Each of the boys like to drive fast.
CORRECT: Each of the boys likes to drive fast.

INCORRECT: Writing letters home are necessary.
CORRECT: Writing letters home is necessary.

INCORRECT: Who are coming tonight?
CORRECT: Who is coming tonight?

INCORRECT: Everybody in the class want to come to the party.
CORRECT: Everybody in the class wants to come to the party.

No Main Clause

A sentence must have one main clause.

INCORRECT: The girl who works where I work.
CORRECT: The girl works where I work.

No Connecting Word Before a Subordinate Clause

INCORRECT: It is necessary I leave.
CORRECT: It is necessary that I leave.

Faulty Word Order

The normal word order is subject — verb — object/complement — adverbials of manner, place, and time (MPT). After an intransitive verb, the adverbial of place precedes the adverbial of time. Adverbials of frequency usually precede the primary verb, and there is inversion after a negative word at the beginning of the sentence.

INCORRECT: I read yesterday a book.
CORRECT: I read a book yesterday.

INCORRECT: I went yesterday to the store.
CORRECT: I went to the store yesterday.

INCORRECT: I go to the library always.
CORRECT: I always go to the library.

INCORRECT: Only if you study you will pass the test.
CORRECT: Only if you study will you pass the test.

Superfluous or Faulty Capitalization and Punctuation

Only the first word of a sentence and proper nouns (names of people and things) are capitalized. Do not capitalize the first word of each line.

INCORRECT: The girl working at the library
            Is my friend.
CORRECT: The girl working at the library
            is my friend.

The final exercises in this chapter are summary exercises. When you work on them you will be applying the knowledge gained in studying this chapter.

Exercise 26 Each sentence contains one of the errors described under the heading Solving Problems. Locate each error. In the space between the lines, make your corrections.

In the 1940s Swiss scientist Auguste Piccard invented the deep sea Diving vessel called the bathyscaphe. Not until twenty years later, on January 23, 1960, his own son gave it the ultimate test. At 8:23 A.M. that day, climbed Jacques Piccard and United States Navy lieutenant Donald Walsh into the bathyscaphe *Trieste* and sealed it shut. Their goal located nearly seven miles below. They wanting to reach the bottom of Mariana Trench, the deepest known spot in the Pacific Ocean.

The *Trieste* were lowered into the water and slowly began its descent. Before noon had reached a depth greater than the height of Mount Everest. One small outside window under the tremendous water pressure of nearly eight tons per square inch cracked, but Piccard and Walsh kept going. They touched at 1:06 P.M. the bottom: 35,800 feet below the surface of the sea.

For twenty minutes each of them were able to observe the fish that swam into the paths of the bathyscaphe lights. Then began on their long trip back. It was at 4:56 P.M. the *Trieste* broke through the ocean's surface. Jacques Piccard and Donald Walsh who had conquered the ocean's greatest depth.

Exercise 27   Read the paragraph below at least three times for general understanding. After the paragraph is a set of unfinished sentences. Complete these sentences with information from the paragraph. Be sure your answers are grammatically correct. Each sentence of the paragraph is numbered. The same numbers are used on the unfinished sentences below.

(1) Modern materials technology is going to take a great weight off the space shuttle. (2) Each of the spacecraft's present solid rocket boosters has something called a motor case, now made of steel, which takes up most of the booster's 150-foot length. (3) And each of these steel motor cases weighs about 100,000 pounds.

(4) Now, however, NASA is testing motor cases made from a composite material — plastic reinforced with carbon fibers. (5) Segments of the new motor case, twelve feet wide by thirty feet long, are being fabricated by winding the composite filament around a cylinder, using both hoop and helical windings. (6) Motor casings made of the new material will weigh about 30,000 pounds less than the old steel ones and thus will confer greater cargo capacity on shuttle missions. (7) The cases, manufactured under the direction of the Marshall Space Flight Center, are due to fly by the end of the year.

1. Modern materials technology will be beneficial to the space shuttle because _____ .

2. The spacecraft has several _____ . These _____ have something called motor cases. These _____ are made of _____ . These motor cases are about _____ long.

3. _____ weigh about 100,000 pounds each.

4. Now, however, NASA is testing a new _____ . This material is composed of _____ . This material is used for _____ .

5. _____ are twelve feet wide and thirty feet long. To make these segments, people _____ around a cylinder. They _____ both hoop and helical windings.

6. Because these motor casings _____ ,

   they will enable the shuttle to carry more _____ .

7. The cases _____ manufactured under the direction of the

   Marshall Space Flight Center. By the end of this year, these _____

   _____ .

Now try something more ambitious: studying an advertisement, discussing it, and writing something like it on your own.

Assignment for Writing

Reading

Read through the ad from International Paper Company. Try to get a general understanding of the contents. Do not worry if you cannot understand every word. Look up in a dictionary only those words that are absolutely necessary for a general understanding of the selection.

Group Discussion

1. Why, do you believe, did International Paper Company use the article "How to write a business letter" as an advertisement? Is the company trying to sell a particular product? Is the company trying to create goodwill?
2. Who is the author of this article?
3. Do you believe that the author is a writing expert? Why, or why not?
4. In what style is this article written: formal, informal, or colloquial?
5. Is this the kind of style that you would use in a business letter? Why, or why not?
6. The article is divided into six major parts. What is the purpose of the first part?
7. In one sentence, summarize the second part, "Know what you want."
8. What are the two important points made in the third part, "Plunge right in"?
9. What does the author mean by the phrase *in the round file*?
10. In the fourth part, "Write so he'll enjoy it," the author gives seven specific suggestions for writing a letter from the reader's point of view. Think of a specific example for each suggestion.
11. In the fifth part of the article there are several proofreading suggestions. Which ones have to do with the physical appearance of the

(*text continues on page 42*)

How to write a business letter

Some thoughts from Malcolm Forbes

President and Editor-in-Chief of Forbes Magazine

International Paper asked Malcolm Forbes to share some things he's learned about writing a good business letter. One rule, "Be crystal clear."

A good business letter can get you a job interview.

Get you off the hook.

Or get you money.

It's totally asinine to blow your chances of getting *whatever* you want—with a business letter that turns people off instead of turning them on.

The best place to learn to write is in school. If you're still there, pick your teachers' brains.

If not, big deal. I learned to ride a motorcycle at 50 and fly balloons at 52. It's never too late to learn.

Over 10,000 business letters come across my desk every year. They seem to fall into three categories: stultifying if not stupid, mundane (most of them), and first rate (rare). Here's the approach

I've found that separates the winners from the losers (most of it's just good common sense)—it starts *before* you write your letter:

Know what you want

If you don't, write it down—in one sentence. "I want to get an interview within the next two weeks." That simple. List the major points you want to get across—it'll keep you on course.

If you're *answering* a letter, check the points that need answering and keep the letter in front of you while you write. This way you won't forget anything—*that* would cause another round of letters.

And for goodness' sake, answer promptly if you're going to answer at all. Don't sit on a letter—*that* invites the person on the other end to sit on whatever you want from *him*.

Plunge right in

Call him by name—not "Dear Sir, Madam, or Ms." "Dear Mr. Chrisanthopoulos"—and be sure to spell it right. That'll get him (thus, you) off to a good start.

(Usually, you can get his name just by phoning his company—or from a business directory in your nearest library.)

Tell what your letter is about in the first paragraph. One or two sentences. Don't keep your reader guessing or he might file your letter away—even before he finishes it.

In the round file.

If you're answering a letter, refer to the date

it was written. So the reader won't waste time hunting for it.

People who read business letters are as human as thee and me. Reading a letter shouldn't be a chore—*reward* the reader for the time he gives you.

Write so he'll enjoy it

Write the entire letter from his point of view—what's in it for *him*? Beat him to the draw—surprise him by answering the questions and objections he might have.

Be positive—he'll be more receptive to what you have to say.

Be nice. Contrary to the cliché, genuinely nice guys most often finish first or very near it. I admit it's not easy when you've got a gripe. To be agreeable while disagreeing—that's an art.

Be natural—write the way you talk. Imagine him sitting in front of you—what would you *say* to him?

Business jargon too often is cold, stiff, unnatural.

Suppose I came up to you and said, "I acknowledge receipt of your letter and I beg to thank you." You'd think, "Huh? You're putting me on."

The acid test—read your letter *out loud* when you're done. You

"Be natural. Imagine him sitting in front of you—what would you say to him?"

might get a shock—but you'll know for sure if it sounds natural.

Don't be cute or flippant. The reader won't take you seriously. This doesn't mean you've got to be dull. You prefer your letter to knock 'em dead rather than bore 'em to death.

Three points to remember:

Have a sense of humor. That's refreshing *anywhere*—a nice surprise in a business letter.

Be specific. If I tell you there's a new fuel that could save gasoline, you might not believe me. But suppose I tell you this:

"Gasohol"–10% alcohol, 90% gasoline–works as well as straight gasoline. Since you can make alcohol from grain or corn stalks, wood or wood waste, coal– even garbage, it's worth some real follow-through.

Now you've got something to sink your teeth into.

Lean heavier on nouns and verbs, lighter on adjectives. Use the active voice instead of the passive. Your writing will have more guts.

Which of these is stronger? Active voice: "I kicked out my money manager." Or, passive voice: "My money manager was kicked out by me." (By the way, neither is true. My son, Malcolm Jr., manages most Forbes money–he's a brilliant moneyman.)

"I learned to ride a motorcycle at 50 and fly balloons at 52. It's never too late to learn anything."

Give it the best you've got

When you don't want something enough to make *the* effort, making *an* effort is a waste.

Make your letter look appetizing –or you'll strike out before you even get to bat. Type it–on good-quality 8½″ x 11″ stationery. Keep it neat. And use paragraphing that makes it easier to read.

Keep your letter short–to one page, if possible. Keep your paragraphs short. After all, who's going to benefit if your letter is quick and easy to read?

You.

For emphasis, underline impor-

tant words. And sometimes indent sentences as well as paragraphs.

Like this. See how well it works? (But save it for something special.)

Make it perfect. No typos, no misspellings, no factual errors. If you're sloppy and let mistakes slip by, the person reading your letter will think you don't know better or don't care. Do you?

Be crystal clear. You won't get what you're after if your reader doesn't get the message.

Use good English. If you're still in school, take all the English and writing courses you can. The way you write and speak can really help –or *hurt*.

If you're not in school (even if you are), get the little 71-page gem by Strunk & White, *Elements of Style*. It's in paperback. It's fun to read and loaded with tips on good English and good writing.

Don't put on airs. Pretense invariably impresses only the pretender.

Don't exaggerate. Even once. Your reader will suspect everything else you write.

Distinguish opinions from facts. Your opinions may be the best in the world. But they're not gospel. You owe it to your reader to let him know which is which. He'll appreciate it and he'll admire you. The dumbest people I know are those who Know It All.

Be honest. It'll get you further in the long run. If you're not, you won't rest easy until you're

found out. (The latter, not speaking from experience.)

Edit ruthlessly. Somebody ~~has~~ said that words are ~~a lot~~ like inflated money–the more ~~of them that~~ you use, the less each one ~~of them~~ is worth. ~~Right on.~~ Go through your entire letter ~~just~~ as many times as it takes. ~~Search out and~~ **A**nnihilate all unnecessary words, ~~and~~ sentences–even ~~entire~~ *paragraphs*.

"Don't exaggerate. Even once. Your reader will suspect everything else you write."

Sum it up and get out

The last paragraph should tell the reader exactly what you want *him* to do–or what *you're* going to do. Short and sweet. "May I have an appointment? Next Monday, the 16th, I'll call your secretary to see when it'll be most convenient for you."

Close with something simple like, "Sincerely." And for heaven's sake sign legibly. The biggest ego trip I know is a completely illegible signature.

Good luck.

I hope you get what you're after.

Sincerely,

Printed in U.S. on International Paper Company's Springhill® Offset, basis 60 lb.

letter? Which ones with style? Which ones with content? And which ones with writing mechanics?

12. What does the author describe in the last part, "Sum it up and get out"?

13. One very important part of culture is the way we deal with people. Americans like to be polite but informal and direct. This trait is also expressed in their business letters. However, not every culture is the same. The people of other countries may write different kinds of letters. In some cultures, for example, business letters are often formal and full of business jargon. Can you find some points made in this article that would not apply to your culture? Which points, in your opinion, would apply to any culture?

Writing Topics

On a separate piece of paper, write a business letter. Choose one of the following topics, or think of one that applies to your own interest.

1. You rented an apartment, paying a deposit of $100.00. The apartment had several problems before you moved in. When you moved out, you cleaned up the apartment very well, but the owner has not returned your deposit. He believes you caused the problems that were already there when you moved in. You want your money back. Write a letter explaining your position.

2. You are a business person. You want to get a free copy of the *Business Survival Kit*. Write to International Paper Company and request a *Business Survival Kit*.

3. You would like to transfer to another college or university. Write to the head of the department in which you would like to study. Tell him or her your qualifications and explain why you want to transfer. Ask if you can be admitted to that department's program.

Some Writing Suggestions

When you first begin to write, do not worry much about grammar. Get your ideas on paper. Work on the general organization first. Are the paragraphs in a logical order? If so, work on each paragraph separately. Can your reader clearly understand your main point? Ask a friend to read your rough copy. He or she may have some questions or suggestions.

Reread the article on how to write a business letter. Have you followed all the suggestions in it? Here is a review of them:

1. Did you call the person by name?
2. Does your first paragraph tell what your letter is about?
3. Is the letter written from the reader's point of view?
4. Is the letter positive, nice, natural, polite, humorous, specific?

5. Did you use the passive voice and descriptive adjectives judiciously?
6. Is the letter short?
7. Is the letter perfect?
8. Is the letter clear?
9. Have you exaggerated, put on airs, or given opinions as facts?
10. Have you eliminated unnecessary words?
11. Does your last paragraph sum up your request or information?
12. Is your closing appropriate?

Proofreading

After you have written and rewritten your essay and you are satisfied with its content, organization, and supporting details, it is time to start worrying about the grammar. Read through your composition several times, each time looking for one of the following grammatical points.

1. Is each sentence capitalized and punctuated? Is there any super-fluous capitalization?
2. Does each sentence and each clause have a subject and a finite verb? Do all verbs agree with their subjects?
3. Does each sentence have a main clause?
4. Does each subordinate clause have a connecting word?
5. Is each sentence ordered correctly? Is the position of adverbials, adjectivals, and objects correct? Do you need inversion in any sentence?
6. Are there any spelling errors?
7. Have you made any errors in the use of articles?

After you have checked on both the content and grammar, copy your letter neatly according to your instructor's specifications.

2

Verb Forms and Their Uses

Review/Preview

In Chapter 1 you studied the sentence as a whole. In this chapter you will take a closer look at the central component of the sentence, the verb phrase, which tells us many important things in the sentence. Here is a list of five things the verb phrase does.

1. The verb phrase tells us what the subject does or is. Example: in *I wrote a letter* the verb *wrote* tells what the subject *I* did.
2. It tells us if the subject is performing the action or if the subject is acted upon. Contrast, for example, *I wrote the letter* with *The letter was written by me.* In which sentence was the subject acted upon?
3. It tells us if an action is going on at a specific point of time or not. Contrast, for example, *I wrote a letter* with *I was writing a letter.* In which sentence did the action take place at a particular time?
4. It tells us if the action itself or the result of the action is more important. Contrast, for example, *I wrote the letter* with *I have already written a letter.* In which sentence is the result more important?
5. It tells us if the speaker is certain or not about something, or it tells us what the speaker's opinion is. Contrast, for example, *He wrote a letter* with *He may write a letter.* In which sentence is the speaker certain about the action? Sometimes a verb phrase tells us several of these things at the same time. For example, what things does the verb phrase tell us in *The letter may have been written?*

Later in this book, you will study each type of verb phrase separately. Chapter 4 explains when to use the progressive and the perfect aspects (Example: I *was writing* a letter/I *have written* a letter). Chapter 6 explains when to use the passive voice (Example: The letter *was written*). Chapter 8 explains when to use mood (Example: I *may write* a letter).

The purpose of this chapter is to explain how these different verb phrases are formed, what helping verbs are needed to form them, and what verb forms are used with these helping verbs.

Then a brief overview will show you how these verb forms can also be used as other parts of the sentence.

Grammar and Meaning

Forms of the Verb

There are four basic verb forms: *infinitive, present participle, past participle,* and *finite.* Study the next diagram, which compares these four basic types and also lists the present and past forms of several finite verbs.

infinitive	present participle	past participle	finite	
			present	past
(to) go	going	gone	go/goes	went
(to) write	writing	written	write/writes	wrote
(to) talk	talking	talked	talk/talks	talked
(to) be	being	been	am/is/are	was/were
(to) have	having	had	have/has	had

Each one of these four basic forms will be discussed here.

Infinitive

The *infinitive* form of the verb, which is also called the *base* form, can occur with or without *to.* It is called the base form because it has no ending and it usually serves as the base for the other verb forms. It is the form of the verb that you can find in a dictionary. If you didn't know the meaning of *seen,* for example, you would have to look up *see* in a dictionary.

Now you will practice selecting infinitive or base forms.

Exercise 1   Examine each of the verb forms below. See if you can tell what its infinitive or base form is. If you are unsure, check a dictionary. Write each answer on the appropriate line.

1. traveled _____   11. wanted _____

2. being _____   12. loaded _____

3. written _____   13. receiving _____

4. seen _____   14. rose _____

5. scheduling _____   15. was _____

6. done _____   16. hacking _____

7. had _____   17. headed _____

8. reaching _____   18. providing _____

9. used _____   19. lifted _____

10. makes _____   20. becomes _____

Exercise 2   Read the story that follows. Then fill in each blank with any appropriate verb in the infinitive form. You may want to use some of the verbs mentioned in Exercise 1.

A Dangerous Journey

Before this, expeditions had been made to the North Pole by dogsled, airplane, airship, submarine, icebreaker, and snowmobile. But no one had ever been able to _____ this dangerous journey alone.

The Japanese explorer Naomi Uemura wanted to _____ the first to take this journey. On March 5, 1978, he headed north from Canada's Cape Columbia with a team of dogs and a sled loaded with half a ton of provisions. During his journey he was scheduled to _____ five airlifts of food and supplies. The rest of the time he would _____ entirely on his own.

An attacking polar bear nearly put an end to his expedition only four days after it had begun. Uemara had to _____ his way through ice ridges nearly thirty feet tall, with temperatures as low as −38 degrees Celsius. Later, as temperatures rose, cracks in the ice became a problem. Uemura had to _____ for iceblocks he could

_____ as bridges across the open water. On April 29, after fifty-five days and 600 miles of travel, Naomi Uemura reached the North Pole. He had been able to _____ what few men had done before him — and he had done it alone.

The infinitive is the base form of the verb, but another form that is often used is the present participle, or *-ing* form.

Present Participle

The *present participle* form, also called the *-ing form,* is the form that ends in *-ing*. Usually the *-ing* ending is added to the infinitive form. Example: *talk/talking; read/reading; say/saying.* However, sometimes spelling changes occur.

The diagram below compares the base form of several verbs with the present participle, or *-ing* form. It also gives spelling rules for making the *-ing* form from the base form.

	Base	-*ing* Form		Spelling Rules
	talk	talking	RULE:	Usually the *-ing*
	go	going		is added to the base
	read	reading		form of the verb. Note
	carry	carrying		that final *y* does
	play	playing		not change. However,
BUT:	lie	lying		*ie* is changed to *y*.
	note	noting	RULE:	A silent *e* is
	leave	leaving		dropped before the
	sue	suing		*-ing* suffix.
	issue	issuing		It is not dropped
BUT:	shoe	shoeing		after an *o*.
	stop	stopping	RULE:	After a short
	fit	fitting		stressed vowel the
				consonant must be
				doubled.
	offer	offering	RULE:	The consonant is not
				doubled after an
				unstressed vowel.

After studying this diagram, you should understand how to change the infinitive or base forms of many verbs to the present participle or *-ing* form.

Exercise 3   Read each of the following verbs. On the line next to each one, write its present participle.

1. shiver_____   7. helped _____

2. make _____   8. felt _____

3. run _____   9. relax _____

4. works _____   10. thought _____

5. want _____   11. warm up _____

6. plays _____   12. exercise _____

Exercise 4   Read the following passages. Then fill in the blanks with any appropriate verb in the present participle form. You may want to use some of the verbs mentioned in Exercise 3.

Why Do You Shiver on a Cold Day?

_____ helps you on a cold day by _____ you feel warmer. When you are _____ , some of your muscles tighten and relax very quickly, over and over again. The muscles are _____ hard without your _____ about them and without your really _____ them to. While your muscles are _____ hard, you are _____ up.

If you are _____ ball or _____ a lot on a cold day, it is unlikely that you will be _____ at all because by _____ you are already _____ your muscles work very hard. The exercise warms you up.

You learned earlier that there are four basic verb forms. You have just studied the infinitive or base form and the present participle or *-ing* form. Now you will learn about the third verb form.

Past Participle

When you look at a list of irregular verbs you will notice that the *past participle* often ends in *-en*. Example: *write — wrote — written; see — saw — seen; ride — rode — ridden*. However, not every one ends in *-en*. Example: *read — read — read; go — went — gone*. But we will refer to this form as the *-en* form of the verb.

The formation of the *-en* form is a little more complicated than the *-ing* form because the English language has many irregular verbs, such as *write, go, be,* and *see.* You probably already know the forms of these verbs, but if you do not, you should memorize them because they occur often. You will find a list of irregular verbs in Appendix C.

There are also many verbs that are regular. These verbs form their past participle by adding an *-ed* ending to the base. Sometimes spelling changes occur.

The diagram below shows you many base verb forms with their past participles.

- -

	Base	*-en* Form (Past Participle)		Spelling Rules
	talk	talked	RULE:	Usually an *-ed*
	help	helped		ending is added to
	discover	discovered		the base.
	miss	missed		
	push	pushed		
	crowd	crowded	NOTE:	If the base ends in
	head	headed		a *d* or *t* the
	want	wanted		suffix is pronounced "id"
	hope	hoped	RULE:	If the base ends in
	schedule	scheduled		a silent *e,* only
	suppose	supposed		a *d* is added.
	judge	judged		
	drop	dropped	RULE:	After a short
	omit	omitted		stressed vowel, the
	pot	potted		consonant must be
	occur	occurred		doubled.
BUT:	whisper	whispered		The consonant is not doubled after an unstressed vowel.
	carry	carried	RULE:	A *y* changes to *i* if
	apply	applied		it is preceded by a
	study	studied		consonant.
BUT:	play	played	RULE:	The *y* does not
	stay	stayed		change to an *i* if it is preceded by a vowel. However,
BUT:	say	said		*say* is an exception.

- -

Exercise 5   Examine each of the verb forms below and on the next page. See if you can tell what its past participle or *-en* form is. If you are unsure, check a dictionary. Write each answer on the appropriate line.

1. cover _____   2. relate _____

3. blossom _____

4. eat _____

5. ripens _____

6. peel _____

7. find _____

8. growing _____

9. has _____

10. look like _____

11. call _____

12. are _____

13. seeing _____

Exercise 6   Read the passage. Fill in the blanks with any appropriate verb in the *-en* form. You may want to use some of the verbs mentioned in Exercise 5.

Have you ever_____ an almond tree? It is a tree that grows in warm climates, and it is _____ to the peach tree. Many almonds are _____ in the warm valleys of California. After an almond tree has _____ , it produces a fruit that looks like peaches. However, the outside of the fruit cannot be _____ . Inside each fruit is a nut that is _____ by a shell. So far, two kinds of almonds have _____ found. One is sweet and the other is bitter. The bitter almond is like the nut that is _____ inside a peach pit. It should not be _____ .

Finite Form

In Chapter 1 the finite form was mentioned in connection with subject/ verb agreement. The finite verb is the first verb in the verb phrase, and it agrees with the subject of a sentence or a clause. (Remember, though, that a phrase doesn't have a finite verb.) The finite verb has two basic forms: a present tense form and a past tense form.

The following diagram shows a group of sentences in the present tense and another group in the past tense. In each sentence the subject of the main clause is italicized. If there is a subject in a subordinate clause, that is italicized too. Look for the finite verb for each italicized subject.

Present tense

The almond tree is a tree *that* grows in California.
Almond trees have light-pink blossoms.
They are grown in California.
An almond is really the seed of a fruit.

Past tense

Uemara was able to make the dangerous journey alone.
He had to hack his way through ice ridges.
He was scheduled to receive more food.
An attacking polar bear nearly put an end to his expedition.

Present Tense

The present finite verb form usually looks exactly like the base form. (*Note:* Usually the present finite form can be distinguished from the base form only by the way it is used in the sentence, not by the way it looks.) However, when the subject is third person singular, an *s* ending is added. Example: find — *find(s);* write — *write(s)*. A few spelling changes may occur, and there are a few irregular verbs.

The diagram below shows you the present tense form of many verbs, comparing each with its base form and giving the rules for spelling.

Base	-s form	Other Forms	Spelling Rules
write read speak	writes reads speaks	write read speak	RULE: Usually an *-s* is added to the base form in the 3rd person singular.
miss push teach rush	misses pushes teaches rushes	miss push teach rush	RULE: When the base form ends in a sibilant (an *-s* sound) an *-es* ending is added. It is pronounced "iz."
do go	does goes	do go	RULE: *es* is added to *do* and *go*.
carry study try	carries studies tries	carry study try	RULE: A final *y* preceded by a consonant is changed to an *ie* before the *-s* ending.
say play	says plays	say play	NOTE: If a final *y* is preceded by a vowel, it does not change. *Say* is irregular in the *-en* form, but not in the present tense form.
be	is	am/are	NOTE: *Be* is very irregular and has a separate form for *I*.
have	has	have	*Has* is an irregular spelling.
	will can must may	will can must may	NOTE: The modal helping verbs have no base form, and they do not add an *-s* ending in the third person singular form.

Exercise 7   Give both present-tense verb forms for the verbs below and on the next page. (*Note:* be has three forms.)

EXAMPLE:

write *write writes*

1. be ＿＿＿＿＿ ＿＿＿＿＿ ＿＿＿＿＿   2. calling ＿＿＿＿＿ ＿＿＿＿＿

3. stood _____ _____

4. differing _____ _____

5. took _____ _____

6. had _____ _____

7. develop _____ _____

8. got _____ _____

9. put _____ _____

10. drew _____ _____

11. beginning _____ _____

12. coming _____ _____

13. may _____ _____

14. to name _____ _____

Exercise 8   Read the passage below. Fill in the blanks with any appropriate verb in the present finite form. Make sure that it agrees with the subject. You may want to use some of the verbs mentioned in Exercise 7.

An alphabet _____ a system of using certain marks, which we _____ letters, to stand for particular sounds. There _____ many different alphabets in the world today, and it _____ taken thousands of years to develop them. The English alphabet of twenty-six letters _____ also be called the Roman alphabet because it _____ been passed down by the ancient Romans, who had _____ it from the Greeks. We _____ it an alphabet because the first two letters of the Greek alphabet were alpha and beta — in other words, calling it the alphabet then _____ exactly the same as calling it the ABCs today.

Have you thought much about the alphabet you have used for many years? Is your alphabet the same as the one used for English, or different?

Exercise 9   On a separate piece of paper, describe in a short passage how the writing symbols in your language differ from the English writing symbols. If your language uses the same alphabet as English, describe how the same symbols may be used for different sounds. Give specific examples to support your statements.

You have learned about the present tense of finite verbs. Now you will see how the past tense is formed.

Past Tense

The past finite verb form is usually the same as the -en form. It is formed by adding an -ed ending to the base form. Example: talk — *talked;* laugh — *laughed.* (*Note:* See the spelling rules above under Past Participle.) Some irregular verbs have different forms for the past finite form and the -en form. Example: write — *wrote* — written; see — *saw* — seen.

Usually, the past finite form does not have a special form for the third person singular. However, the verb *be* has a special form for the first and third person singular. Below is a diagram showing these special forms for *be*.

----

base: *be*
-ing form: *being*
-en form: *been*

finite {
present: I *am,* you *are,* he *is,* we *are,* they *are*
past: I *was,* you *were,* he *was,* we *were,* they *were*

Exercise 10   Give the past finite forms of the following verbs. A couple of these are irregular. You may need to check a dictionary.

1. be _____   9. call _____
2. live _____   10. rebel _____
3. beginning _____   11. attacks _____
4. fight _____   12. capture _____
5. done _____   13. shouting _____
6. offer _____   14. surrender _____
7. go _____   15. declare _____
8. building _____   16. to farm _____

Exercise 11   Read the passage below. Fill in the blanks with any appropriate verb in the past finite form. You may want to use some verbs mentioned in Exercise 10.

Ethan Allen _____ an American hero in the Revolutionary War. He _____ the leader of the Green Mountain Boys from Vermont, and he is remembered as Vermont's greatest man of his time, but he _____ not born there. Vermont _____ not a state (or separate colony) then and very few people _____ there. Ethan Allen _____ born in Litchfield, Connecticut, on January 10, 1738, nearly forty years before the Revolutionary War _____ .

He _____ the British in the French and Indian War, just as George Washington _____ . After this fighting, when the governor of New Hampshire _____ good farmlands "across the Green Mountains" to some of the soldiers, Ethan Allen _____ one of those who _____ there and _____ himself a home in what now is Vermont. These settlers, although they _____ themselves the Green Mountain Boys, _____ really men.

You have learned about several verb forms: the infinitive or base form, the present participle or *-ing* form, the past participle or *-en* form, and the finite verbs, past and present. Now try a summary exercise using all these forms.

Exercise 12 Read through the following passage. Try to identify the form of each verb in italics. Then do the following:

Put a 1 over each infinitive or base form.
Put a 2 over each present participle or *-ing* form.
Put a 3 over each past participle or *-en* form.
Put 4a over each present finite verb and 4b over each past finite verb.
Note: The answers are given in Exercise 13.

Thomas Young, an English scientist and physician who *lived* from 1773 to 1829, *became* interested in sound and light when he was in medical school. He had *made* studies of the human eye while still an undergraduate, and for his thesis he *decided* to write on the human voice. This interest led him *to do* a great deal of research in the physics of sound waves and physical optics, as the study of light was termed. He *read* all of Newton's published work on light and became convinced that all that was known of light at that time could *be* explained by *using* the idea of waves.

In one experiment Young *provided* the answer to the question of the *alternating* bands of light around certain light images. He took a single source of light and arranged it so that it would *pass* through slits in an opaque screen. The slits were narrow and placed close together. Beyond the two slits he *set up* a reflecting screen. When he *turned on* his light and it passed through both slits, the diffraction image was interrupted by a series of dark lines parallel to the image. They *looked* like black sticks in a picket fence. Young *found* that if he covered one of the slits, the diffraction remained but the series of dark lines disappeared.

What was *happening* was this: With both slits open, the light *going* through each one *spread out* or diffracted. But the light from one slit overlapped the light coming from the other.

An interference pattern was set up that was immediately visible on the screen as a series of dark lines where a wave trough and crest *canceled* each other upon arriving at the screen.

The importance of Young's experiment was that no particular theory of light could *account* for the interference pattern he had observed.

The next exercise is related to the one you just worked on. It is a chart that is partly filled in. The chart has blanks for the verb forms that you have just studied.

Exercise 13   Provide the remaining verb forms. Write them on the blanks.

infinitive	present participle	past participle	present finite forms	past finite form(s)
EXAMPLE:				
write	*writing*	*written*	*write/writes*	*wrote*
1. _____	_____	_____	_____	lived
2. _____	_____	_____	_____	became
3. _____	_____	made	_____	_____
4. _____	_____	_____	_____	decided
5. to do	_____	_____	_____	_____
6. _____	_____	_____	_____	read
7. be	_____	_____	_____	_____
8. _____	using	_____	_____	_____
9. _____	_____	_____	_____	provided
10. _____	alternating	_____	_____	_____

11. pass _____	_____	_____	_____	_____
12. _____	_____	_____	_____	set up _____
13. _____	_____	_____	_____	turned on _____
14. _____	_____	_____	_____	looked _____
15. _____	_____	_____	_____	found _____
16. _____	happening _____	_____	_____	_____
17. _____	going _____	_____	_____	_____
18. _____	_____	_____	_____	spread out _____
19. _____	_____	_____	_____	canceled _____
20. account _____	_____	_____	_____	_____

Exercise 14   Read the following passage.

Situation: You traveled from one country to another by plane. You arrived at an airport. Then you had to transfer to another plane.

Now, on a separate piece of paper, write meaningful English sentences to explain what you did between the time you arrived at the airport and the time you left. Here is a list of words and phrases that will help. You may use any verb with or without helping verbs. Be sure to use the right tense.

1. get off the plane	9. departure gate
2. arrival gate	10. connecting flight
3. follow signs	11. boarding pass
4. passport check	12. waiting area
5. claim luggage	13. snack bar
6. customs	14. board the plane
7. customs officer	15. stewardess
8. transfer	

Now that you have learned about verb forms, you will see them in action inside verb phrases.

Uses of Verb Forms in the Verb Phrase

In Chapter 1 you learned that the verb phrase may consist of either one or several verbs: one primary verb sometimes preceded by one or more auxiliary verbs. Here again, for easy reference, is a list of the different types of auxiliary verbs. Study the diagram of auxiliary verbs.

Auxiliary or helping verbs

modals	semi-modals	perfect aspect	progressive aspect	passive voice	negation/interrogation
will	to be going to	have	be	be	do
would	used to			get	
shall	to be about to				
should	to be to				
	to be supposed to				
may	to be allowed to				
might	to be permitted to				
can	to be able to				
could					
must	to have to				
need	to need to				
dare	to dare to				

- -

Now look at the following diagram to see how these helping verbs are used with other verb forms. Which two types of helping verbs are followed by the plain infinitive form of the verb? Which verb form follows a semi-modal?

You can see that the helping verb *be* may be followed by either the *-en* form or the *-ing* form. What is the difference in meaning? Besides *be,* which other helping verb is followed by the *-en* form?

Each of the following example sentences has one finite form. Can you identify each one?

- -

Verb form	Examples:	When to use the verb form
infinitive	I can *speak* English.	after a modal
	We must *speak* English.	after a modal
	Do you *speak* English?	after *do*
to-infinitive	We are supposed *to speak* English in class.	after a semi-modal
	We are *to speak* English at home, too.	
	We have *to speak* a lot of English.	
-en form	I have *spoken* English for three years.	after *have* to form the perfect aspect
	He may have *spoken* Chinese.	
	English is *spoken* in this class.	after *be* to form the passive voice
-ing form	I am *speaking* English at this moment.	after *be* to form the progressive aspect
	They were *speaking* Arabic when I came into the room.	
finite form	He *speaks* English every day.	first verb in the verb phrase
	He *spoke* English yesterday.	

- -

You can see now that in verb phrases, only certain verb forms fit with certain auxiliary verbs. The following diagram is a summary showing you which auxiliary or helping verb goes with each type of verb form.

Auxiliary		Form of the verb that follows
modals	+	plain infinitive or base form
semi-modals	+	*to*-infinitive
do	+	plain infinitive
perfect *have*	+	*-en* form
progressive *be*	+	*-ing* form
passive *be*	+	*-en* form

Exercise 15   Fill in the blank with an appropriate auxiliary verb. (In some cases more than one auxiliary is correct.) Then explain your choice(s) on a separate piece of paper.

EXAMPLE:

I *have* spoken English for three years.

(*Spoken* is a past participle; only *have* or *be* may be followed by a past participle. This is not a passive sentence, so I must use *have*.)

1. The thermometer _____ invented by a German inventor, Gabriel Fahrenheit.

2. Sound _____ not travel in a vacuum.

3. The highest number of which a human _____ think is a centillion.

4. A horse _____ sleep either standing up or lying down.

5. The earth _____ traveling through space at the rate of 72,600 miles an hour.

6. Synthetic diamonds _____ successfully produced for the first time in 1954.

7. The game of basketball _____ been played for almost a hundred years.

8. Basketball _____ invented by James Naismith of Springfield, Massachusetts, in 1891.

Sometimes there is more than one auxiliary or helping verb in a verb phrase. If there are two or more helping verbs in the verb phrase, they follow a specific pattern. The next diagram shows you the pattern in which auxiliary or helping verbs are used when there is more than one in the verb phrase.

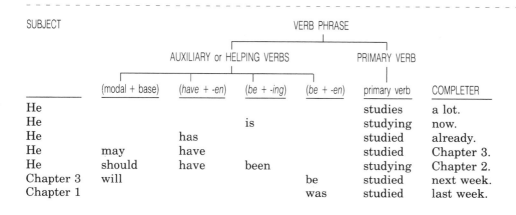

SUBJECT	VERB PHRASE					
	AUXILIARY or HELPING VERBS			PRIMARY VERB		
	(modal + base)	(have + -en)	(be + -ing)	(be + -en)	primary verb	COMPLETER
He					studies	a lot.
He			is		studying	now.
He		has			studied	already.
He	may	have			studied	Chapter 3.
He	should	have	been		studying	Chapter 2.
Chapter 3	will			be	studied	next week.
Chapter 1				was	studied	last week.

As you can see from the sentences in the diagram, the helping verbs come before the primary verb. If there are two or more helping verbs, the following rules apply:

1. Whichever verb comes first has the finite form.
2. Modals occur before the other helping verbs.
3. *Have* comes after a modal, but before the other helping verbs.
4. Progressive *be* comes after a modal or *have,* but before passive *be.*
5. Passive *be* is the last helping verb before the primary verb.

Special rules apply to the auxiliary or helping verb *do,* which is not listed in the diagram above. The helping verb *do* is followed by the base form of a verb. It is used to make a sentence interrogative (a question), negative (with *not*), or emphatic. When a sentence has no helping verb, it must use the helping verb *do* to form a question or a negative. The only exception in American English is the linking verb *be.*

EXAMPLES:
Did he go to the library? (question)
He didn't attend class yesterday. (negative)
He does like ice cream. (emphatic)

The next seven short exercises all give practice in working with auxiliary or helping verbs. Make sure that you use the correct verb form after each one.

Exercise 16   Change each of the following sentences to a sentence with a modal. The auxiliary or helping verb you should use is given in parentheses after the sentence.

EXAMPLE:
He is here. (*might*)
He might be here.

1. Ducks and geese fly at a speed of seventy miles per hour. (*can*) ___

_____ .

2. Each year, only about one person out of a million is killed by lightning. (*might*) _____ .

3. Arabic numerals have first been used in India, not in Arabia. (*must*)

_____ .

4. All the instruments in an orchestra are tuned to the note of middle A. (*should*) _____ .

5. A notch in a tree remains the same distance from the ground as the tree grows. (*will* — main clause only) _____

_____ .

6. Flax is harvested only once in seven years. (*can*) _____

_____ .

7. Even a fish gets seasick. (*might*) _____

_____ .

8. The average housewife washes two and a half million cooking and eating utensils in her lifetime. (*will*) _____

_____ .

Exercise 17   Change the following sentences to questions beginning with *do, does, did,* or another verb.

EXAMPLE:
He left an hour ago.
Did he leave an hour ago?

1. Most snakes travel only a few miles from the place where they were born. _____ .

2. No part of a snake's body leaves the ground when it moves from place to place. _____ .

3. An ear of corn always has an even number of rows of kernels. ____ _____ .

4. Malaysia is the world's largest rubber producer. _____ _____ .

5. Only five percent of the people of the United States dream in color. _____ .

6. The venomous rattlesnake always gives warning before it strikes. _____ .

7. Scientists cannot reliably predict earthquakes. _____ _____ .

8. Cutting hair does not make it grow faster. _____ _____ .

Exercise 18   Change the following sentences to sentences containing a semi-modal.

EXAMPLE:

He may leave now.
He is permitted to leave now.

1. You must help. _____ .

2. You should be on time. _____ .

3. He can jump over that fence. _____ _____ .

4. When he was young, he would ride his bike to school. _____ _____ .

5. We may go out tonight. _____ .

6. They may not smoke in the classroom. _____ _____ .

7. They can analyze sentences. _____ _____ .

8. My grandfather would tell me stories when I was little. _____

_____ .

9. He will go to the store this afternoon. _____

_____ .

10. He always went to the library. (*use:* He used to . . .) _____

_____ .

Exercise 19   Change the following sentences to sentences with *have.*

EXAMPLE:
He is here.
He has been here.

1. He is studying. _____ .
2. He may leave. _____ .
3. He may be studying. _____ .
4. He was hurt in the accident. _____ .
5. He may be hurt. _____ .
6. He studies every day. _____ .

Exercise 20   Change the following sentences to passive sentences.

EXAMPLE:
I am building the house.
The house is being built (by me).

1. We are watching a movie. A movie _____

_____ .

2. We may like this movie. This movie _____

_____ .

3. They have shown this movie before. This movie _____

_____ .

4. We might have heard this story before. This story _____

_____ .

5. We should have studied our lessons. Our lessons _____

_____ .

Exercise 21   Change the following sentences to sentences with the progressive *be* auxiliary.

> EXAMPLE:
> He has studied.
> *He has been studying.*

1. He may have studied. _____ .
2. He studied last night. _____ .
3. The house is built. _____ .
4. He might leave. _____ .
5. He has attended class regularly. _____

    _____ .

6. He may have lived here for three years. _____

    _____ .

Since *be* and its forms are so important in English, it will be wise to study *be* more closely.

Functions of the Verb Be

As you can see from the diagram of auxiliary or helping verbs on page 57, the verb *be* has several functions. The word or verb form that follows *be* will depend on what function *be* has in the sentence:

1. If *be* is a linking verb, it is followed by a complement. Examples: *I am busy. I am a student.*
2. If *be* is an intransitive verb, it is followed by an adverbial of place. Example: *I am in the classroom.*
3. If *be* is an auxiliary verb of the progressive aspect, it is followed by a present participle. Examples: *I am working. I am studying English. I am reading.*
4. If *be* is an auxiliary verb of the passive voice, it is followed by a past participle. Examples: *The letter was written. The house has been built.*
5. If *be* is a semi-modal, it is followed by a *to*-infinitive. The semi-modal *to be to* has a meaning similar to *to be supposed to* or *to be destined to*. Examples: *I am to study hard. Before he left Portugal, Columbus did not know he was to discover a new continent.*

Exercise 22   Read the following passage. In the passage each use of a form of *be* is in parentheses.

Put a 1 over it if it is a linking verb.
Put a 2 over it if it is an intransitive verb.
Put a 3 over it if it is an auxiliary verb of the progressive aspect.
Put a 4 over it if it is an auxiliary verb of the passive voice.
Put a 5 over it if it is a semi-modal.

In 1898 a perplexing manuscript (was) received by the editors of the Russian magazine *Science Survey*. Not only (was) it full of mathematical equations and chemical formulas, but it also proposed an idea that (was) both daring and original. The article said it (was) possible for a rocket-powered vehicle to escape from earth and travel through space.

The author (was) Konstantin Tsiolkovsky, who had (been) teaching mathematics at a secondary school that (was) located in the provincial city of Kaluga. He (was) not completely unknown, however. In the past he had written a few newspaper and magazine articles. In one of those the possibility of space travel had (been) mentioned.

Now he claimed that the problem of space travel had (been) solved at least on paper. The *Science Survey* editors (were) not sure how to react. They read Tsiolkovsky's article carefully. His calculations (were) checked and rechecked.

Then his article (was) put aside. However, five years later, in 1903, it (was) published.

Today that article (is) recognized as the first truly scientific study of space travel. Tsiolkovsky had stated clearly that a rocket could achieve its thrust in airless space. As proof he pointed to Newton's third law of motion, which had (been) published more than 200 years earlier.

Besides *be*, there is another verb that requires special attention: the verb *have*.

Functions of the Verb Have

Have is a commonly used verb with several functions:

1. If it is an auxiliary of the perfect aspect, it is followed by a past participle. Example: I have *written* a letter.

2. If it is a semi-modal, it is followed by a *to*-infinitive. *To have to* has a meaning similar to *must*. Example: I have *to write* a letter. Sometimes the noun, adjective, or adverb precedes the *to*-infinitive. Examples: I have a letter *to write*. I have a lot of work *to do*.
3. If it is a transitive verb, it is followed by a direct object and has a meaning similar to *own*. Example: I have *a letter*.
4. If it is a transitive verb meaning *order* or *cause to happen*, it is followed by a noun and a plain infinitive phrase. Example: I have *him paint* the house. This structure may also be passive. Example: I have *the house (to be) painted*.

Now you know that *have* may convey four different meanings. The following exercise will give you practice in sorting them out.

Exercise 23   Read the passage. In the passage each use of a form of *have* is in parentheses.

> Put a 1 over it if it is an auxiliary of the perfect aspect.
> Put a 2 over it if it is a semi-modal.
> Put a 3 over it if it is a transitive verb meaning *own*.
> Put a 4 over it if it is a transitive verb meaning *order* or *cause to happen*.

Tsiolkovsky's theories (had) provided a firm basis for practical space rocket research. Yet practical research still (had) far to go in the future. Men (had) been talking about space travel for centuries, but no one (had) ever been able to do anything about space travel. Apparently, Tsiolkovsky (had) his readers believe that he was just another impractical dreamer. His 1903 article was greeted with such complete indifference that no one even bothered to (have) it reviewed and criticized.

Quietly, Tsiolkovsky continued to teach in Kaluga and work on his theories. Between 1911 and 1914 he (had) several more technical articles published on space travel. Gradually, Russian scientists began to (have) an interest in his work. But the First World War and the Russian revolution were fast approaching, and the government (had) to prepare for them, so after 1914 Russia (had) no time to worry about space travel, and Tsiolkovsky receded into his accustomed obscurity.

Then, by 1924, the Soviet government realized that they (had) a neglected pioneer who lived within its own borders. The government (had) all of Tsiolkovsky's technical articles reprinted, and the retired schoolteacher, now nearly seventy, received his first real recognition. He was hailed as a national hero and a prophet of the future.

The following exercise has been adapted from a newspaper column by Ann Landers.

Exercise 24   Choose the appropriate auxiliary verb or the right form of the primary verb given in parentheses.

The Chronicle of Higher Education (has/was) reported that the University of Colorado Board of Regents (has/was) voted to allow professional note-takers to sell classroom notes, at the discretion of individual instructors. The board (acted/acting) after several students at the university's Boulder Campus set up a commercial note-taking service.

Ann Landers (has/was) disturbed by what appeared to be the triumph of crass commercialization over personal initiative.

She (write/wrote) to the heads of several highly respected institutions of learning. Here you (can/are able) find excerpts from the responses:

A. Bartlett Giametti, president of Yale: "If the news report (is/are) accurate, we have another instance of education construed as a consumer item. Education (is/can) not something to be (buying/bought) or (selling/sold) like a toaster or a municipal bond."

G. Armour Craig, acting president of Amherst: "Your clipping about paid note-takers at Boulder (has/was) stopped me dead in my tracks. I (have/am) astounded that any such act of piracy (can/has) be legalized, and I (do/have) not understand why any college teacher (had/would) permit such a practice."

From Derek Bok, president of Harvard: "Without knowing more of the facts, I would (had/have) thought that the proper course would (being/be) to ban professional note-taking. It (is/be) conceivable that there are special considerations not mentioned in the brief article. Having often (be/been) criticized by trigger-happy people who (do/have) not know all the facts, I (have/do) not wish to pass judgment on the situation."

Donald Kennedy, president of Stanford University: "Any student who wants to (has/can) find the relatively easy road to an undergraduate education: and it is the student who (will/is) lose. I wish the faculty (could/had) decided to ban professional note-taking. I believe it is a matter for the faculty and not a governing board to decide, so I (have/do) not blame the regents."

Uses of Verb Forms as Other Sentence Parts

Many sentences contain verb forms as subjects, objects, adjectivals, and adverbials. Although these verb forms sometimes seem to be used at random, the rules for using them are very specific. Later in this book, you will learn in detail under what circumstances these verb forms are used, but here you will find a general overview that will enable you to recognize them.

Plain Infinitive

The plain infinitive, the base form without *to,* is used only in a few specific cases as part of the direct object of a sentence. However, these particular uses are quite common, so you may want to memorize the next small groups of verbs.

SUBJECT	VERB PHRASE	OBJECT		(ADVERBIAL[S])
		noun	base form	
	make			
	have			
	let			
We	make	him	*study*	in the library.
They	have	the painter	*paint* the house.	
She	let	the children	*stay* up late.	
		noun	base form / to- infinitive	
	help			
We	help	him	*study* for his test.	
			to *study* for his test.	

	verbs of perception	noun	base form -ing form	
We	saw	him	*study*	in the library.
We	saw	him	*studying*	in the library.
They	heard	the children	*leave* the house.	
They	heard	the children	*leaving* the house.	

- -

As shown in the diagram above, *make, have,* and *let* are used with a noun or pronoun followed by a plain infinitive when they mean *force, cause,* or *allow* someone to do something. The verb *help,* however, is different. It can be followed by a noun and either a plain infinitive or a *to*-infinitive.

Another type of verb is called a *verb of perception*. Verbs like *see, hear, watch, notice, observe,* and *feel* may be followed by a noun and a plain infinitive or an *-ing* form.

Exercise 25   Below are some questions. Answer each one with one of the kinds of sentences in the example. Then underline the plain infinitive and the *-ing* form in each answer.

EXAMPLE:

What did you hear your roommate do?
I heard my roommate close the door.
I heard my roommate closing the door.

1. What did the mother let the children do? _____

_____ .

2. What does the teacher usually have you do? _____

_____ .

3. What did you observe the policeman do? _____

_____ .

4. What did the policeman make the burglar do? _____

_____ .

5. What did you overhear him say? _____

_____ .

6. What did your mother make you do? _____

_____ .

7. What did you listen to? _____ .

8. What did the little boy help his father do? _____

_____ .

9. What did you watch the athletes do? _____

_____ .

10. What did the president have his cabinet do? _____

_____ .

To-*Infinitive*

The *to*-infinitive is more versatile than the infinitive without *to*. Look at the diagram. How many functions of the *to*-infinitive can you find?

SUBJECT	VERB PHRASE	OBJECT/COMPLEMENT	(ADVERBIAL[S])
To leave immediately	is	necessary.	
To see	is	*to believe.*	
This lesson	is	easy *to understand.*	
I	don't know	*what to do.*	
I	want	*to leave*	now.
I	am going		to the store *to buy some rice.*
I	am	too tired	*to run a mile.*
I	am	energetic enough	*to run a mile.*
I	would like	a hamburger *to go.*	

From the diagram above you can see that the *to*-infinitive may be used as subject or complement. When it is used as subject, it often occurs with a temporary *it* construction. Example: It is necessary *to go.*

Sometimes the *to*-infinitive occurs after an adjective without temporary *it*. Examples: 1) *To understand* this lesson is easy. 2) It is easy *to understand* this lesson. 3) This lesson is easy *to understand.*

The *to*-infinitive may be used in a reduced *Wh*-clause, *what I should do* or *what to do,* and it may be used as direct object after certain transitive verbs. For more on this, see Chapter 10.

A *to*-infinitive phrase may be used as adverbial to express purpose. Example: *Why are you going to the store? I am going (in order) to buy some rice.*

The *to*-infinitive is also used as an adverbial after a *too* or *enough* phrase to express either positive or negative result. Examples: *I am too tired to run* means *I am so tired that I cannot run.* The sentence *I am energetic enough to run a mile* means *I am so energetic that I can run a mile.* The formation of these adverbials will be discussed in Chapter 5.

The *to*-infinitive may be used as adjectival after a noun. Example: In the sentence *I would like a hamburger to go,* the infinitive *to go* modifies the noun *hamburger.* (See Chapter 7 for more details.)

Exercise 26 Read the passage below. Find each *to*-infinitive phrase and decide how it is used.

Put a 1 over it if it is used in the verb phrase after a semi-modal.
Put a 2 over it if it is used as subject after temporary *it*.
Put a 3 over it if it is used as complement after a linking verb.
Put a 4 over it if it is used as object after a transitive verb.
Put a 5 over it if it is used as adverbial after an adjective.
Put a 6 over it if it is used as an adjectival after a noun.

The Rosetta Stone

The meaning of ancient Egyptian writing puzzled scholars for a long time. Translators needed a key *to unlock the mystery*.

In 1798 in Rosetta, Egypt, French soldiers found a stone that had three different kinds of inscriptions: one in Greek and two in ancient Egyptian writings. All three messages appeared *to say the same thing*. The Greek was easy *to translate*, and it seemed it was possible *to translate the Egyptian writings* by using the Greek as a key. But no one was able *to solve the puzzle*.

Many scholars tried *to solve the puzzle*, but it was not until 1818 that the twenty-eight-year-old Jean Francois Champollion discovered that, in the Egyptian writing called hieroglyphics, some pictures stand for sounds. By 1822 the French scholar had solved the mystery of language that had baffled experts for so long. The Rosetta stone could be read. But Champollion was not *to receive credit for his stunning achievement until thirty years after his death*.

Present Participle

Like the *to*-infinitive, the *-ing* form of the verb has various uses. Study the diagram to see what they are.

ADVERBIAL of TIME or REASON	SUBJECT	VERB PHRASE	COMPLEMENT or OBJECT	(ADVERBIAL[S])
	Seeing	is	believing.	
	Studying hard	is	necessary.	
	I	heard	him singing.	
	He	stopped	talking.	
	We	enjoy	reading.	
Being sick,	Mary	stayed		at home.
Having finished their work,	they	left.		
After finishing their work,	they	left.		
While working	they	heard	a loud noise.	

From the diagram above, you see that the *-ing* form may be used as subject, complement, or object with certain verbs (for more details on this see Chapter 10). The *-ing* form is most commonly used with the verb *be*.

Another use of the *-ing* phrase is as adverbial of time or reason. When a sentence begins with an *-ing* phrase set off with a comma from the rest of the sentence, it usually expresses why or when something happened. Example: In the sentence *Being sick, Mary stayed home,* the phrase *being sick* explains why Mary stayed home.

The *-ing* form is also frequently used as an adjectival. In the diagram below, can you explain why the *-ing* form comes before the noun in the first two sentences and after the noun in the last two sentences?

	NOUN	
The *frightening*	movie	lasted two hours.
The *daring*	boy	jumped over the ditch with his motor bike.
The	movie	*frightening me most* was *Jaws.*
The	boy	*daring to jump over the ditch with his motor bike* won the prize.

In the diagram above, you saw the *-ing* form used as an adjectival. When the *-ing* form is a single-word adjective, it comes before the noun, but when it is part of a phrase, it follows the noun.

Exercise 27   Read the passage below. Find each *-ing* phrase and decide how it is used.

Put a 1 over it if it is used in the verb phrase after progressive *be*.
Put a 2 over it if it is used as a subject.
Put a 3 over it if it is used as a complement.

Put a 4 over it if it is used as a direct object.
Put a 5 over it if it is used as an adverbial.
Put a 6 over it if it is used as an adjectival.

What Happens During Breathing?

When you breathe in, air goes through *breathing* passages in your nose. From your nose, the air goes into a tube called your windpipe and then down into your lungs. There, *having been taken from the air,* oxygen passes into your bloodstream, and your blood keeps on *carrying the oxygen around your body* to all your cells.

While carrying the oxygen around your body, your blood is *picking up* a gas called carbon dioxide. *Ridding all your cells from this gas* is necessary because it is a waste gas.

The task of the muscles between your ribs and under your lungs is *tightening and relaxing to pump these gases in and out* so that your heart, *pumping constantly,* can carry the carbon dioxide to your lungs. Finally, *breathing out,* you get rid of this carbon dioxide along with leftover air.

Past Participle

In the verb phrase, the past participle has two functions. Examples: *I have written a letter* (after *have* to form a perfect tense) and *The letter was written* (after *be* to form the passive voice). However, outside the verb phrase the past participle has only one meaning.

When the *-en* form is used outside the verb phrase, it is derived from *be* + *-en*. In other words, it is derived from a passive construction; therefore, it has a passive meaning.

In the sentence in the following diagram, who *introduced* and who *read*?

SUBJECT	VERB PHRASE	COMPLETER
The student *introduced to you yesterday*	is	from Honduras.
The student (who was) introduced to you yesterday	is	from Honduras.
The book *read by me*	is	on the table.
The book (which was) read by me	is	on the table.
He	bought	a *used* car.
The *hurt* boy	cried	for help.

Like the *-ing* form, the *-en* form is often used as an adjectival before or after a noun. The difference between the use of the present participle and the past participle phrase as adjectives is that the present participle is active in meaning and the past participle is passive in meaning.

Compare the *-ing* forms and the *-en* forms in the diagram below.

The student (who is) sitting next to me is from Honduras.
       he is sitting — active
The student (who was) introduced to you is from Honduras.
       he was introduced (by someone) — passive
       someone introduced him to you — active
The book belonging (= which belongs) to me is on the table.
       it belongs to me — active
The book (which was) read by me is on the table.
       it was read by me — passive
       I read the book — active

On page 71, you saw that an *-ing* phrase at the beginning of a sentence set off with a comma may have a *because* meaning. An *-en* phrase at the beginning of a sentence has a similar meaning.

Study the following diagram. Why did the room look cheerful?

ADVERBIAL	SUBJECT	VERB PHRASE	COMPLETER
Painted bright yellow,	the room	looked	cheerful.
Being painted bright yellow			
Because it was painted bright yellow — passive			
Because someone painted it bright yellow — active			

In the English language, the verb *be,* when it is not a finite verb, is frequently omitted. Also, the present participle *being* may be omitted. Therefore a past participle phrase at the beginning of a sentence is often really a *being* phrase in which the *being* is omitted.

In the next exercise you will practice using past participle phrases with a *because* meaning.

Exercise 28   Complete each of the following sentences with a meaningful main clause. Be sure that your main clause expresses action that is caused by the past participle phrase.

EXAMPLE:

Stung by a bee, *I had a swollen arm.*

1. Hurt in the accident, he _____

2. Called by her mother, the little girl _____

_____ .

3. Caught by the police, the burglar _____

_____ .

4. Spoken by many people on earth, English _____

_____ .

5. Caught in a snowstorm, the driver _____

_____ .

6. Cured from his sickness, the patient _____

_____ .

7. Used by people all over the world, the computer _____

_____ .

8. Left behind by his master, the puppy _____

_____ .

Exercise 29   Complete the following sentences. After each blank is a verb form. Use a form of that verb, either the *-ing* or the *-en* form, to fill in each blank.

The Magic Eye

In a large store or in a railroad station, you may find a door _____ (control) by a "magic eye." When someone approaches the door, the door opens by itself. Here is how it works. The magic eye is a phototube _____ (mount) in front of the door, at one side of the approach to the door. A lamp _____ (locate) on the other side of the approach shines a beam of light onto the phototube. As long as the light falls on the tube, a current flows through it. A person _____ (approach) the door passes between the lamp and the phototube. The _____ (block) beam of light _____ (direct) towards the phototube stops the _____ (flow) current. The interruption of this current operates a relay, which closes the switch of the mechanism _____ (swing) the door open.

Solving Problems

Here again is a brief summary of those points that you have to think about when you are proofreading something that you have written. Verb forms are probably the most confusing part of the English language because they occur both inside and outside the verb phrase.

In the verb phrase the form of the verb depends on whether it is the first verb or not, or on what helping verb precedes it.

Outside the verb phrase the form depends on function (subject, object, complement, adverbial, or adjectival) and on meaning. The forms outside the verb phrase will be discussed in greater detail in Chapters 5, 7, and 9, but some pointers are given here.

More Than One Finite Verb

Each verb in the verb phrase has a specific form. The first verb has the finite form and agrees with its subject. There is only one finite verb in each verb phrase.

INCORRECT: What did he wants?
CORRECT: What did he want?

INCORRECT: Can he goes with us?
CORRECT: Can he go with us?

Confusion of Past Tense and -*en* Form

The past finite form and the -*en* form are very often the same (Example: *talk — talked — talked*), but in the case of irregular verbs they are sometimes not. (Example: *write — wrote — written*). Make sure you use the correct form.

INCORRECT: He has ate all his dinner.
CORRECT: He has eaten all his dinner.

INCORRECT: He swum in the river yesterday.
CORRECT: He swam in the river yesterday.

Confusion of Forms after *Be*

Each helping verb is followed by a specific verb form. The helping verb *be* is followed by an -*ing* form to form a progressive and a -*en* form to form a passive.

INCORRECT: Amsterdam is locating in the Netherlands.
CORRECT: Amsterdam is located in the Netherlands.

INCORRECT: The boy is watched TV.
CORRECT: The boy is watching TV.

Confusion of *-ing* and *-en* Forms as Adjectivals

When an *-ing* form is used as an adjective it is active in meaning. An *-en* form as an adjective is passive in meaning.

INCORRECT: Amsterdam, locating in the Netherlands, has a lot of canals.
CORRECT: Amsterdam, located in the Netherlands, has a lot of canals.

INCORRECT: The boy watched TV is my friend.
CORRECT: The boy watching TV is my friend.

Confusion of Infinitive and *-ing* Forms

The use of the infinitive or *-ing* form outside the verb phrase is a very confusing topic. It will be discussed in detail in Chapter 10, but there are two simple rules that usually apply: After an adjective, the infinitive form is usually used, but after a preposition, the *-ing* form is common.

INCORRECT: This lesson is *easy* understanding.
CORRECT: This lesson is *easy* to understand.

INCORRECT: I am interested *in* to study grammar.
CORRECT: I am interested *in* studying grammar.

The two exercises that follow cover what you have learned in this chapter.

Exercise 30 Each of the sentences below contains one of the errors mentioned above. Identify each error and explain what is wrong. Then rewrite the passage correctly on a separate piece of paper.

This riddle will shows how good a detective you are. Four men, Jim, John, Jack, and George, went off one day on a hunting trip, suggesting by John. Unfortunately, a quarrel sprung up and one of these law-abiding citizens shot and killed another. Each of the facts in the case are given below. See if it can been determined from these facts who the murderer and his victim were.

1. Jim did not exposed his brother's guilt.
2. George had just left the hospital on the day of the murder, after to have been in it for three days.
3. Jim had taken special care of Jack, who was handicapped and was accustomed to ride in a wheelchair. He even employing it while out in the open.

4. George had met John only five days before the murder taken place.
5. Jack had meet Jim's father only once.
6. The man who had suggested the hunting trip up was willing giving evidence against the murderer, whom he disliked.
7. The murdered man had eaten dinner on the previous night with one of the men who did not customarily played golf with John.

Note: To find out who the murderer and his victim are, do Exercise 31.

Exercise 31

The following exercise tests your ability to relate structure to meaning. Read the passage at least three times. Following the passage are some incomplete sentences. Complete the sentences with information from the passage. Your answers should be true according to the information and grammatically correct.

From the first statement, it is clear that Jim's brother is the murderer, and Jim himself is therefore innocent. Who is Jim's brother?

Having met Jim's father only once, Jack cannot be Jim's brother, so Jack is not guilty. Willing to give evidence against the murderer, John, the leader of the trip, cannot be the murderer. Therefore George must be the murderer.

Now let's track down the victim.

John, the leader, is still alive, since he wanted to convict the murderer. George, the murderer, obviously cannot be the victim. This means that the murdered man must have been either Jim or Jack.

Since Jack is handicapped and since George has known John for only five days, they are the men with whom John did not customarily play golf. Consequently, one of them must have eaten with the murdered man on the previous night. George was in the hospital, so it was not he. Therefore Jack must have eaten with the victim. This makes it clear that Jack is not the victim. Since George and John have already been eliminated, this leaves only Jim to be the man who was murdered. In short, George shot Jim.

1. Jim's brother is guilty because _____

_____ .

2. Because his brother is guilty, Jim is _____

_____ .

3. Jack cannot be Jim's brother because _____

_____ .

4. Because Jack is not Jim's brother, he _____

_____ .

5. Because _____ , John cannot be the murderer.

6. Having eliminated Jim, Jack, and John, we _____ _____ .

7. The fact that John is willing to convict the victim proves that _____ .

8. George is still alive because _____ _____ .

9. Either _____ or _____ was the victim.

10. Being handicapped, Jack does not _____ _____ .

11. Having met John only five days before the murder, George _____ _____ .

12. Because _____ , George had not eaten with the victim the night before the murder.

13. Because we know that George did not eat with the victim the night before the murder, we know that _____ _____ .

14. Having eaten with the victim, Jack cannot _____ _____ .

15. Having eliminated George, John, and Jack, we know _____ _____ .

Assignment for Writing

Reading

Read the ad called "Road Test" several times until you have a general understanding about its content. Do not look up words in a dictionary unless it is necessary for a general understanding of the content.

Group Discussion

1. Who wrote this advertisement?

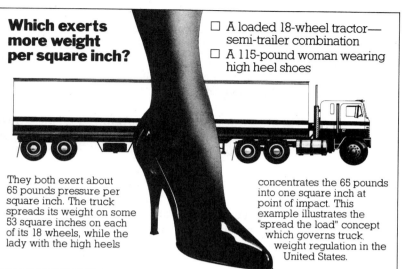

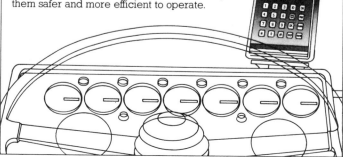

2. Why, in your opinion, did this foundation put this ad in many American magazines?
3. Do you believe that some Americans may complain about big trucks on the road? Why, or why not?
4. Some people might complain about trucks damaging the roads. Which part of the ad tries to convince the reader that trucks do not damage roads?
5. Some people might complain about truck drivers driving fast and wildly. Which part of the ad tries to convince the reader that this is not so?
6. There are also two parts that try to convince the reader that trucks are necessary for the American economy. Which parts are they?
7. Which ones of the following pairs of sentences are general statements and which ones give specific facts and details? Which ones are the most convincing to the reader? Why?

   a. A loaded eighteen-wheel tractor semi-trailer combination distributes its weight equally on its eighteen wheels.
   b. A truck spreads its weight on some fifty-three square inches on each of its eighteen wheels, while a woman in high heels concentrates sixty-five pounds into one square inch at point of impact.

   a. Trucks transport a lot of food items.
   b. Trucks transport virtually all raw milk from farm to processing dairy.

   a. Trucks are monitored by computers for driver performance, vehicle performance, miles per gallon, average miles per hour, total trip time, and gross weight.
   b. Trucks are monitored closely.

   a. The American trucking industry employs 7,000,000 people.
   b. Many people are employed by the American trucking industry.

8. In two sentences, state why the trucking industry is essential to the American economy, in the opinion of the ad writer.
9. At the bottom of the ad, there is a part that sums up most of the facts. Note that it uses many strong adjectives, such as *finest* and *vital*. Which other adjectives are used?

Writing

Pretend that you are a public relations officer at the American Trucking Association Foundation. You have just received a letter from an angry citizen who complains about trucks. He says that trucks damage the roads and that all truck drivers are wild. He wants to get rid of most of the trucks in the United States.

Write a polite letter to this person. Try to convince him that trucks do not really damage the roads and that not all truck drivers are wild. Also convince him that the trucking industry is essential to the American economic system.

Make sure that you sound convincing by supporting your general statements with enough examples, facts, and details. Then write a strong and convincing conclusion.

Suggestions for Writing

Not every writer writes in the same way, but probably most writers do a lot of rewriting before they are satisfied with the final product. (This textbook, for example, has been rewritten at least five times.)

Writing in your own language and writing in a foreign language are probably very similar. However, there is one major difference: In your language you don't have to think about each little detail so much. The spelling, the grammar, and the sentence structure come naturally to you. In a foreign language, each of these points can be a major obstacle. You should not let these obstacles bother you during the whole writing process. The following suggestions may be helpful to you in your writing assignment.

First of all, try to think in English, but when you first start writing, you should not worry about finding the right words, phrases, and expressions. You might even want to jot down some unfamiliar expressions in your own language. It is not even important to have good grammar at this point. The main thing is to get your ideas on paper.

After you have a general idea about what you are going to write, you should plan the organization. Like the first paragraph in a business letter, the first paragraph should get the attention of the reader. Those first few lines are very important. Your reader will either want to go on reading or want to stop reading. What do you want your reader to do? Your last paragraph should sum up your information.

Each of the remaining paragraphs should be logically organized. You don't want to confuse your reader by talking about three or four different things at the same time. However, you do want your reader to learn something. Look at each paragraph separately and ask yourself two questions: (1) Can my reader easily figure out what I am talking about? (2) Are there enough details and facts to sound convincing to my reader?

Proofreading

After you have written and rewritten your essay and you are satisfied with its content, organization, and supporting details, it is time to proofread carefully. Read through the composition several times, each time looking for one or two specific errors. The points below are important.

1. Is each sentence capitalized and punctuated correctly?

2. Is each sentence a complete sentence? Does each sentence have a subject and a finite verb? Does it have an object?
3. Look at each verb form that you have used. Identify it (infinitive, *-ing, -en,* or finite) and make sure that you have used it correctly.
4. Are the articles used correctly?
5. How about the prepositions?
6. Is the spelling correct?

When you are sure that there are no grammar errors, rewrite the composition according to your instructor's specifications.

3

The Compound Sentence

Review/Preview

In Chapter 1 you saw that longer sentences are often made up of two or more short sentences. In this chapter you will see how two or more sentences may be combined to form a *compound sentence*. A compound sentence is a sentence that consists of two or more main clauses. These main clauses are joined in one of two basic ways: with a conjunction or with a semicolon.

- -

Main Clauses Joined with a Conjunction

	SENTENCE 1	SENTENCE 2
	John went to class every day.	He studied very hard.
Coordinate conjunction	John went to class every day,	*and* he studied very hard.
Correlative conjunction	*Not only* did John go to class every day,	*but* he *also* studied very hard.

- -

Two main clauses (or parts of main clauses) can be joined with a *coordinate conjunction* or a *correlative conjunction*.

	SENTENCE 1	SENTENCE 2
	John went to class every day.	He studied very hard.
Semicolon	John went to class every day;	he studied very hard.
Semicolon + conjunctive adverb	John went to class every day;	*moreover,* he studied very hard.

Main clauses can be joined with a semicolon (;). In this case a conjunctive adverb is used to make clear the relationship between the clauses.

Grammar and Meaning

Coordinate and Correlative Conjunctions

There are only a few coordinate and correlative conjunctions, so you may want to memorize them so that you will be able to recognize them and distinguish them easily from other types of connecting words.

Coordinate conjunctions:	and, but, or, nor, for, so, yet
Correlative conjunctions:	not only . . . but also, both . . . and, either . . . or, neither . . . nor

Although the seven coordinate conjunctions and four sets of correlative conjunctions are grammatically similar, these conjunctions express different meaning relationships between clauses or parts of clauses.

First we will examine their grammatical similarities, mainly the punctuation mechanics, and then we will discover their differences in meaning.

Punctuation Rules for Compound Sentences

Most of the coordinate and all of the correlative conjunctions may connect either complete main clauses or parts of main clauses, for example: two subordinate clauses, two phrases, or two words. In the examples below, the sentence parts being connected are in italics.

Two complete main clauses are separated with a comma.	*John went to school,* but *Mary stayed at home.* Not only *did I read the material,* but *I* also *memorized it.*

Two parts of main clauses (subjects, predicates, completers, and so on) are not separated with a comma.

I *studied very hard* yet *failed the test.*
Both *John* and *Mary* went to school.
Neither *John* nor *Mary* stayed home.
What you do or *what you say* is your own business.
John stayed home because he wanted to *study* and *take a nap.*

If more than two parts are joined, there is a comma between items and a conjunction and a comma between the last two items.

John, Mary, and *Peter* went to the movies.
Please explain *what your plans are, where you are going,*
    and *how you are going to travel.*
X, Y, and *Z* are letters frequently used in algebra.
The colors of the American flag are *red, white,* and *blue.*

- -

The rules are as follows: (1) two complete main clauses joined by these conjunctions have a comma before the conjunction; (2) if the conjunction joins two parts of a clause, there is no comma; (3) however, if more than two parts are joined, for example three or more items, there is a comma between items, and a comma and a conjunction between the last two items. This is called *items-in-a-series.*

Exercise 1   Punctuate and capitalize correctly.

baboons live on the ground during the day but at night they sleep high up in the trees they have not only strong arms and legs but also sharp teeth so they are ready to fight off enemies baboons live in troops and they hunt together for food the babies either cling underneath their mother or ride on her back both the mother and the other grownups in a troop help look after the young ones

Exercise 2   Punctuate and capitalize correctly.

the roly-poly, black-and-white giant panda looks like a walking toy and many toys have been made to look like it it is related to both bears and raccoons but it comes from only one place in the world it can be found only in a bamboo forest in China and there it eats nothing but bamboo shoots

Agreement Rules for Compound Subjects

As you know, the finite verb must agree with the subject. If the subject is compound, you must examine the meaning of the conjunction to see whether the subject is singular or plural.

ADDITION	John *and* Mary are students.	two persons
	Both John *and* Mary attend a university.	two persons
BUT:	My roommate *and* friend is from Venezuela.	my roommate and friend refer to the same person
CHOICE	John *or* Mary is going to help.	one person is going to help
	Either John *or* Mary is going to help.	
	Neither John *nor* Mary is going to help.	
BUT:	*Either* my parents *or* my sister is coming to visit.	the finite verb agrees with the subject nearer to it
	Neither my sister *nor* my parents are coming to visit.	

When the conjunction expresses addition, the subject is of course plural. When the conjunction expresses a choice, the finite verb usually agrees with the item nearer to it.

Exercise 3   Find the subject in each sentence and fill in the blank with the correct form of the finite verb in the present tense. Use a form of the verb that is in parentheses.

Soundproofing (be) _____ a type of insulation. For example, either sound-absorbing or sound-deadening materials (be) _____ placed on walls and ceilings to reduce echoes. Both the quality of a speaker's voice and the quality of music (be) _____ improved by reducing objectionable echoes. For this purpose, hair felt covered with burlap, perforated fiberboard, corkboard, or a special type of acoustical plaster and tile (can) _____ be used. Heavy cloth curtains and upholstered furniture (be) _____ also effective. Each of these materials (work) _____ to reduce echoes because each (contain) _____ a large number of small air passages. As sound waves (penetrate) _____ these passges, a part of their energy (be) _____ converted by friction into heat energy.

Parallelism

In the English language, it is important to achieve overall balance in any written entity, not only in a book, chapter, composition, or letter but also in each paragraph and each sentence.

In order to achieve balance in a compound sentence, you must join items that are *parallel,* which means they have to be of the same grammatical construction. For example, both parts must be sentences, clauses, phrases, gerunds, *to*-infinitives, nouns, adjectives, adverbs, and so on.

- -

John and Mary are students.	and	‖ John ‖ Mary
Not only do they study, but they also work part-time.	not only but also	‖ (do) they study ‖ they work part-time
John is a good student and works hard.	and	‖ is a good student ‖ works hard
Mary enjoys both studying and working	both and	‖ studying ‖ working
They hope to graduate next year and find a job.	and	‖ graduate next year ‖ find a job
Mary wants to work in a large company or in a small retail business.	or	‖ in a large company ‖ in a small retail business.
John doesn't know what he wants to do or where he wants to work.	or	‖ what he wants to do ‖ where he wants to work

- -

One unusual construction may occur with the conjunction *and.* If *and* connects two sentences in which the verb phrases are the same, the verb phrase in the second clause may be deleted. Usually there is a comma to replace the verb.

- -

Mary *studies* French, and John *studies* Spanish.
Mary *studies* French, and John, Spanish.

I *wanted to go* swimming, and my friend *wanted to go* sailing.
I *wanted to go* swimming, and my friend, sailing.

- -

Exercise 4   Underline the parallel items in the following passage, as in the first sentence.

Another type of soundproofing reduces the sound transmitted from room to room by vibration of the <u>walls</u> and <u>floors</u>. Sound waves make these surfaces vibrate and produce other sounds. This type of sound transmission is difficult to overcome. In general, such heavier building materials as brick, stone, and concrete produce less vibration than lighter materials like wood and fiberboard. Fiberboard reduces echoes, but it does not effectively stop the passage of sound from room to room.

Floor coverings like thick carpet, heavy linoleum, rubber tile, and cork tile help insulate against sound-producing vibrations. In factories, steel springs and rubber or cork pads supporting machinery greatly reduce sound transmission through a building by vibration.

Exercise 5   In the following sentences correct the items that are not parallel.

1. His job is teaching the advanced classes, coordinating the program, and selection of teaching materials.
2. My roommate wants to move to an apartment with more living space and having more closet space.
3. My history class was interesting, exciting, and could be easily understood.
4. Our instructor told us to prepare this exercise for tomorrow and that we should be ready for a quiz.
5. I don't care about his private life and what he does in his free time.

Exercise 6   Complete the following sentences in your own words. Make sure you use parallel structure.

1. What you do or _____ is your own business.
2. I like ice-skating, and my friend _____ .
3. Not only the class but also _____ was difficult.
4. To lose weight, you must either _____ or _____
   _____ .
5. I didn't enjoy the movie, nor _____ .
6. Both my parents and _____ are coming to visit me.
7. He is crying either because he hurt himself or _____ .
8. Not only _____ the course, but I also learned from it.

Meanings of Coordinate Conjunctions

You have just seen the basic similarities in structure among the coordinating conjunctions and correlative conjunctions. In this section, we will examine the differences in meaning among these conjunctions.

Some of the coordinate conjunctions (*and, but,* and *or*) have more than one meaning, and some of their meanings overlap.

And and So

Addition	I bought two shirts, *and* Mary bought a skirt. This week we had one test *and* two quizzes. John *and* Mary are going to the movies.
Time sequence	We went to the store *and* the movies. John entered, *and* Peter left the room.
Result	He fell down *and* broke his arm. I studied hard, *and* I passed the test.
	The weather is bad, *so* we will stay home. I have a class in a few minutes, *so* I must hurry.

And may express addition, time, and result. *So* expresses only result. It has basically the same meaning as *therefore*.

Exercise 7   Complete the sentences in your own words.

1. I wanted to make a long distance call, so _____

_____ .

2. I dialed 0, and _____ .

3. I wanted to make a collect call, so _____

_____ .

4. The operator asked me if it was a person-to-person call, and _____

_____ .

5. No one answered the phone, so _____

_____ .

For

Reason	We must hurry, *for* we are late. We cannot buy a house, *for* we are poor. I am tired, *for* I went to bed late last night.
NOTE:	I am tired *because* I went to bed late last night. *Because* I went to bed late last night, I am tired.
INCORRECT:	*For* I am tired, I went to bed late last night.

The coordinate conjunction *for* does not occur much in everyday American English, but it does occur occasionally in the formal written language.

For has the same meaning as *because,* but grammatically it is different. *For* introduces a main clause, and *because* introduces an adverbial clause of reason. An adverbial clause can come at the beginning of a sentence, but a *for*-clause cannot.

Sometimes international students confuse the meanings of *for* and *so.* Remember that they are coordinate conjunctions and can occur only between two related main clauses. In other words, there is only one possible way of ordering the clauses. The clause after *for* expresses a reason and the clause after *so* expresses a result. The clauses may therefore be ordered only as follows:

[result],	*for*	[reason]
I am studying hard,	for	I will have a test tomorrow.

[reason],	*so*	[result]
I will have a test tomorrow,	so	I am studying hard.

Note: And, but, yet, or, and *nor* are frequently used to connect parts of clauses, but *for* and *so* can connect only complete main clauses.

Exercise 8   Complete the following sentences in your own words.

1. I am happy, for _____ .

2. I am homesick, so _____ .

3. _____ , so I got an A on the test.

4. _____ , for I studied very hard.

5. I will write my parents today, for _____

_____ .

6. I will write my parents today, so _____

_____ .

7. I did not attend class yesterday, for _____

_____ .

8. I did not attend class yesterday, so _____

_____ .

But and Yet

- -

Concession   I felt sick, *but* I went to school.
                  I studied hard, *but* I failed the test.

                  I am very tired, *yet* I cannot sleep.
                  He is poor *but* happy.
                  He is poor *yet* happy.

Contrast   This room is not dark *but* light.
                  John went to school, *but* I stayed home.

INCORRECT: John went to school, *yet* I stayed home.

- -

But can express both concession and contrast. A concession expresses something that is different from what one expects. If a person is very poor, for example, you expect him or her to be unhappy, not happy. In a contrast expression, something is basically restated in a negative or opposite expression. Example: not rich = poor. Note that *yet* can express only concession, not contrast.

Exercise 9   Complete the following sentences in your own words.

    1. The sun is shining, yet _____ .

    2. I wanted to go on a picnic, but _____

       _____ .

    3. The park is not very far away, but _____

       _____ .

    4. I like to ride my bike, yet _____ .

    5. There is a thunderstorm watch, but _____

       _____ .

Exercise 10   Complete the sentences meaningfully from information in the following situation: You went to the bank yesterday. You could not cash a check because you left your I.D. at home.

    1. Yesterday I went to the bank, for _____

       _____ .

    2. I walked up to the window, and _____

       _____ .

3. The teller wanted to see my driver's license, so ＿＿＿＿＿＿＿＿＿＿

＿＿＿＿＿＿＿＿＿＿＿＿＿＿＿＿＿＿＿＿＿＿＿＿ .

4. When I put my hand in my pocket, I noticed that I had forgotten my
I.D., and ＿＿＿＿＿＿＿＿＿＿＿＿＿＿＿＿＿＿＿＿ .

5. I was not able to cash a check, for ＿＿＿＿＿＿＿＿＿＿＿＿＿＿＿

＿＿＿＿＿＿＿＿＿＿＿＿＿＿＿＿＿＿＿＿＿＿＿＿ .

6. I needed some cash, but ＿＿＿＿＿＿＿＿＿＿＿＿＿＿＿＿＿＿ .

7. I knew the teller was not allowed to cash my check without a proper
I.D., yet ＿＿＿＿＿＿＿＿＿＿＿＿＿＿＿＿＿＿＿＿ .

8. I was angry at the teller, but ＿＿＿＿＿＿＿＿＿＿＿＿＿＿＿＿

＿＿＿＿＿＿＿＿＿＿＿＿＿＿＿＿＿＿＿＿＿＿＿＿ .

Or and Nor

Choice	John may be in the library, *or* he may be home.
	John *or* Mary *is* going to the store.
	John *or* his parents *are* at home.
Negative choice	Mary does not know where John is, *nor do I.*
	We will not call them, *nor will we* write them.
Negative condition	John must study, *or* he will fail the course.
	Don't drive so fast, *or* you will get a ticket.
	Don't drive so fast, *or else* you will get a ticket.

After *nor,* there is inversion of the subject and the finite verb (*we do* becomes *do we*). (See Chapter 1.)

When *or* expresses a negative condition, it is also followed by *else*. *Or else* expresses a meaning similar to *otherwise*.

Exercise 11   Complete the following sentences in your own words.

1. Do you want to go to the movies, or ＿＿＿＿＿＿＿＿＿＿＿＿

＿＿＿＿＿＿＿＿＿＿＿＿＿＿＿＿＿＿＿＿＿＿＿＿ .

2. Mary did not want to eat in the cafeteria, nor ＿＿＿＿＿＿＿＿

＿＿＿＿＿＿＿＿＿＿＿＿＿＿＿＿＿＿＿＿＿＿＿＿ .

3. John wanted to eat at Peking Restaurant or ＿＿＿＿＿＿＿＿＿

＿＿＿＿＿＿＿＿＿＿＿＿＿＿＿＿＿＿＿＿＿＿＿＿ .

4. Neither John nor _____ has arrived yet.

5. Neither John nor _____ have arrived yet.

Exercise 12   Rewrite the following passage and combine the sentences into compound sentences where possible.

The tiniest of all birds is the hummingbird. Princess Helena's hummingbird is the smallest. It is less than three inches long. A hummingbird's nest is no bigger than half a walnut shell. The eggs are no bigger than peas.

These beautiful little creatures feed on insects. They feed on the nectar from flowers. These birds are very small. They can go deep inside a flower. They have very long beaks and coiled tongues. Hummingbirds move their wings very fast. The wings make a humming sound. These tiny creatures can stay still in the air. They can move backward. They can move forward. They can move sideways. They are like helicopters.

Their feathers are very beautiful. People compare them to jewels. They may also have long tails. They may have crests. They may have ruffs.

Exercise 13   From the following information, compose a few paragraphs describing the mockingbird. Try to use as many coordinating conjunctions as possible. Make sure you punctuate correctly and keep items parallel. Also make sure that subjects and verbs agree and are inverted where necessary.

Topic	
sentence	The song goes "Listen to the Mockingird...."
Song	worth listening to, imitates other birds' songs, something original is added
Built	slender, gray, white patches on the wings and tail
Length	9–11 inches
	adult bird and young similar
Location	common in most of the South of the United States
	nest around homes
Nests	bulky, made of coarse twigs, weed stems, shreds, string, rags; in shrubs, thickets, vines; near houses; 1–15 ft. off the ground, rarely higher
Food	beetles, grasshoppers, and other insects; some wild fruit in season, grape and holly preferred

Meanings of Correlative Conjunctions

The four sets of correlative conjunctions (*both ... and, not only ... but also, either ... or, neither ... nor*) have meanings and grammatical properties that are very similar to those of the coordinate conjunctions that were just discussed. They may be used to connect complete sentences or parts of sentences. These conjunctions consist of two parts, and they are used instead of the coordinate conjunctions for more emphasis.

Both...And and Not Only...But Also

Addition   *Both* John *and* Mary are going to the movies.
They hope that *both* the story *and* the acting are good.
The movie *both* interested *and* fascinated them.
Both jogging *and* swimming are my hobbies.

Not only did they like the acting, *but* they *also* liked the story.
The movie was *not only* interesting *but also* fascinating.

In the first sentence the verb is plural because the subject is compound. Note that the items joined are parallel and that there is inversion of subject and finite verb after *not only* when it precedes a complete main clause.

Either...Or and Neither...Nor

Choice   *Either* John *or* Mary was at home.
Either John *or* his parents were at home.
Either his parents *or* John was at home.

Negative choice   *Neither* John *nor* Mary wants to go to the movies.
I want *neither* to see him *nor* speak to him.
I like *neither* jogging *nor* swimming.

Can you explain the *subject-verb agreement* rules in the first three sentences? How are the items *parallel* in all the sentences?

Exercise 14   Combine the following sentences with the correlative conjunction given in parentheses. Make sure (1) that you use parallel structures, (2) that your verb agrees with the subject, and (3) that you invert the subject and verb when necessary.

Note: You may change some words if it is necessary.

1. I want to take Math 105 next semester. I want to take Economics 103 next semester. (either...or)

2. Math 103 is not a required course for my major. I do not need Economics 102. (neither . . . nor)

3. I want to take some required courses. I want to take some elective courses. (both . . . and)

4. I want to live off-campus next semester. I want to find a comfortable apartment. (not only . . . but also)

5. My friend is looking for an apartment within walking distance. I also want to find an apartment within walking distance. (both . . . and)

6. I do not like living in the dorms. I am not happy with the food in the cafeteria. (neither . . . nor)

7. My friend wants to cook his own meals. I want to cook my own meals. (both . . . and)

8. We are going to cook food from our native country. We are going to invite friends to have dinner with us. (not only . . . but also)

9. However, I am not looking forward to doing the dishes every night. My friend does not enjoy cleaning up the apartment every day. (neither . . . nor)

10. We will take turns doing the work we don't like. We will do the dishes and the housework together. (either . . . or)

Exercise 15   The ad on page 96 for *The Atlantic,* a current events magazine, contains many incomplete sentences. Rewrite the ad with complete sentences. Use as many compound sentences as you can. Use each coordinate conjunction (*and, but, or, nor, for, so, yet*) and each pair of correlative conjunctions (*not only . . . but also; both . . . and; either . . . or; neither . . . nor*) at least once.

Semicolon and Conjunctive Adverbs

When two sentences are closely related in meaning, they may be separated by a semicolon instead of a period. Like a period, a semicolon indicates that a sentence is complete, but unlike a period, a semicolon indicates that the sentence before the semicolon and the sentence after the semicolon have something in common in meaning. The sentences are logically related. Note that the sentence after the semicolon does not start with a capital letter.

CURRENT EVENTS

You've read the paper and your weekly newsmagazines. But still, you want more than reporting...more than quick commentary.

You turn to The Atlantic.

Independent. Intelligent. Interested, as you are, in understanding tough issues. World economy, US-Soviet relations, Lebanon — the whole kaleidoscope of current events.

Explore new perspectives on Freud and psychoanalysis, the latest wave of immigration, raising children, and more. Examine issues with important writers and thinkers like Jane Jacobs, James Fallows, Mario Vargas Llosa.

The Atlantic is challenge, excitement.

Plus fiction, humor, and superb coverage of the arts. Every month The Atlantic delivers it all in stimulating, clear prose.

Subscribe now and save 50% off the single copy price and 34% off the basic subscription rate. Just fill out the order card in this issue and mail today.

Don't miss out on quality coverage of the important events and ideas of our time.

The Atlantic
Ahead of the times

EXAMPLE:

The washing machine broke; she called the repair man.
John fell down; he broke his arm.

INCORRECT: The washing machine broke; she went to school.
INCORRECT: John fell down; it started to rain.

Exercise 16   If the sentences are logically related, replace the period with a semicolon and the capital letter with a lower-case letter.

1. Babies are born with the sense of touch. The sense of smell develops immediately after birth.

2. A fly is not a fly, nor is a glowworm a worm. They are both beetles.

3. Unidentical twins are called fraternal twins. Quadruplets occur only once in every million births.

4. Halloween is a popular holiday in the United States. Children especially enjoy it.

5. School chalk is not chalk. It is plaster of Paris.

6. Water literally runs off a duck's back. It takes seven billion fog particles to make a teaspoon of water.

7. The weasel, a small, reddish-brown animal, turns white in frigid, cold climates. The cheetah is the world's speediest four-legged animal.

8. Celluloid was the first plastic. It was used to make billiard balls.

Note: When the second main clause amplifies or explains the first clause, a colon may be used instead of a semicolon.

EXAMPLE:
Punctuation marks are important: they help us understand a sentence.

Punctuation Rules and Position of Conjunctive Adverbs

To make the logical relationship between two thoughts or ideas more clear, certain adverbs can be used. These adverbs are often called *sentence adverbs* or *conjunctive adverbs* because they modify a whole sentence and show a meaning relationship between two sentences. Conjunctive adverbs are words or expressions like *however, therefore, moreover, besides, in addition,* and *indeed.* Although conjunctive adverbs and coordinate conjunctions are grammatically different, they often have similar meanings, for example, *so/therefore, and/besides, but/however.*

John went to school, so he was not home yesterday.
John went to school; therefore, he was not home yesterday.

John went to school, and he studied hard.
John went to school. Besides, he studied hard.

John went to school, but Mary stayed home yesterday.
John went to school; however, Mary stayed at home yesterday.

Grammatically, there are two main differences between coordinate conjunctions and conjunctive adverbs. First, the punctuation rules are different. Second, the position of adverbs is flexible, but the position of conjunctions is not. Look at the following diagram. As you can see, sentences with conjunctive adverbs are much more flexible in both punctuation and position of the adverb than sentences with coordinate or correlative conjunctions.

Summary of Punctuation Rules for Compound Sentences

- -

	Explanation
He did not attend the meeting, *but* he did send a report. *Not only* did he attend the meeting, *but* he *also* gave a report.	The coordinate or correlative conjunction comes between the two main clauses. A comma usually precedes the conjunction.
He did not attend the meeting. He sent a report. He did not attend the meeting. *However,* he sent a report. He did not attend the meeting. He sent a report, *however.* He did not attend the meeting. He did, *however,* send a report.	Two closely related sentences may be separated by a period. A conjunctive adverb may come at the beginning, at the end, or in the middle of the second sentence.
He did not attend the meeting; he sent a report. He did not attend the meeting; *however,* he sent a report. He did not attend the meeting; he sent a report, *however.* He did not attend the meeting; he did, *however,* send a report.	Two closely related sentences may also be separated by a semicolon. Note that the word at the beginning of the second clause is not capitalized.

- -

Note: To avoid stringy sentences, it is best to use a semicolon only once in a sentence.

Exercise 17   Punctuate and capitalize correctly.

alabaster is a kind of stone it looks like marble however it is much softer it is used for both statues and vases

there are two kinds of alabaster on the one hand there is a white or delicately shaded variety it is semi-translucent besides it has a pearly luster this variety is a kind of gypsum and is chiefly found in Italy however some comes from Spain England and elsewhere on the other hand there is the variety called *Oriental alabaster* or *onyx marble* this kind is deposited as stalagmites in caves it is a calcium carbonate mineral and is found in Italy and in other countries on the Mediterranean Sea it is much harder than the other variety it was therefore often used in sculpture by the ancient Greeks and Romans

Meanings of Conjunctive Adverbs

There are many conjunctive adverbs that are used often, and you probably are familiar with their meanings. Other conjunctive adverbs, however, express very limited and specific logical relationships between sentences. Below you will find examples of conjunctive adverbs that occur frequently in American English.

Addition, Similarity, and Specification

- -

Addition   I write my parents every week; *moreover,* I call them once a month.
I prefer to write letters; *besides,* it is a lot cheaper.
Telephone calls are very expensive; *in addition,* the connection is not always good.
I can express myself better in writing; *furthermore,* it is a lot cheaper than calling.
I like to write letters; I *also* like to receive them.
I like to write letters to my parents, *but* I *also* like to call them.

- -

All the conjunctive adverbs above express the same relationship as *and,* but they have a more specific or stronger meaning. They are synonyms, so they may be interchanged. *Note: Also* is often used together with other conjunctions.

- -

Similarity   He did not do very well in his math course; *similarly,* he did very poorly in chemistry.
He did not attend his math classes very regularly; *likewise,* he was reported for excessive absences in his chemistry class.

- -

When we want to express not only that two things are added together but also that they are very similar or parallel to each other, we may use *similarly* or *likewise*. These adverbs mean *and in exactly the same manner....* These adverbs are therefore much more limited in meaning than *moreover, furthermore,* and so on.

Specification   He is a superior student; *in fact,* he has a 4.00 average.
He never relaxes; *as a matter of fact,* he doesn't even watch television.
He studies very much. *Indeed,* he never goes out. (*Indeed* is not used much in this sense in American English.)

When a general statement is followed by a specific statement that supports the general statement, the specific one may be introduced by one of the above adverbs. In other words, these adverbs are very limited in meaning, and can be used only when the second sentence gives some specific proof that the first one is true.

Contradictory   He looks very honest; *actually,* he is a thief.
specification   He looks very poor; *actually,* he is the wealthiest man in this city.
He looks very honest; *in fact,* he is a thief.
He looks very poor; *in fact,* he is the wealthiest man in this city.
INCORRECT: He is a superior student; *actually,* he has a 4.00 average.

When a general statement is followed by a specific statement that contradicts the general statement, the specific one is introduced by *actually,* which means *but the real truth is that.... In fact* may also be used in this case, but *actually* cannot be used to express specification.

Exercise 18   Complete the following sentences in your own words.

1. When Mohammed arrived in America, he felt homesick; moreover,

_____ .

2. He had trouble adapting to the climate; furthermore, _____

_____ .

3. He did not like American food; in fact, _____

_____ .

4. He found everything very expensive here; as a matter of fact, ____

_____ .

5. He was afraid that his English was not good enough; actually, _____

   _____ .

6. Fortunately, he has gotten used to living in America; in fact, _____

   _____ .

7. He has made friends with a lot of American students; besides, _____

   _____ .

8. He wants to finish his studies here; in addition, _____

   _____ .

Exercise 19   In a few paragraphs, describe the adjustments you had to make when your life changed, for example, when you moved to America or started college. Try to use as many conjunctive adverbs of addition, similarity, specification, and contradictory specification as you can. Make sure you use the adverbs logically and punctuate the sentences correctly.

Concession and Contrast

- -

Concession   This car is very old; *however,* it runs well.
This car does not look very pretty; *nevertheless,* I am very proud of it.
The seats of the car are torn; *nonetheless,* they are very comfortable.
I can afford to buy a new car; *still,* I want to keep this old one.
I can afford to buy a new car, *but* I *still* want to keep my old one.

- -

The concession adverbs have a meaning similar to *but* and *yet.* Concession means that something is different from what one would normally expect. If the weather is cold, for example, we normally expect people to wear a coat outside. To go outside without a coat is different from what one would normally expect.

Note: The adverb *still* may be used together with other conjunctions.

- -

Contrast   *On the one hand,* he is trying to save money.
On the other hand, he buys a lot of new tapes each week.
His roommate, *in contrast,* never spends money carelessly.
On the contrary, he has been able to save enough money to buy a new car soon.

- -

There are several adverbs that express a kind of opposite, just as does the second meaning of *but.* Usually *on the one hand* and *on the other hand* are used together.

Result

The dorms are very noisy; *therefore,* I would like to move off campus.
There are no kitchens in our dorms; *as a result,* we must eat in the cafeteria.
My native food is very spicy. *Consequently,* I find American food very bland.
I am still a freshman; *thus* I am not allowed to move off-campus.
My friend is a graduate student; *hence* he is allowed to live off-campus.
We are students at this university; *in consequence,* we must obey its rules.

The result adverbs have meanings similar to *so.*
Notes: Hence and *in consequence* are very formal and not used much in everyday American English. *Thus* may be used together with other conjunctions.

Exercise 20   Rewrite the following passage. Try to use different conjunctive adverbs of addition, concession, and result. You must use at least five conjunctive adverbs.

Annie Oakley was the world's most famous sharpshooter. Her father died when she was young. She helped support the family by hunting rabbits and quail. By the age of fifteen she was able to outshoot professional marksmen. She became a star with Buffalo Bill's Wild West Show in 1885. She could do all sorts of tricks. For example, from a distance of thirty paces, she could shoot a playing card in two with the thin edge held toward her. She could hit dimes that had been thrown in the air. She once shattered 4,772 out of 5,000 glass balls before they touched the ground.

When she was touring Europe, Kaiser Wilhelm, the emperor of Germany, lit a cigarette and asked Annie to shoot it from his lips. The Kaiser's aides were horrified. Annie stayed calm. She stepped back 100 paces. She took careful aim and fired. She didn't miss!

Negative Condition

Like the second meaning of *or,* the conjunctive adverb *otherwise* explains what will happen if a certain condition is not met.
Note: The comma after *otherwise* is generally omitted.

You must attend class; *otherwise* you will be reported for excessive absences.
You must put on a warm coat; *otherwise* you will catch a cold.

Time

There are many adverbs that show a time relationship. They may show what happened next, before, or at the same time; they may also express a relative order. Some of these are not really adverbs but adverbial time phrases.

Note: Many adverbs of time, especially those of subsequent time, do not need to be set off with commas.

- -

Subsequent time

Boil the water; *next* add the rice.
Cut up the meat; *then* clean the vegetables.
Stir-fry the meat; *later* add the vegetables.
A few minutes later, turn down the fire.
Subsequently, add the spices.
After that, stir in the cooked rice.
Afterwards, you can eat a delicious meal.

Previous time

He lived in New York for three years. *Before that* he lived in Washington.
He is now attending Harvard. *Previously,* he was enrolled at Princeton.
He is now a law student. *Formerly,* he majored in political science.

Simultaneous time

He was working as a bookkeeper. *Meanwhile,* he went to school to get a degree in business.
He attended university from 1981 to 1985. *During the same time,* he worked as a bookkeeper.
He majored in business. *At the same time,* he took some courses in computer science.
He graduated last fall. *In the meantime,* he has found a better job.

Relative order

First of all, you pick up your registration packet.
In the first place, it is important that you fill out the trial schedule.
Secondly, you go see your advisor.
In the second place, you go see your advisor.
In the last place, you must go to the coliseum.
At the end, you have your I.D. picture taken.
Finally, you pay your fees.

- -

Exercise 21

Look at the diagram on page 104 showing how to tie a four-in-hand knot and explain to your classmates how to do it. Use as many conjunctive adverbs of time as possible. Some helpful vocabulary is given below:

1. place tie around your neck; narrow end shorter than wide end
2. cross wide end over narrow end
3. move wide end around narrow end
4. move wide end behind narrow end
5. continue wrapping wide end
6. bring it over narrow end

7. bring it up under the neckband
8. pull the wide end through the center loop
9. shape the fullness of the wide end just below the knot to form a "dimple" or small pleat
10. slide up the knot to tighten it/the knot becomes smoother and neater

Follow these steps to tie a four-in-hand knot

Example and Paraphrasing

In an example, a general statement is illustrated. In a paraphrase, the same thing is said with different words. Sometimes, when the speaker or writer is not sure that a sentence is clear by itself, the same information can be restated with different words. Such a restatement is often introduced by *in other words.*

- -

Example   There are many ways to improve your English; *for example,* you can watch television. There are many good programs on television; *for instance,* PBS has many educational programs.

Paraphrase   Attending class is mandatory; *in other words,* a student will be penalized for absences.

- -

Exercise 22   The following passage contains short, choppy sentences. Rewrite it, including at least five transition words (coordinate conjunctions, correlative conjunctions, or conjunctive adverbs) to make the passage more coherent.

Academy Awards are prizes given each year by the Academy of Motion Picture Arts and Sciences for the best performances. They are given for other work contributing to motion pictures.

The Academy has other purposes. It represents to the public the point of view of the creators of films. It promotes the art and science of films. It focuses public attention on the best in motion pictures. It is best known for its Academy Awards.

The Academy has eighteen branches (actors, art directors, cinematographers, directors, executives, film editors, musicians, producers, public relations, short subjects, sound, writers, and so on). Each branch is represented on the eighteen-member Board of Directors.

Candidates for Academy Awards are nominated by the producers. About twenty-five awards are made each year, for best motion picture, best actor and actress in leading and supporting roles, best direction, and so on. Awards are made for technical advances. Special awards are sometimes given for contributions that do not fit any particular classification. The Irving Thalberg Award may be given for outstanding contributions over a period of years.

The board of governors of the Academy elects the prizewinners. Every year they have a big banquet at which the prizes are awarded to these winners. A television broadcast of this banquet pays most of the Academy's expenses. Each prize is a little statue with the figure of a man on top of it. One of the first actresses who won one of these statues nicknamed the little man "Oscar." The name has stuck. Ever since, winning an Academy Award has been know as "winning an Oscar."

Solving Problems

Probably the detailed punctuation rules cause the most problems in the formation of compound structures. Here these rules are briefly reviewed. There are three kinds of connecting words: coordinating conjunctions, correlative conjunctions, and conjunctive adverbs. The first two kinds have similar punctuation rules. The third kind does not.

Conjunctions		Adverbs
coordinating	correlative	conjunctive
and, but,	both .. and	however, therefore,
or, nor,	not only ... but also	nevertheless, besides,
for, so,	either ... or	also, on the other hand,
yet	neither ... nor	for example, and so on

Main clause, *and* main clause.
part of main clause *and* part of main clause
item, item, *and* item

Sentence. *However,* sentence.
Sentence. Sentence, *however.*
Sentence. Sen-, *however,* -tence.
Sentence; *however,* sentence.
Sentence; sentence, *however.*
Sentence; sen-, *however,* -tence.

Fused Sentence

Many people make the following error: They write two or more sentences in a row without properly separating or joining them. When two sentences are written together as one without a conjunction or punctuation mark, the result is called a *fused sentence*.

INCORRECT: Bats are flying mammals they are not birds.
CORRECT: Bats are flying mammals. They are not birds.
CORRECT: Bats are flying mammals; they are not birds.

Comma Splice

Another common error, a *comma splice,* is the result of punctuating two or more sentences as if they were one, with only a comma separating them. Remember that a comma is used with a conjunction or phrase. It cannot be used to indicate that a sentence is finished. When a sentence is finished, we must use a period or a semicolon.

INCORRECT: Bats are flying mammals, they are not birds.
CORRECT: Bats are flying mammals, so they are not birds.
CORRECT: Bats are flying mammals; therefore, they are not birds.

Faulty Internal Punctuation and Capitalization

INCORRECT: Baboons live on the ground during the day but at night they sleep high up in the trees.
CORRECT: Baboons live on the ground during the day, but at night they sleep high up in the trees.

INCORRECT: John, Mary and Peter went to the movies.
CORRECT: John, Mary, and Peter went to the movies.

Note: Many authors do not use the comma before a conjunction, but most standard handbooks advocate its use before the conjunction and the last item, especially if the items are long.

INCORRECT: Neither my sister, nor my parents are coming to visit.
CORRECT: Neither my sister nor my parents are coming to visit.

INCORRECT: I write my parents every week; moreover I call them once a month.
CORRECT: I write my parents every week; moreover, I call them once a month.

INCORRECT: He majored in business. He took some courses in computer science; at the same time.
CORRECT: He majored in business. He took some courses in computer science at the same time.

Lack of Agreement

INCORRECT: John and his friend is coming over.
CORRECT: John and his friend are coming over.

INCORRECT: John or his friends is coming over tonight.
CORRECT: John or his friends are coming over tonight.

Lack of Parallelism

INCORRECT: I don't like jogging or to swim.
CORRECT: I don't like jogging or swimming.

INCORRECT: Not only do I want to pass this course but also get a good grade.
CORRECT: Not only do I want to pass this course, but also I want to get a good grade.

INCORRECT: We saw Mr. Johnson, my advisor and who teaches math.
CORRECT: We saw Mr. Johnson, who is my advisor and who teaches math.
CORRECT: We saw Mr. Johnson, my advisor and a math teacher.

Lack of Inversion

INCORRECT: I don't want to play tennis, nor I want to go to the movies.
CORRECT: I don't want to play tennis, nor do I want to go to the movies.

Confusion of *For* and *So*

INCORRECT: I did well on my test, so I studied hard.
CORRECT: I did well on my test, for I studied hard.

INCORRECT: My shoes are too small, for my feet hurt.
CORRECT: My feet hurt, for my shoes are too small.

Illogical Use of Conjunctive Adverbs

INCORRECT: I write my parents every week; likewise, I call them once a month.
CORRECT: I write my parents every week; moreover, I call them once a month.
CORRECT: I write my parents every month; likewise, they write me regularly.

INCORRECT: He is a superior student; in fact, he is a good athlete.
CORRECT: He is a superior student; besides, he is a good athlete.
CORRECT: He is a superior student; in fact, he has a 3.8 average.

INCORRECT: He asked me to help him; on the other hand, I did not have time.
CORRECT: He asked me to help him; however, I did not have time.

Now that you have reviewed the trouble spots in forming compound sentences, see if you can identify them in the following passage about Charles Lindbergh, a famous American aviator.

Exercise 23 In the following passage, each sentence contains one of the errors mentioned above. Identify each error and rewrite the passage correctly.

In the early 1900s many aviators wanted to fly nonstop across the Atlantic Ocean; however, a prize of $25,000 was offered by a New York hotel owner in 1919 to the first aviator who could fly across the Atlantic Ocean nonstop between New York and France. Many fliers tried to claim the prize even a few lost their lives in the attempt. Not only Charles Lindbergh was a flier with a dream, but he also had great skill. Likewise, he climbed aboard "The Spirit of Saint Louis" early in the morning of May 20. All he brought with him to eat and drink during the flight were five chicken sandwiches, and a canteen of water. However, the specially built plane was heavily loaded with a huge supply of fuel for the long journey, for the wheels just barely managed to clear the telephone wires at the end of the runway.

Feeling drowsy and finding himself dozing off was his biggest problems as he reached the halfway point.

After twenty-five hours in the air, he passed over a fishing boat; A few minutes later, he saw the coastline of Ireland on the horizon. Lindbergh was neither surprised nor was he terribly excited, for he was exactly where he had planned to be at that hour.

After thirty-three hours alone in the air, he had conquered the Atlantic yet he was worried that he would be in trouble with the French customs because he had forgotten to apply for an entry visa.

Therefore, he was surprised, relieved and excited when a cheering crowd greeted him when he landed.

Exercise 24 The following exercise tests your ability to relate structure to meaning. Read the passage at least three times. Then complete the sentences below with information from the passage. Your answers should be true according to the information and grammatically correct.

Radar uses pulses of radio waves in an echo system for locating objects and measuring how far away they are. If you shout toward a cliff, the sound of your voice moves to the cliff, strikes it, and then bounces back as an echo. A radar transmitter sends out a pulse of radio waves instead of a sound. If the pulse strikes an object in its path, it bounces back as an echo, which can be picked up by a radio receiver.

A radar transmitter sends out pulses in a narrow beam. The beam reaches out like a probing finger in one direction at a time, so that if an echo comes back we can tell which direction it came from. To change the direction in which a beam travels, the radar antenna keeps turning. In this way, it scans the space surrounding it.

It takes time for a radar pulse to travel. It travels with the speed of light, which is 186,000 miles per second. When a pulse strikes an object and comes back as an echo, there is an interval between the time that the pulse left the antenna and the time that it came back. The length of this interval is the amount of time it takes for the pulse to make a round trip from the antenna to the object and back again. By measuring this interval, we can calculate how far away the object is.

1. Radar uses pulses of radio waves in an echo system not only for

   _____ but also ____

   _____ .

2. An echo is a sound that has bounced back. For example, _____

   _____ .

3. Similarly, a radar transmitter _____

   _____ .

4. A pulse of radio waves strikes an object in its path. Then _____

   _____ .

5. A radar transmitter sends out pulses in a narrow beam in one direction at a time; therefore, _____ .

6. The radar antenna keeps turning to change the direction in which a beam travels; in other words, _____ .

7. _____ , for it travels with the speed of light; therefore, _____

   _____ .

8. The length of this interval is the amount of time it takes for the pulse to make a round trip from the antenna to the object and back again; in other words, _____ .

Assignment for Writing

The following advertisement, entitled "Technology and Jobs," is by *United Technologies*. First read the advertisement, then answer the questions below.

(1) If you wanted to phone someone about 50 years ago, you had to go through the operator. The dial telephone was a rarity in those days. When the phone company began introducing dial telephones, there was a great fear among telephone operators that they would be thrown out of work.

(2) Workers formed "dial conversion committees" to slow down or stop the introduction of the dial telephone. These committees failed. Dial telephones were introduced. But — operators were not thrown out of work. In fact, the opposite happened. Their numbers increased substantially.

(3) Why? The new technology allowed the telephone system to expand more rapidly than anyone ever expected.

(4) The fear that technology would eliminate jobs is not peculiar to our century. It goes back at least to the first part of the last century. It was then that groups of English workers tried to prevent the industrialization of Britain by wrecking factories and machinery. They thought the machines were going to take away their jobs. In fact, the machines increased the number of jobs well beyond anyone's wildest dreams.

(5) One of the few things on which economists of all different schools agree is that the idea that technology reduces jobs is a fallacy. It's a fallacy because it assumes that the total amount of work to be done in any economic system is fixed.

(6) It's really not fixed at all. It's changing constantly. And for many reasons. New consumer demands, population increases, technology — they all work to increase employment.

(7) In the last 30 years, for instance, America has added 30 million people to the ranks of the employed. Many of them work in industries that only came into being because of new technology.

(8) In fact, high-technology industries create jobs eight times as fast as low-technology industries. And a U.S. Commerce Department study finds that from 1957 to 1973, the output of technologically-intensive industries grew 45 percent faster than that of other industries. Employment increased 88 percent faster.

(9) The microelectronics industry is an obvious example. This industry did not even exist 30 years ago. Today it's the world's ninth largest industry. And it's growing. It's expected to be the fourth largest by the end of this decade. Certainly any industry with this kind of record has a positive impact on jobs. In fact, in the past decade the rate of job growth in microelectronics has been twice as fast as the national average. And the industry is giving rise to entirely new kinds of service jobs that rely on microelectronic products. They're all part of our growing information society.

(10) The greatest threat to the labor force today is — lack of technology. Business faces international competition. And technology is international. Preventing or delaying its introduction in one country would mean its even more successful introduction in other countries. Companies need to invest aggressively in technological innovation if they are to remain competitive — and create new jobs.

Class Discussion

1. Who, in your opinion, is United Technologies, the writers of the ad used in the writing assignment?
2. Why did they write this advertisement?
3. Does United Technologies want to describe something, inform people of something, or convince people of something?
4. Paragraph five presents the main argument. Restate the argument in one sentence.
5. Which two paragraphs give historical evidence to support the main argument?
6. Which two paragraphs give recent facts to support the main argument?
7. How many examples have the authors used to support their argument?
8. In which paragraphs have the authors used specific facts, numbers, and statistics?
9. Paragraph ten is the conclusion. Restate it in one sentence.
10. Do you agree or disagree with the authors? Why?
11. Was this passage convincing? Why, or why not?

Small-Group Discussion

Divide yourselves into small groups of three or four students with the same nationality (or from the same general area). Together, "brainstorm" the following issues — that is, make general lists to answer the following questions. (These general lists will help you later to form some ideas for your composition.)

1. In what ways has technology helped your country?
2. In what ways has technology hurt laborers in your country?
3. In what ways may technology help your country in the future?
4. In what ways may technology hurt your country in the future?
5. In what fields (for example, communication, transportation, agriculture, energy, and so on) has technology been or will technology be the most useful or harmful for your country?
6. On the whole, do you believe that technology will help or hurt your country?
7. In one sentence, state your opinion.

Writing

You are a board member of United Technologies in your country. You have to give a report to the board. Write a short report (of about 350 words) to convince the other board members that technology is good or bad for the people in your country. It is best to limit yourself to one field in which technology may be helpful or harmful: for example, transportation, industry, business, communication, or agriculture. Make sure that one paragraph develops your main argument, and that you have at least three examples (each one developed into a paragraph) to support your argument. One of the examples should contain specific facts, details, or statistics. Your conclusion should tell the reader what might happen if technology were, or were not, stopped.

Suggestions for Writing

Have you ever read a paragraph or composition and wondered, "What is the author trying to tell me? What is the main idea?"

When you write, it is important that you stay to the point. For example, when writing about technology, you should not insert a paragraph about a decline in the food supply because of climate changes or another about an increase in taxes because of changes in the economy.

When you look back over the previous passage, you will notice that the author stayed to the point. He or she had one goal in mind: to convince people that technology was useful and necessary, and that technology did not take jobs away but actually created more jobs.

Paragraphs 1 and 2 give examples of ways people were frightened that they would lose their jobs because of technology. However, the number of jobs was increased. Paragraph 3 explains why jobs increased.

Paragraphs 4, 5, and 6 give facts and statistics to show how technology has increased jobs.

Paragraph 7 explains that fighting technology is harmful to the economy.

Every paragraph, sentence, and word is about the topic under discussion. Can you find any sentence that strayed from the topic?

Before you start writing, you should clearly set your goals. Ask yourself, "What do I want to tell my reader?" You should be able to answer that question in no more than two sentences. These two sentences state your topic.

When you start writing, you will probably come up with many different ideas. Jot them down, but before you start rewriting, you should ask yourself with every idea, "Does this item support my topic?" If it does not, you should either change the item or delete it completely. Before you start proofreading for grammatical errors, read through your entire composition again and try to find a paragraph or sentence that strayed from your topic.

You could also exchange papers with a classmate and ask him or her to write down what your topic is. If your classmate cannot discover your topic, you probably have items in your composition that do not support it. However, do not get discouraged. Remember that rewriting and rewriting is the key to good writing.

Proofreading

After you have written and rewritten your report, and you are pleased with the general content and organization, it is time to make sure that your report does not contain errors of the following type.

1. Is each sentence a sentence? (Capitalization? Punctuation: periods, semicolons, commas?) No fused sentences or comma splices?
2. Are ideas connected logically with conjunctive adverbs or other conjunctions? Have you used enough transitions? Are items parallel?
3. Subject-verb agreement? Pronoun reference? Consistency in use of pronouns?
4. Verb forms? Consistency in the use of tenses?
5. Spelling? Use of articles?

When you are sure that there are no grammar errors, rewrite the composition according to your instructor's specifications.

Tense and Aspect

Review/Preview

In Chapter 2 you saw how different verb forms are combined with auxiliaries to show differences in tense, aspect, voice, and mood. In this chapter you will see how the different verb tenses and aspects are used.

In English, there are three basic tenses: past, present, and future. Each of these tenses has a perfect form: past perfect, present perfect, and future perfect. All six of these tenses have progressive forms: past progressive, present progressive, and so on. In other words, there are twelve tenses altogether.

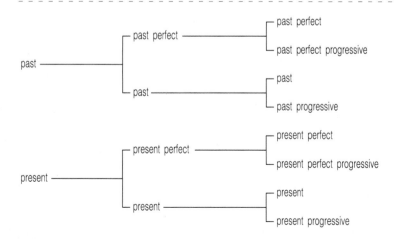

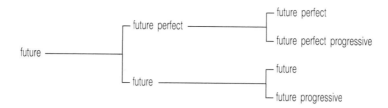

- -

Each one of these twelve tenses has a specific function, and usually only one of these tenses is correct in a sentence. We may also have to change the tense when we use a different mood (indicative or subjunctive) or a different type of clause (main clause or subordinate clause). Therefore, the use of tense is often confusing to both native and non-native speakers.

In this chapter, you will first learn about four general situations:

1. When is the progressive aspect used?
2. When is the perfect aspect used?
3. In what types of clauses is the use of tense affected?
4. How does mood affect the use of tenses?

Then, at the end of this chapter, diagrams will give you an overview of the uses of each tense.

Grammar and Meaning

The Use of the Progressive

The progressive is formed with the auxiliary *be* followed by the *-ing* form of the verb.

- -

John *is studying* English now.	present progressive
John *has been studying* English for three years.	present perfect progressive
John *was studying* when I walked in.	past progressive
John *had been studying* English before I came.	past perfect progressive
John *will be studying* tonight.	future progressive
John *will have been studying* before he comes to visit.	future perfect progressive

- -

The progressive is used to indicate that an action is in continuous progress at a specific point in time or during a limited period of time.

When you examine this definition carefully, you will see that a verb must fulfill three main requirements before it is used in the progressive.

1. The verb has to express an *action,* not a state.

2. The action has to be in *continuous progress;* it cannot be interrupted.
3. The action has to be in continuous progress *at a specific point in time or during a limited period of time,* not at an unspecified point of time.

Each of these requirements will be presented separately in the following sections.

Active versus Stative Verbs

To be used in the progressive, the verb has to express an *action;* in other words, the verb has to express what a subject *does.* Verbs that express not an action but a state of inaction aren't used in the progressive. There are also some verbs that aren't used in the progressive because they express an involuntary action. These verbs are so-called *stative* verbs. There are several general categories of stative verbs:

1. linking verbs
2. verbs expressing possession
3. verbs expressing a state of mind or attitude
4. verbs that express an involuntary mode of perception.

Linking Verbs

- -

John *is* a student.
He *remained* still.
She *seemed* sad.

The strawberries *taste* good.
He *weighs* 125 pounds.

BUT: I *am tasting* the soup.
He *is weighing* the potatoes.

INCORRECT: He is seeming sad.
INCORRECT: The strawberries are tasting good.

- -

As you saw in Chapter 1, linking verbs convey a meaning similar to the mathematical symbol = (equals). In these sentences, the verbs do not express an action, but they describe the state of the subject. Verbs that may be used either as a linking verb or as an action verb may be used in the progressive when they are used as action verbs.

Note: In spoken English, some linking verbs are used in the progressive.

EXAMPLE:

He is feeling weak. He is becoming lazy.

Verbs of Possession

- -

John *has* a car.
This book *belongs* to me.
He *owns* three houses.
This book *contains* ten units.

NOTE: He *is having* a party.
He *is having* a good time.

INCORRECT: John is having a car.
INCORRECT: The book is belonging to me.

- -

In a sentence like *I have a car,* the subject is not doing anything; the predicate describes not an action but a state of possession. When *have* expresses not possession but a meaning similar to *give, enjoy,* or *experience,* it may be used in the progressive.

Verbs Expressing a State of Mind or Attitude

- -

I *love* you.
She *hates* him.   an emotional state
They *like* to swim.

We *admire* his courage.
I *regret* my mistake.
His mother *trusts* him.
He *appreciates* your help.   the opinion of the subject
He *says* that this is a useful book.
He *means* that we learn a lot from it.
He *thinks* that you are right.

BUT: I am thinking now.   an action of the brain
I am admiring your dress.   to look at admiringly
I am loving this book.   to enjoy

Children *depend* on their parents.
Children *need* discipline.   a need of the subject
This situation *indicates* immediate action.
I *want* to help you.

I *know* the answer to this question.
I *understand* the problem.   a state of mind
I *see* what you mean.

INCORRECT: He is needing discipline right now.
INCORRECT: I am wanting to help.

- -

Verbs that express how a person feels about something or what his opinion is about something do not express what a subject *does*. They do describe the subject's state of mind (that is, his emotion, opinion, need, or understanding).

Verbs Expressing an Involuntary Mode of Perception

- -

	We *hear* the cars driving in the street. She *sees* him raising his hand. I *notice* the dirty carpet.	
BUT:	We *are listening* to the teacher. We *are watching* the teacher write.	
BUT:	He *is seeing* a psychiatrist. She *has been seeing* him a lot lately.	seeing means *getting therapy from.* seeing means *visiting with* or *dating.*
INCORRECT: INCORRECT:	We are hearing the cars. She is seeing him raise his hand.	

- -

Such verbs as *hear, see, behold, notice,* and *observe* express a mode of perception in which the subject of the verb is not making a deliberate effort. For example, when we are in a classroom, we subconsciously *hear* many sounds like the running of the air conditioner, the coughing of people, and the fluttering of papers. On the other hand, we probably make a special effort *to listen* to the instructor. Similarly, we *see* many things, such as the walls, the windows, and the carpet. But we have to alert our sense of sight *to watch* or *to look at* the instructor write on the board.

Now that you have learned that verbs that express a state, not an action, are not used in the progressive, try to do the following exercise.

Exercise 1　　(1) Identify the following verbs as stative verbs or action verbs. (2) Then, on a separate piece of paper, use the following situation to create an English sentence with each one of the verbs below. Use the simple present tense with stative verbs and the present progressive tense with action verbs. *Note:* Some verbs may be used as both.

Situation: You are in a classroom. You describe the people, things, classroom procedures, and so on, in this class.

EXAMPLE:
like (stative) *I like the color of the carpet in this room.*

1. like _____　　　3. have _____

2. sit _____　　　4. love _____

5. learn _____   18. admire _____

6. watch _____   19. appear _____

7. hate _____   20. listen to _____

8. study _____   21. require _____

9. own _____   22. remain _____

10. see _____   23. raise hand _____

11. know _____   24. seem _____

12. believe _____   25. appreciate _____

13. hear _____   26. weigh _____

14. regret _____   27. consider _____

15. need _____   28. pay attention _____

16. understand _____   29. stand _____

17. depend _____   30. think _____

Exercise 2   Read over the following passage. Fill in the blanks with stative verbs like *be, seem, involve, mean, have,* and *become.* Be sure you use the correct form.

There _____ no single Indian language. Some of the several hundred Indian tongues _____ to be quite different from all the rest. Others form language families because they _____ similar grammars and many words from the same roots. There _____ no general characteristics that make American Indian languages different as a group from languages elsewhere.

Indian languages, like all others, _____ their share of grunts and gestures. But they _____ more than the simple collection of "ughs" and "hows" heard in motion-picture and television Westerns. The number of words may _____ smaller than in English, but Indians often lump a number of ideas onto one word, so that it _____ practically a whole sentence. Wintun, the language of a California tribe, _____ one short word that _____ *she-is-dress-striped.* English would use six words, *she* _____ *stripes in her dress.*

Continued versus Interrupted Time

A continued action	A repeated action or a habit
We *are attending* class now.	We *attend* class three times a week.
He *was laughing* when I saw him.	He *laughed* two times.
He came in while I *was reading* a book.	I *read* a lot when I was in high school.

	He *is arriving* now.	present
	He *is leaving* right now.	present
BUT:	He *arrived* at three o'clock.	past
BUT:	He *will arrive* at three o'clock tomorrow.	future

The progressive is used when the action of the verb is continued, so it can't be used when an action is repeated (that is, started and stopped several times). For example, something that happens frequently (often, sometimes, once a week, twice, now and then) is not a continued action but a repeated action. Also a habit is not a continued action but a repeated action.

Note: When a verb describes a continued action of very short duration, the progressive *must* be used in the present. However, in the past or future a progressive is usually not used with an event of short duration.

Exercise 3   Create English sentences with the following sentence parts.

EXAMPLES:

listen to the teacher (now)
I am listening to the teacher.
listen to the teacher (usually)
I usually listen to the teacher.

1. study English grammar (now) _____

_____ .

2. study English grammar (three hours a day) _____

_____ .

3. talk to my classmates (at this moment) _____

_____ .

4. talk to my classmates (usually/before class) _____

_____ .

5. copy from the chalkboard (presently) _____

_____ .

6. copy from the chalkboard (whenever it is necessary) _____

_____ .

7. do an exercise (right now) _____

_____ .

8. do an exercise (for homework/every day) _____

_____ .

9. practice English (at this very moment) _____

_____ .

10. practice English (whenever I have a chance) _____

_____ .

Specific versus Non-specific Time

The progressive is used when the action is continued either at a specific point in time or during a limited period of time. Of course, *now* or *at this moment* is a specific point in time. Therefore, in the present tense, the progressive is used when a speaker or writer describes an action that is in progress at the moment of speaking or writing.

Note: Usually the words *now* or *at this moment* are not expressed but understood. (Example: *I am reading [now].*) On the other hand, the simple present tense is usually accompanied by an expression of frequency. (Example: *I read frequently.*)

- -

A specific or limited time	A non-specific time / A general truth
I am reading a book *(now).*	
I will be swimming *at seven in the morning.*	I will swim *tomorrow.*
While I was reading, the telephone rang.	I read a good book *yesterday.*
Johnny is drinking a glass of milk. *(now)*	American children *drink* a lot of milk. *(always)*
I was studying in the library *between four and five yesterday.*	I studied in the library *yesterday.*
I will be studying *all afternoon tomorrow.*	I will study *tomorrow.*
UNIDIOMATIC: He reads a book.	UNIDIOMATIC: I was reading a book last week.
UNIDIOMATIC: I sit in a chair.	UNIDIOMATIC: I will be reading tomorrow.

- -

If there is no time expression in a present-tense sentence, the specific time *now* is usually understood. It is therefore unidiomatic to use an action verb in a simple present tense if it is not clearly expressed or understood that the action is habitual.

On the contrary, in the past or future tense the specific time must be clearly expressed or clearly understood from the context. If the specific time is not expressed or clearly understood, the simple future or simple past should be used.

Exercise 4

On a separate piece of paper, create English sentences based on the following situation with the time expressions given in the *simple past* or *progressive past tense*.

Situation: You are a businessperson with a busy schedule. You have to visit clients, dictate letters, make telephone calls, make sure your employees do their work, and so on.

> EXAMPLES:
>
> at eight this morning
> *At eight this morning, I was driving to work.*
> this morning
> *This morning I met with a client.*
> all morning
> *The secretary was typing all morning.*

1. last week
2. all last week
3. when my supervisor came in
4. at five o'clock yesterday
5. yesterday
6. two minutes ago
7. yesterday afternoon
8. yesterday noon
9. last night
10. at midnight last night

Exercise 5

Change the verbs in parentheses to the simple past tense or the progressive past tense.

One day, while he (stay) at Campobello, Roosevelt (go) sailing with his wife and sons in a small boat. He (teach) his boys to sail the boat. Then a forest fire (break out) on a nearby beach, and the whole family (go) to help put out the fire. The fire, however, (prove) to be more serious then they first (suppose). For three hours, they (work on) putting it out. Later, to cool off, they (go) for a swim in a nearby lake. Then, while Roosevelt and his sons (go) home, they (run) part of the way — a distance of about a mile and a half. After he (reach) home, Roosevelt (decide) to go swimming again even though the water in the Bay of Fundy, where the island of Campobello is located, is ice-cold all year round. Next, Roosevelt (sit) for half an hour in his wet bathing suit while he (read) through some mail that had recently arrived. It (be) then that he (feel) a bad chill. His wife, Eleanor, finally (persuade) him to go to bed, but by this time he (feel) so weak that his sons (have) to help him up the stairs. The next day, Roosevelt (have) a high temperature. His left leg (feel) uncomfortably heavy, and it also (hurt) him. A local doctor (be) called in. As Roosevelt (get) worse, other doctors (be) called. After two weeks, it (be) decided that Roosevelt (have) poliomyelitis.

Exercise 6   Change the verbs in parentheses to the simple past or past progressive tense. Explain your choices.

On an October afternoon in 1899, 17-year-old Robert Goddard (sit) in the living room of his Worcester, Massachusetts, home. He (read) a new book, *The War of the Worlds,* by H. G. Wells. He finally (put) the book aside, (go) out to the backyard, (climb) a tall cherry tree, and (begin) to prune away some dead limbs.

"It (be) one of those quiet, colorful afternoons of sheer beauty which we have in October in New England," he later (write), "and as I (look) toward) the fields to the east, I (imagine) how wonderful it would be to make some device which (have) even the possibility of ascending to Mars and how it would look on a small scale if it (go up) from the meadow at my feet."

While young Goddard (climb down) from the tree, he (realize) that he had become, in his words, "a different boy." He (feel) that life now (have) a purpose for him.

Robert Goddard never (lose) sight of that purpose. During his college years, he (fill) notebook after notebook with ideas relating to high-altitude flight. In 1911, he (receive) his Ph.D. from Clark University in Worcester, where he (become) a physics professor. Then he (begin) to work with a device that he (know) (have) "the *possibility* of ascending to Mars."

Exercise 7   Write a paragraph of about 75 words describing an important event in your life. Try to use the past progressive at least three times.

The Use of the Perfect

As you learned in Chapter 2, the perfect tense is formed with the helping verb *have*.

- -

I *have lived* here for ten years.	present perfect
I *have been living* here for ten years.	present perfect progressive
I *had lived* there for ten years before we moved.	past perfect
I *had been living* there for ten years before we moved.	past perfect progressive
I *will have lived* here for ten years by fall.	future perfect
I *will have been living* here for ten years by fall.	future perfect progressive

- -

A perfect tense indicates that something is completed before another point in time and that it is relevant to that point in time.

As you can see, this definition has two main elements:

1. The action or state has to be *completed* before another point in time.
2. The action or state has to be *relevant* to that point in time.

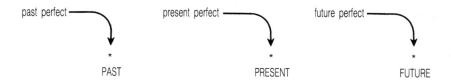

A verb in the perfect tense shows that something is completed or finished before another moment and gives emphasis to the *result* of the action. Look at the following three examples:

I have bought a car. This sentence really means: *I have a car now.* Not the action of *buying* but the result of this action, *having a car,* is important to the speaker.

Your friend is about to leave in a car and you want to warn him or her that the streets are wet and slippery. You might say, *Be careful! It has rained.* This sentence does *not* express that it is raining but that as the result of rain, the streets are slippery.

You have a test today and you are well prepared, so you are very confident that you will do well. You might say to your classmate, *I am not nervous at all because I have studied.* This sentence expresses not that you have studied up to now, but that the result of studying is important: I know my lesson now!

	RESULT
Be careful! It *has been raining*.	The streets are wet.
I am not nervous about the exam because I *have studied*.	I know my lesson.
The police cannot catch the thief because he *has escaped*.	The thief is gone.
I was careful because it *had been freezing*.	The streets were icy.
I was not nervous about the exam because I *had studied*.	I knew my lesson.
The police could not catch the thief because he *had escaped*.	The thief was gone.
I will be careful because it *will have been freezing*.	The streets will be icy.
I will not be nervous because I *will have studied*.	I will know my lesson.
The police will not be able to catch the thief because he *will have escaped*.	The thief will be gone.

As with the progressive, a present moment is automatically understood in the present. Example: *I have bought a car.* In this sentence, it is clear that this action took place before now.

However, in the past and future, the other moment must be expressed in the sentence (or be clearly understood from the context). Example: He had just bought a car *when he won another one in the lottery.* As in the previous sentence, the time point is often defined in (or established by) a subordinate clause.

Exercise 8   Read the following passage and underline each perfect verb phrase.

Many people have sailed around the world. Some have even done it alone. But, until 1968, no one had done it single-handedly without stopping. That summer, ten sailors entered a contest hoping to be the first to succeed.

After nine of the contestants had dropped out during the trip, Robin Knox-Johnston was the only remaining contestant after almost a year. The thirty-year-old sailor had covered more than 30,000 miles before he docked his thirty-two foot yacht *Suhaili* in Falmouth, England. He had sailed around the world and had come back to his home port. It must have felt wonderful to be back because it was the first time he had set foot on land in 313 days.

To make the completion and relevance clear and to indicate that a perfect tense must be used, there is often a specific time word or expression in the sentence. There are two such groups of expressions: those that express a recent past and those that include the present.

After Adverbs Expressing a Recent Past

Certain adverbs in the English language express a very recent past. They show that an action has just been completed and that the result of that action is clearly felt.

Example: *Where is John? He has* just *arrived.* (Meaning: He is here now.)

Another example: *You must do your homework. No, I have* already *done it.* (Meaning: It is finished.)

- -

	EXPRESSIONS
He has *just* arrived.	just
He has been very sick *of late*.	of late
He hasn't arrived in the United States *yet*.	yet
He has done a lot of work *lately*.	lately
I had *already* done my homework before you came in.	already
He had *finally* finished washing his car when it started to rain.	finally
Just when he had hung up the phone, it rang again.	just
I will have left *by* the time he gets here.	by....
We will have finished this book *before* the end of the school year.	before...
No sooner had he left the house *than* it started to rain.	no sooner...than...
His English had not improved much *until* he started reading a lot.	until...

INCORRECT: He had hung up the phone.
INCORRECT: He had left the house.
INCORRECT: His English had not improved much.
INCORRECT: We will have finished this book.
INCORRECT: He will have left.

- -

As you can see from the diagram, the perfect tense is used with adverbs like *just, already, finally,* and so on. Notice that the present perfect tense is often used in simple sentences, but the past perfect and future perfect tenses usually occur in complex sentences. As you saw earlier, in a present-tense sentence, a present point in time (now) is automatically understood, but in a past or future tense sentence, the moment to which an event is related is usually expressed in the subordinate clause.

After Time Expressions That Include the Present

Certain time expressions express two points in time at once. Example: I have lived here *for* three years. The preposition *for* shows us (1) that the action began three years ago and (2) that the action has continued up to now. (It does not necessarily mean that it will stop now.) Therefore, these time expressions show that there is relevance between a continued action and another point in time.

He has lived here *since* 1984.	since
He has visited three times *so far*.	so far, up until now/then, and so on
He had always wanted to buy a car *until* he realized how expensive one was.	until now/then
He has been living here *since* 1984.	since
INCORRECT: He has been visiting *three times* so far.	repeated action
INCORRECT: He had always been *wanting* a new car until...	stative verb

---

The adverbs *so far, up to now/then,* and *until now/then,* the conjunction *since,* and the prepositions *for* and *since* are usually used with the perfect tense. These words express not only relevance but also a limited period of time; therefore, the progressive may be used to emphasize the duration of the action. Of course, if the action is not continuous, or if the verb is a stative verb, the progressive cannot be used.

In the following diagram you can see that such adverbs as *never, always, this week, this month,* and *sometimes* may be used with different tenses. They are used with the perfect tense if another point in time is understood in the sentence.

If the past tense is used with these expressions, the event is not relevant to the present. In these sentences, *in the past* is understood.

	MEANING:
He *has* always *wanted* a new car.	He has always wanted a car *up to now*.
He always *wanted* a new car.	He does not want a new car anymore.
He *has visited* us three times this week.	The week is not over. Up to now he has visited three times.
He *has* never *seen* the Statue of Liberty.	He has not seen it up to now, but he still has an opportunity to see it.
He never *saw* the Statue of Liberty.	He will not see it in the future (because he will not have an opportunity anymore).
We *have studied* three chapters this semester.	This semester is not over yet. We have covered three chapters *up to now,* and we will probably cover more chapters.
We *studied* three chapters this semester.	We will not study any more chapters.
He always *walks* to school.	custom or habit
He never *arrives* late.	custom or habit

Exercise 9   On a separate piece of paper, create English sentences in the perfect tense with the following sentence parts. You may use a progressive where possible.

1. already/study perfect tense
2. recently/receive a letter
3. finally/clean up my room
4. just/enter the classroom
5. lately/not receive a newspaper
6. scarcely/enter the house/when it started to rain
7. feel lonely/of late
8. go shopping/not yet
9. buy new clothes/already
10. no sooner (answer the telephone)...than the doorbell rang
11. live here/for
12. be in class/since
13. read five books/up to now
14. by the end of this week/spend...days studying the verb tenses
15. by the time this semester is over/finish the grammar book
16. never/see such a good movie before
17. always/remember to do my work
18. I was very careful because/rain
19. scarcely/arrive at the airport/when my name was called
20. by next month/stay here for...months

Exercise 10   Create an English sentence, on a separate piece of paper, with each of the following time expressions based on the following situation.

Situation: You are a famous tennis player. You practice a lot. You train a lot. You eat well. You win many famous tournaments. (Wimbledon, United States Open, and so on) You win a lot of money. You buy a lot of things. And so on.

1. already	6. just
2. recently	7. lately
3. for	8. up to now
4. always	9. since
5. never	10. this year

Tense Changes in Subordinate Clauses

Usually we use the past tense for a past situation, the present tense for a present situation, and the future tense for a future situation. However, there are some cases in which we must use a different tense from the one we expect. For example, there are certain kinds of subordinate clauses in which the use of tense is affected. Let's review briefly the different types of clauses.

In Chapter 1, the different types of clauses were discussed. You learned about main clauses and subordinate clauses. Among the subordinate clauses were subject, object, complement, adverbial, and adjectival clauses. The first three types of clauses are grouped together as noun clauses.

What you do is your own business.	subject ⎫
I don't know *where he is*.	object ⎬ noun
The important thing is *that you study hard*.	complement ⎭
The boy *who was here yesterday* is from Saudi Arabia.	adjective
He is tired *because he studied all night*.	adverbial

There are two types of clauses in which we might have to use a different tense than we expect: certain noun clauses and certain adverbial clauses. We will discuss below the use of tense in these types of clauses.

In Noun Clauses After Past-Tense Main Verbs

A noun clause is a clause that functions as a subject, object, or complement. Although a tense change, which is called the *sequence-of-tense rule,* occurs in all three types of clauses, it occurs most often in object clauses.

    a. John *says* that he *is* tired.
    b. John *said* that he *was* tired.

Note: Both sentences *a* and *b* mean that John *is* tired right now, but the past tense is used in sentence *b* because the verb in the main clause (*said*) is in the past tense.

If a main clause that contains a past tense is followed by a noun clause, it is necessary to apply the so-called sequence-of-tense rule in the noun clause.

Another example: Your instructor comes into the room and says, "I am going to give you a quiz." One of the students is not sure what was said, so he asks his classmate, "What did he say?" His classmate answers, "He *said* he *was* going to give us a quiz." *Is going* is changed to *was going* because of *said. Note:* The formation rules for noun clauses are discussed in Chapter 9.

The following diagrams show you how the verb tense changes in the noun clause if the verb in the main clause has a past tense.

A Present Finite Verb Becomes a Past Finite Verb

    He works here.   present
    I think that he works here.
    I thought that he *worked* here.   past

	Is he working?	present
	She wants to know if he is working.	
	She wanted to know if he *was* working.	past
	How long has he worked?	present
	I am not sure how long he has worked.	
	I wasn't sure how long he *had* worked.	past
	He will work there.	present
	I assume that he will work there.	
	I assumed that he *would* work there.	past
	Water freezes at 32 Fahrenheit.	
	He says that water freezes at 32 Fahrenheit.	
BUT:	He said that water freezes at 32 Fahrenheit.	general truth
NOTE:	She asked how old Dr. Arnold is.	informal
NOTE:	She wanted to know where he works.	informal

- -

If the *finite* verb in the original sentence is in the present tense, it becomes a past tense verb in a noun clause, if the verb in the main clause is in the past tense. However, this change does not take place if the noun clause states a general truth.

To make an event sound more vivid or less formal, or to show that the event is relevant to the speaker at the moment of speaking, the present forms sometimes remain in spoken or written English.

- -

Past Tense Becomes Past Perfect Tense

He worked there last year.	past
They believe that he worked there last year.	
They believed that he *had worked* there last year.	past perfect
Was he working when you saw him?	past
She wants to know if he was working when you saw him.	
She wanted to know if he *had been* working when you saw him.	past perfect

- -

If there is a past-tense verb in the noun clause, it changes to the past perfect tense after a past-tense main verb.

- -

A Past-Perfect Tense Verb or a Past Modal Verb Does Not Change

He had worked there for three years before he moved.	past perfect
She said that he *had worked* there for three years before he moved.	past perfect
He had been working there many years until he was transferred.	past perfect
She said that he *had been working* there many years until he was transferred.	past perfect

He could have worked there longer if he had not moved.   past modal
He said that he *could have worked* there longer if he had not moved.   past modal

- -

If the verb is in the past perfect tense or has a past-tense modal, there is no change after a past-tense main verb. Also note that the tense does not change in clauses that are subordinate to the noun clause. Examples: *before he moved; until he was transferred; if he had not moved.*

Exercise 11   Change the following sentences to noun clauses after *We thought...*

1. They have already painted the house. _____

   _____ .

2. Construction on the house will begin next week. _____

   _____ .

3. The director did not send the report. _____

   _____ .

4. You are allowed to leave now. _____

   _____ .

5. We will have a party for you. _____

   _____ .

6. You can speak three languages. _____

   _____ .

7. You could speak three languages. _____

   _____ .

8. You could have helped me. _____

   _____ .

9. He had already left when I arrived. _____

   _____ .

10. She left yesterday. _____

    _____ .

11. She was playing tennis when I called. _____

    _____ .

Exercise 12   Create English sentences based on the following situation with each of the following main clauses.

Situation: You have just listened to the news on television. Many things were announced. There was a fire in a hotel. The value of the dollar has gone up (or down). The president received the prime minister from another country. There were sports announcements. There were weather announcements. And so on.

1. The news announcer said that _____

   _____ .

2. She also reported that _____ .

3. She stated that _____ recently

   _____ .

4. She said that _____ early this

   morning _____ .

5. She mentioned that _____ now

   _____ .

6. The weather announcer predicted that _____

   _____ tomorrow _____ .

7. He also believed that _____ next

   week _____ .

8. He thought that _____ by the day

   after tomorrow.

9. The sports announcer reported that _____

   _____ .

10. He also announced that _____

    tomorrow.

11. At the end of the news broadcast, the announcer said that _____

    _____ .

Exercise 13   Interview one of your classmates. Find out as many details about his or her home town as you can. For example, you can ask about its location, weather, size, population, historical sites, and so on. First write down your questions and his or her answers as they were said. Then rephrase the information in a passage of about 150 words using such phrases as *I wondered, wanted to know,* and *he or she said, reported, stated, told me,* and so on.

In Adverbial Clauses Expressing Future Time

You probably already know that the auxiliary *will* is often used to express future time. Example: *I will leave tomorrow. He will drive to New York tomorrow.*

However, in an adverbial clause of time or condition, the auxiliary *will* is not used, even if it expresses future time.

- -

You will leave (tomorrow).	future
I will see you before you *leave*.	present
I will see you this afternoon.	future
If I *see* you this afternoon, I will give you the book.	present
You will be driving (all afternoon).	future progressive
I will think about you while you *are driving* all afternoon.	present progressive
You will have arrived (before ten P.M.).	future perfect
I will call you after you *have arrived*.	present perfect

NOTE: If you *will* play the piano, I will sing.   *will = to be willing to*

- -

Exercise 14   Change the following sentences to adverbial clauses of time or condition and add a meaningful main clause. In your adverbial clause, use the word in parentheses.

EXAMPLE:

(if) You will arrive before eight.
I will see you if you arrive before eight.

1. (before) We will have finished studying this book. _____

_____ .

2. (after) We will have been studying the verb tenses. _____

_____ .

3. (if) We will understand all the grammar. _____

_____ .

4. (while) We will be studying the next chapter. _____

_____ .

5. (when) We will understand all the grammar. _____

_____ .

6. (if) We will not learn proper grammar. _____

_____ .

7. (before) The semester will be over. _____

_____ .

8. (after) The papers will be graded. _____

_____ .

The Use of Tense in the Subjunctive Mood

Normally, the present tense is used for a present situation, the past tense for a past situation, and the future tense for a future situation. However, when we want to express something that is not true, we must use a different tense. Look at the following passage, which contains a *contrary-to-fact* statement.

Mary went to the hairdresser yesterday and had her hair cut short. Now she is sorry. She may say, "I wish I *had* long hair. If I *had* not *cut* my hair yesterday, I wouldn't be so unhappy now." The past tense *had* is used for a present situation and the past perfect tense *had cut* is used for a past situation to show that the situations are not true.

Other examples: The fact is that John does *not* have a car. He might say, "I wish I *had* a car" or "If I *had* a car, I would travel around the world." As you can see, the past tense is used to indicate a *present* contrary-to-fact situation.

The fact is that Mary did not come to class yesterday. She missed a test, so she might say, "I wish that I *had gone* to class yesterday" or "If I *had gone* to class, I would not have missed the test." The past perfect tense is used to express a *past* contrary-to-fact situation.

Note: See Chapter 8 for further details on the formation of contrary-to-fact statements.

Contrary-to-Fact Statement	Meaning:
If I *were* rich, I would buy a car.	I am not rich.
If I *had* a car, I would travel a lot.	I do not have a car.
If I *traveled* a lot, I would be happy.	I do not travel a lot.
I wish I *were* happy.	I am not happy.
If John *had studied* last year, he would not have failed that course.	John did not study last year.
If John *had* not *failed* that course, he would not be so unhappy.	John failed that course.
I wish John *had* not *been* so unhappy.	John was very unhappy.

Note: The verb *be* is the only verb that uses a special form in the first and third person singular. Examples: *I/He was sick* (indicative). *I wish I/he were rich* (subjunctive).

Exercise 15   Change the following facts to wishes.

EXAMPLE:
He is sick.
I wish he weren't sick.

1. He doesn't speak the truth. _____
_____ .

2. He doesn't write me a letter every week. _____
_____ .

3. I do not go home every weekend. _____
_____ .

4. I did not go home last summer. _____
_____ .

5. I did not receive a letter today. _____
_____ .

6. We are studying grammar. _____
_____ .

7. We are sitting in class. _____
_____ .

8. It is hot today. _____
_____ .

9. It was raining yesterday. _____
_____ .

10. I have to study tonight. (Use the helping verb *do.*) _____
_____ .

The Use of the Tenses

So far in this chapter you have learned several general rules for using the tenses:

1. The progressive is used to describe an action in progress at a specific point in time or during a limited period of time. Verbs that do not express actions, but states, cannot be used in the progressive.
2. The perfect is used to express that an action is finished before another moment in time and is relevant to that moment in time. The

moment *now* is automatically understood in a sentence in the present tense, but in a past-tense or future-tense sentence, the moment is usually established by a subordinate clause. Several adverbs like *already, just,* and *yet* also usually require a perfect tense.

3. A tense change takes place in noun clauses after a past-tense verb in the main clause or in adverbial clauses of time or condition.
4. A tense change takes place in clauses that express contrary-to-fact situations.

Now that you are familiar with these general rules, we will summarize the use of each tense separately.

The Present Tense

The simple present tense and the progressive present tense are often confused. Remember that in the present tense sentence the time *now* is automatically understood if there is no other time expression. Therefore, if the verb is an action verb, we usually use the progressive tense. The present tense is limited to expressing repeated actions like habits, customs, general truths, and statements with stative verbs.

The main use of the progressive is to indicate that an action is in progress at the moment of speaking or writing and that the action will continue for a limited period of time, which may be very short or long.

Both the simple present and the progressive present may indicate a future event. The main difference is that the simple present indicates a regularly scheduled event, like a train departure, and the progressive present, a planned event, like leaving on a trip. Note that the event is something that can be planned or organized by a human being.

The simple present tense is also used instead of a future perfect to express future time in adverbial clauses. It is also used instead of the past tense in the narrative present to tell a story in a lively manner.

- -

The Simple Present Tense

Repeated actions: habits, customs, general truths

John usually comes late.
I never go to bed late.
I call my parents once a week.

People in America eat hamburgers.
I write many letters.
I drive a car.
John eats breakfast at 7:30 A.M.

The sun rises in the east.
Cows eat grass.

INCORRECT: I write a letter.
CORRECT: I am writing a letter (now).

The Progressive Present Tense

Actions in progress

I am studying the progressive.
I am taking an English grammar course this semester.
I am learning to express my thoughts in English.
Many new inventions are being made in this century.
Technology is making a lot of progress this decade.

INCORRECT: I am often studying in the library.

Stative verbs: linking, possession,
state of mind, perception

Mary *seemed* happy.
John *has* a bicycle.
We *like* to swim.
She *wants* to speak to you.
We *hear* the noise in the hall.

Future scheduled events

The train leaves at 10:15 tomorrow.
I go to class at 11:00 tomorrow morning.
Our club meets next Friday.
The plane from Dallas arrives at 4:06.

Future planned event

I am leaving tomorrow.
I am going to New York.
I am staying at the Hilton.
I am giving a party tomorrow.

INCORRECT: It is snowing tomorrow.

Adverbial clauses of future condition or time

If you *help* me, I will help you.
Before I *leave,* I will clean up my room.
I will call you when I *need* you.
I will ask the teacher when the next
   test *is*.
I will go to the store when I *have* to.

Narration: informal spoken or written English

I *go* to school, and guess what? My car
   has a flat tire, and I *am* 30 minutes
   late for class.

- -

Exercise 16   Make general statements about the following subjects on a separate piece
of paper. (Do not use the verb *be*.)

EXAMPLE:

The sun
The sun rises in the east.

1. dogs
2. fish
3. cows
4. stars
5. the earth
6. coffee
7. computers
8. cars
9. tigers
10. electricity
11. teachers
12. students
13. television
14. microscopes
15. men
16. women
17. children
18. infants
19. toddlers
20. teenagers

WORDLESS WORKSHOP

By ROY DOTY

$50 to Terri McBride of Matthews, N.C., for this idea. Send yours (with Social Security No.) to Wordless, POPULAR SCIENCE, 380 Madison Ave., New York, N.Y. 10017. No ideas will be returned.

Exercise 17   What is going to happen next week? In complete sentences, write down five regularly scheduled activities and five planned activities that will take place next week.

Exercise 18   Look at the Wordless Workshop on page 138. Describe each picure as if it were going on *right now*. Give at least three sentences to go with each picture in either the simple present or present progressive tense.

Some vocabulary you may need includes riding lawn mower; workshop; PCV pipe; two-hole pipe brace; coupler; canopy; canvas cloth; sewing machine; and stitch.

The Past and Perfect Tenses

The past, present perfect, and past perfect tenses are often confused. Remember that the perfect tenses show some relationship between two events, and the past tense does not.

The past tense is used primarily to show that an event took place in the past, is finished, and has no relevance to the present. Usually, it is accompanied by such definite past-time expressions as *yesterday, last week, an hour ago, in 1981,* or *early this morning.* If no such expression is included, it can be clearly understood from the context. (Note that it is wrong to use a present perfect tense with a definite past-time expression.)

The present perfect, on the other hand, shows that there is some relationship between the past event and the present, thus emphasizing the result rather than the action of the verb. It is often accompanied by such time expressions as *already, recently, for,* and *since.*

Both the past and the present perfect tense may be used in the progressive aspect to show that an action was in continued progress at a specific point in time or during a limited period of time in the past.

The simple past, like the simple present tense, can also express a past habit. In this case, a time expression of frequency is usually included. The helping verbs *used to* or *would* are used if there is no time expression.

As you learned earlier in this chapter, the present perfect tense is used instead of the future perfect tense in an adverbial clause of condition or time.

- -

The Past Tense	The Present Perfect Tense
	A past event with relevance to the present
A definite past time	
I went to the store *yesterday.*	I have forgotten my book.
The school was founded *in 1952.*	(I don't have a book now.)
I was late for class *this morning.*	I have written a letter.
	(I expect an answer.)

We have had a test last week.
The school has been founded in 1952.

I have *already* studied three chapters.
Haven't you studied the passive voice *yet?*
Have you *ever* visited New York City?
I have studied *for three hours.*

The past progressive

I was reading a book when you called.
You called while I was reading a book.
I was studying from four until eight P.M.
He was working all day long.
I was sleeping at three A.M.
UNIDIOMATIC: He was working yesterday.

A past habit

When I was young, I went to school *every day.*
I usually rode my bike to school.
Sometimes I took the bus.
BUT: I *used to* ride my bicycle to school.
BUT: I *would* take the bus once in a while.

The perfect progressive

I have been studying since three o'clock.
I have been living here for five years.

Future perfect time in an adverbial clause of time or condition

If I have finished my work, I will visit you tonight.
I will have finished my work before I visit you.

INCORRECT: You must work until you *will* have finished your work.
INCORRECT: I will have finished my work before I *will* stop working.

- -

Exercise 19 Change the verbs in parentheses to the appropriate tenses: simple present, present progressive, present perfect, or simple past. Explain your choices.

1. Iron that (be protected) by a layer of zinc (be called) galvanized iron.

2. The largest blue whale that (be) ever (caught) (weigh) 145 tons.

3. Wine (be used) in medical practice for more than 2,000 years.

4. The capital of the state of Texas (be changed) fifteen times.

5. *Fortnight* (be) a contraction of "fourteen nights." In America, this expression (be replaced) by "two weeks."

6. Twenty years (be added) to the average life expectancy in America since 1900.

7. Volcano ash (be known) to remain hot for a period of nearly a hundred years.

8. A very good way to find out whether or not an egg (be cooked) (be) to attempt to spin it. A raw egg (not spin).

Exercise 20   Write a letter to a friend. Tell him or her what has happened to you over the last two months. Try to use the present perfect tense at least four times.

Exercise 21   Complete the following sentences in your own words. Your sentences should be meaningful, and the use of tense should be correct.

1. Yesterday, the students _____ .

2. While _____ , I heard footsteps in the hall.

3. If _____ , I would ask for help.

4. He said that he _____ today.

5. Yesterday noon, we _____ .

6. I wish _____ today.

7. The teacher believed that _____ .

8. Last week, we _____ .

Exercise 22   On a separate piece of paper, create English sentences with each of the following time expressions based on the following situation.

Situation: You are a commercial airline pilot. During the flight you have many duties. You have to take off safely and land the plane. You have to stay in touch with the control tower. You have to inform the passengers of weather and flight conditions. Because of your work you travel all over the world. Sometimes you spend a few days in a foreign country. You visit many interesting places and meet many interesting people.

1. last week
2. during a flight/usually

3. at 5:03 P.M. yesterday
4. for three days
5. already
6. always
7. sometimes
8. when I flew to Bangkok
9. in 1984
10. early this month
11. from January 3rd to January 5th
12. at noon yesterday

Exercise 23   Write a paragraph in the past tense about the pictures in Exercise 18. Start your paragraph with the following sentence: Last month, when Mrs. Rogers was about to cut the lawn, . . .

The past perfect tense is used primarily to indicate that an event was finished before a moment in the past and that it was relevant to that moment. It is usually accompanied by such time expressions as *already, yet, scarcely, hardly,* and *no sooner . . . than.*

The past tense is used to express a past event that happened before another past event if there is no relevance between the two events.

As you saw earlier in this chapter, the sequence-of-tense rule requires a tense change in a noun clause: if the verb in the main clause is in the past tense, the past tense expresses a present time and the past perfect tense, a past time.

Also, the past tense expresses a present contrary-to-fact situation, and the past perfect, a past contrary-to-fact situation.

- -

The Past Tense	The Past Perfect Tense
A past event without relevance to another moment in the past	A past event with relevance to another moment in the past
After he studied, he went to the movies. Before he studied, he went to the store.	After he had studied, he rested a while. Before he went to the store, he had made a grocery list.
	He had not left yet when they arrived. He had lived there for three years before he moved. He had been living there for three years before he moved.
Present time in a noun clause after a past-tense main verb	Past time in a noun clause after a past-tense main verb
"I am very busy today." John says that he is very busy today. John said that he was very busy today.	"I was very busy yesterday." John says that he was very busy yesterday. John said that he had been very busy yesterday.

"I am leaving tomorrow."
He says that he is leaving tomorrow.
He said that he was leaving tomorrow.

"Mary left yesterday."
He says that Mary left yesterday.
He said that Mary had left yesterday.

A present contrary-to-fact situation

I wish I had blond hair.
If I were rich, I would buy a car.
If I had time, I would help you.
I wish I were living at home.

A past contrary-to-fact situation

If I had paid more attention, I would have done better.
I wish I had gone to class more regularly last semester.
If I had had time last week, I would have helped you.
I wish I had been living at home when I went to college.

- -

Exercise 24   Fill in the blanks below to create good English sentences based on the following situation.

Situation: You are a dentist. Your patients usually make appointments. Then you see them. You first clean their teeth. Then you make x-rays to check the root system. Before you fill a cavity, you give the patient an injection. The injection deadens the nerves. Then you fill the cavities with silver or porcelain.

1. Yesterday I saw a patient after he _____

    _____ .

2. No sooner _____ than he sat down

    in the chair.

3. He had hardly sat down when I _____

    _____ .

4. After I _____ , I made some x-rays.

5. After _____ , I noticed two cavities.

6. Before I started working on his teeth, I _____

    _____ .

7. After _____ , I filled the cavities.

8. _____ hardly _____

    _____ when the patient left.

In 1985 and 1986 a massive campaign was under way to restore the Statue of Liberty. No one could have predicted the generosity of the American people. The fund-raising drive was so successful that it collected $13 million more than was needed to restore the Statue. The following exercises are related to this campaign and the restoration process.

Exercise 25   Change the verbs in parentheses into either the past or past perfect tense. Use the past perfect tense where possible. Adjust the word order where needed. Explain your choices.

The copper skin not (sag), the plated muscles (lose) none of their tone. But a close inspection of the Statue of Liberty's features (show) signs of age. Rust (stain) her cheeks; water (corrode) her features. Worse, the iron armature supporting her 151-foot frame (expand and twist), causing rivets to pop.

The National Park Service (realize) that a drastic overhaul of this most-beloved national monument (be) required. In deference to budget deficits, the NPS (decide) to go to the private sector to raise the millions of dollars it (will take) to heal her, so the newly formed Statue of Liberty-Ellis Island Foundation (create) a campaign and (ask) corporations, citizens, state and local governments for donations and (find) the money and materials to fix the Lady.

It is unlikely that any other structure in America (can elicit) such an enormous response. The elderly, who as young immigrants first (see) the Statue's resolute visage from the decks of inbound ships; children, who (see) her only in photographs; corporations, full of civic fealty and pride — all (contribute).

Repairs (begin) more than two years before the Statue (have) to be ready for her centennial celebration in 1986. For two years, scaffolding (hide) the figure that (symbolize) liberty and a new beginning to more than 17 million immigrants between 1886 and 1986.

The crumbling flame of her 21-foot torch (be) replaced with copper sheeting covered with glittering gold leaf. Stainless steel (take) the place of the rusting iron armature. Her up-held arm, with its faltering supports, (be) strengthened.

That year, in honor of the Liberty's renewal, the Foundation (schedule) a festive July 4 weekend, with a dedication, concerts, meetings, and a fireworks extravaganza; in short a bang-up birthday party for Lady Liberty and the nation.

Exercise 26   Examine the illustration called "Statue of Liberty Restoration" and write a passage describing the restoration process. Use the past perfect tense where necessary.

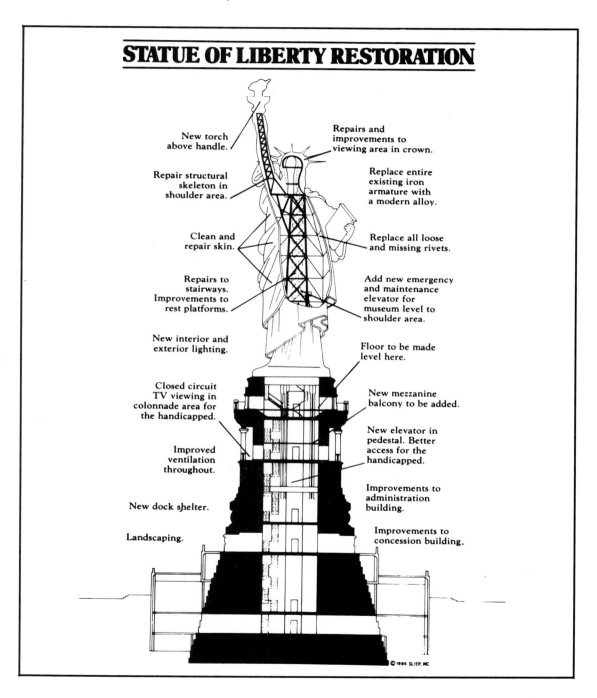

STATUE OF LIBERTY RESTORATION

New torch above handle.

Repairs and improvements to viewing area in crown.

Repair structural skeleton in shoulder area.

Replace entire existing iron armature with a modern alloy.

Clean and repair skin.

Replace all loose and missing rivets.

Repairs to stairways. Improvements to rest platforms.

Add new emergency and maintenance elevator for museum level to shoulder area.

New interior and exterior lighting.

Floor to be made level here.

Closed circuit TV viewing in colonnade area for the handicapped.

New mezzanine balcony to be added.

New elevator in pedestal. Better access for the handicapped.

Improved ventilation throughout.

Improvements to administration building.

New dock shelter.

Landscaping.

Improvements to concession building.

© 1985 SL/EIF, INC.

The Future Tense

The future tense indicates that something will happen some time after the present. The future progressive is used when an action will be in progress at a specific point in time or during a limited period of time in the future.

I will go home after I finish my studies.
I will see you this afternoon.
Shall we leave tomorrow?
I will be studying tomorrow afternoon.
I will help you tomorrow.

Are we going to leave tomorrow?
I am going to help you tomorrow.
I was going to help him, but he wasn't home.

I am about to leave.
He was about to leave when the telephone rang.

To form the future tense, the modal auxiliary *will* is added to the verb phrase. Example: *I will go to the store.* Sometimes a distinction is made between *shall* and *will,* but in modern American English, *shall* is used only for *I* or *we* in questions. Example: *Shall we go now? Shall I help you?* Although these sentences have future meaning, they express a polite suggestion rather than a future question. (Let's go. Would you like for me to help you?)

Besides futurity, *will* may indicate that the subject of the sentence or the speaker wants or is willing to do something. Example: *I will be there.* (I promise that I will be there.) *You will be on time.* (I demand that you come on time.) *Will* is also used to express future probability or prediction. Example: *Boys will be boys.* (Boys will never change.) In other words, the modals *will* and *shall* often express more than just a future.

Therefore, in spoken English, the semi-modal *to be going to* is often preferred to express a definite future event. Example: *I am going to the store this afternoon. I am going to major in engineering.*

The semi-modal *to be about to* expresses an immediate future. Example: *The father grabbed the child because he was about to run in the street. I am about to go to class.*

Note that the semi-modals *to be going to* and *to be about to* can also be used in a past tense.

Exercise 27   On a separate piece of paper, create English sentences with the following sentence parts. Use the most appropriate auxiliary of future tense; *will/shall, to be about to,* or *to be going to.* Use a progressive when possible.

1. I/see/him/later
2. John/study/at five o'clock this afternoon
3. we/ask/him/over for dinner
4. she/work/all morning/tomorrow
5. I/leave
6. they/travel/through Asia/during the month of April
7. the little boy/fall in the pool/when his father grabbed him
8. Michael/go/to first grade/next fall
9. they promise that/they/write/us/many letters
10. the movie/be over/soon

The Future Perfect Tense

The future perfect indicates that something will be finished at a point in the future and that it will be relevant to that point in the future.

- -

I will already have left before you get there.
By the time you get here, I will have left.

Before his vacation is over, he will meet many people.
Before his vacation is over, he will have met many people.

I will go home before John gets here.
Mary will have gone home before John gets here.

I will have been working for three hours by the time you get there.

- -

Again, with certain adverbs like *already* and *yet* the future perfect is required. The future perfect is also required with *by* expressions. With other time expressions, both the future or future perfect may be acceptable, depending on whether the completion and result of the action are more important than the action itself.

The future perfect progressive is used to indicate that an action will be in progress at a specific point or for a limited period of time.

Exercise 28   On a separate piece of paper, create English sentences with the following sentence parts. Use the future or future perfect tense. Use the progressive where possible.

1. I/speak/with him/before he leaves
2. John/arrive/by five o'clock/this afternoon
3. by the time he gets here/I/finish/this assignment
4. next month/I/live/here/for five months
5. she/help/me/tomorrow morning
6. we/ask/him to help us
7. I/stay/here/until I finish my education

8. they/visit/many different countries
9. he/travel/for three hours/before he gets to Los Angeles
10. he/finish/his book/by May
11. I hope that/I/not forget/everything/that I learned this semester/ by this time next year
12. Mary/cook supper/by the time we get to her house
13. The little boy/fall/in the swimming pool/unless his father grabs him
14. by the time he has graduated/he/receive/many job offers

Solving Problems

Verb forms and the use of verb tenses are confusing because there are so many different possible structures. Here you will quickly review the main potential problems.

Inappropriate Tense with Time Expression

Remember that the time expression in the sentence often tells you what tense must be used. The following chart gives a general overview of time expressions and the tenses that are usually used with them.

Note: These are guidelines and not rules, so you may find exceptions to the statements in this chart.

- -

Adverbs of Frequency

always, frequently, usually, never, ever, once a week, once a month, and so on	simple present, simple past, or perfect; no progressive

A Specific Moment or a Limited Duration

now, at this moment, this week, all day all year, and so on	present progressive
for three days, since this morning, and so on	present perfect progressive
yesterday at five o'clock, when I came in, and so on	past progressive
tomorrow afternoon from two to four, all next week, and so on	future progressive
while...., during...from two to four, and so on	different progressive tenses

a few minutes ago, an hour ago, this   simple past tense
    morning, at the beginning of this week,
    yesterday, the day before yesterday,
    last week, last month, last year,
    in 1981, in the 17th century, and so on

A Recent Past or an Expression That Includes the Present

already, recently, just, yet,   a perfect tense
    finally, lately, of late, still,
    since..., so far, up till now, until,
    by... before, no sooner... than,
    hardly, for

- -

INCORRECT: He has gone to the store yesterday.
CORRECT: He went to the store yesterday.

INCORRECT: He already finished his work.
CORRECT: He has already finished his work.

Inappropriate Use of the Progressive

The verb must fulfill several requirements before it can be used in the progressive: it has to show an action in continued progress, at a specific point in time, or during a limited period of time.

INCORRECT: I am liking him.
CORRECT: I like him.

INCORRECT: I have been visiting him three times this week.
CORRECT: I have visited him three times this week.

INCORRECT: I was going to the movies yesterday.
CORRECT: I went to the movies yesterday.

Inappropriate Use of the Perfect

The perfect is used to show a completed event with relevance to another moment. It emphasizes the result of an action, and it must be used with certain time expressions.

INCORRECT: I already ate lunch when he invited me.
CORRECT: I had already eaten lunch when he invited me.

| INCORRECT: | I have eaten breakfast before I went to class. |
| CORRECT: | I ate breakfast before I went to class. |

Faulty Use of *Will* in Adverbial Clauses

The auxiliary *will* is not used in a future adverbial clause of time or condition.

| INCORRECT: | Before I will leave, I will call you. |
| CORRECT: | Before I leave, I will call you. |

| INCORRECT: | If he will help me, I will be finished soon. |
| CORRECT: | If he helps me, I will be finished soon. |

Faulty Use of Tense in Noun Clauses

If the verb in the main clause is in the past tense, the verb in a noun clause must follow the so-called sequence-of-tense rule.

| INCORRECT: | He said that he went to the store yesterday. |
| CORRECT: | He said that he had gone to the store yesterday. |

| INCORRECT: | I asked if he is sick. |
| CORRECT: | I asked if he was sick. |

Faulty Use of Tense in Contrary-to-Fact Statements

The past tense is used for a present contrary-to-fact situation and the past perfect tense for a past contrary-to-fact situation.

| INCORRECT: | I wish I have a lot of money now. |
| CORRECT: | I wish I had a lot of money now. |

| INCORRECT: | If you did not miss the class, you would not have missed the test. |
| CORRECT: | If you had not missed the class, you would not have missed the test. |

Inconsistent Use of Tense

Do not shift tenses unnecessarily.

| INCORRECT: | I watched a movie last night. The movie is good. |
| CORRECT: | I watched a movie last night. The movie was good. |

Now that you have studied the verb tenses and have reviewed the trouble spots, see if you can find the errors in the passage about the Carolina Raptor Center, a place where wounded birds of prey are cared for.

Exercise 29   Each sentence in the following passage contains one of the errors mentioned above. Identify each error and explain why it is wrong. Then rewrite the passage correctly. *Note:* The sentences in quotation marks give the words as they were spoken, so these sentences may require different tenses from the tenses used in the remainder of the passage.

A Place for Birds of Prey

Even though the vulture's wounds healed, it wasn't ready to leave. Again and again, the large black bird was taking to the blue North Carolina sky, circled the chain-link pen and landed nearby. Inside the pen, the rest of the flock watched their newly freed member, who is one of nearly two hundred birds at the Carolina Raptor Center.

"That is sometimes creating a problem," said Sylvia Larson, a center volunteer. She explained that they don't always want to leave the rest of the flock behind even after they had gotten well.

Since it opened two years ago in the Latta Plantation Park north of Charlotte, the center treated and released hundreds of raptors, or birds of prey. Those who were already restored to health are returned to the wild, usually to the place where they were found. Others, with more permanent wounds, are remaining at the center.

"If we will be able to, we treat and release them. Otherwise, they were kept for breeding or educational purposes," Larson said. She then explained that they got birds that have been shot, hit by cars, or those with a number of injuries.

Most of the raptors are native to the Carolinas, but the center is also including birds from other parts of the country, such as Zlaty, a golden Eagle from the West.

Dan Swicegood, a volunteer, said that about thirty raptor centers were existing around the country. He continued, "They send us a bird they may not have room for and didn't want to put to sleep." He added that besides local people, game wardens, and area museums bringing in birds, the volunteers at the center also often have gone to pick them up.

Every weekend, visitors can watch the birds in the center where the birds flew around in roped-off enclosures. In one, a group of hawks and falcons usually has stared with dark, unblinking eyes at the visitors. Some of the falcons are having no physical ailments; instead, the birds suffer from an identity problem known as "imprinting." "If it will have been taken too soon from its parents, a raptor will imprint on the humans around him and not know it's a bird," Larson explained. "The process was known to be irreversible. We have gotten some severely emaciated falcons who have been released in the wild and nearly starved because they didn't know how to hunt. If we release them again, they would not survive."

Exercise 30   The following exercise tests your ability to relate structure to meaning. Read the passage at least three times. Then complete the sentences below by using information from the passage. Your answers should be true according to the information and grammatically correct.

Mary, a high-school drama teacher, and her husband-to-be made an appointment to be married at the county courthouse. Everything went according to schedule until the judge asked, "Will you take this man to be your wedded husband?"

"I do," said Mary.

"The proper response," whispered the judge, "is *I will.*"

"But in all the shows that I have seen and been in," Mary insisted, "they always say *I do.*"

The judge and Mary stared at each other and the groom grew increasingly nervous. The impasse was broken when the witness, an English teacher, announced in an authoritative voice that could be heard at the rear of the chamber, "If you wish to be absolutely correct, the response should be *I shall.*"

The judge searched the room in an appeal for help. Finding none, he snapped his book shut and declared, "Whatever, I now pronounce you husband and wife."

1. Mary and her husband-to-be were at the county courthouse because

_____ .

2. Everything _____ during the first

part of the ceremony.

3. Then the judge asked if Mary _____

   _____ .

4. Mary answered that she _____ .

5. The judge thought that the proper response _____

   _____ .

6. However, Mary insisted that in all the shows she _____

   _____ .

7. While the judge and Mary _____ ,

   the groom _____ .

8. The witness, an English teacher, broke the impasse because she

   announced that the correct _____ .

9. The judge searched the room because he _____

   _____ .

10. Because he _____ , he snapped his

    book shut and declared that he _____

    _____ them husband and wife.

Assignment for Writing

Reading

Read through the following advertisement a few times so you understand the general contents. Do not worry if you do not understand each word. Only look up words that are absolutely necessary for an understanding of the selection.

Group Discussion

1. Who wrote this advertisement?
2. Why, in your opinion, did this center put this advertisement in many American magazines?
3. What is the center's main argument for air bags? State the argument in one sentence.
4. How do air bags work?
5. What protection does an air bag give that a seat belt does not?

THIS COULD SAVE YOUR LIFE.
BUT YOU CAN'T HAVE IT.

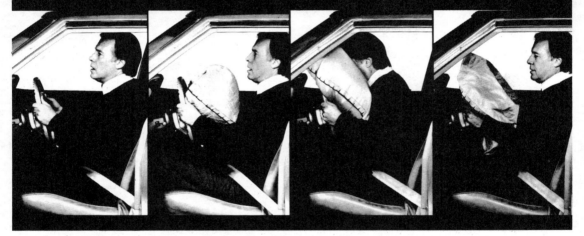

Today people died who shouldn't have. People who would have been saved by air bags.

In an accident, air bags automatically provide a cushioning buffer between you and the car. They protect occupants' necks, heads and faces from flying glass and other debris. They're most effective in front and front-angle collisions, the deadliest kinds of crashes.

Today you can't have this protection. Except for a few luxury imports, cars with air bags are not available.

The auto industry has opposed air bags for years. They claim they would cost twice what the government's independent experts have testified. And they say car buyers don't want

to pay for the extra protection air bags provide.

We think they're wrong.

In the property and casualty insurance industry, we've studied air bags for a long time. Experts tell us they would prevent thousands of deaths a year, and eliminate hundreds of thousands of serious injuries.

How much would air bags actually cost? As standard equipment, they would add about three percent to the price of the average automobile. It sounds like a bargain, and it is.

Right now in Washington, Secretary of Transportation Elizabeth H. Dole is reviewing possible safety requirements for all new cars. And most car companies are trying to keep air bags right where they are

today. Nowhere.

Do something about it while there's still time.

Send for a free copy of our new report, *Air Bags: A Matter of Life or Death.* It sums up the latest facts and tells how you can get involved.

Help save air bags and help save lives. One could well be your own.

ttt Insurance Information Institute
A nonprofit action and information center

6. Why, in your opinion, is the auto industry opposed to air bags?
7. Do you think car buyers want to pay for the extra protection air bags provide? Why or why not?
8. If a new car costs about $10,000, how much would an air bag cost?
9. Why, in your opinion, is the Secretary of Transporation reviewing possible safety requirements for all new cars?
10. Do you believe the government should make air bags mandatory? Why or why not?

Writing

Write an essay of about 450 words in which you state your opinion about airbags.

In your introductory paragraph, state your opinion for or against airbags. Then briefly state three main arguments to support your opinion.

Then expand each argument into a full paragraph. Each paragraph should contain specific facts; in other words, it should contain at least one example, some statistics, or specific details that support your argument.

In your conclusion, state how your reader can get involved.

Proofreading

After you have written and rewritten your essay and you are satisfied with its content, organization, and supporting details, it is time to start worrying about the grammar. Read through your composition several times, each time looking for one of the following specific errors.

1. Is each sentence a sentence? (No fused sentences? Punctuation? Capitalization?)
2. Have you used the correct tense? Find the verb phrase in each sentence and clause. Identify the tense and explain to yourself why you have used that particular tense. Should it be progressive? Should it be perfect? Have you followed the sequence-of-tense rule? Does the sentence express a fact or is it contrary to fact? Have you used the correct verb forms?
3. Have you used tense consistently?
4. Does each finite verb agree with its subject?
5. Have you used enough transitions (conjunctive adverbs, coordinate conjunctions, correlative conjunctions)?
6. Are there any errors in spelling or in the use of articles?

5

The Adverbial Clause

Review/Preview

In Chapter 1 you saw that adverbials express *when, where, why, under what condition,* and so on, something takes place. Adverbials often modify whole sentences, but they may also modify verbs, adjectives, or other adverbs.

Adverbials may occur in all sentence patterns: those with transitive, intransitive, and linking verbs.

They may have several forms: They may be single words, phrases, clauses, or reduced clauses.

Functions

Surely, John will read this book.	modifies a sentence
He can *swim fast*.	modifies a verb
He is an *extremely* good swimmer.	modifies an adjective
He can swim *very fast*.	modifies an adverb

Sentence patterns

John *read* a book *in the library*.	with a transitive verb
Mary *walked fast*.	with an intransitive verb
Peter *seems* tired *today*.	with a linking verb

Forms

John came *yesterday*.	single word
John came *a few days ago*.	phrase
John came *before he left for New York*.	clause
John came *before leaving for New York*.	reduced clause

When a clause functions as an adverbial, it is called an adverbial clause. It is formed by putting an appropriate connecting word, a *conjunction* or a *conjunction phrase,* before a simple sentence. Remember that a clause is like a sentence in that it has a subject and a finite verb. The main difference between a clause and a sentence is that a clause has a connecting word. (See Chapter 1.)

| I studied the lesson. | (I will have a test.) |
| I studied the lesson | *because* I will have a test. |

| I studied the lesson. | (I went to class) |
| I studied the lesson | *before* I went to class. |

A simple sentence explaining *why* is changed to an adverbial clause of reason with the conjunction *because,* and a simple sentence explaining *when* to an adverbial clause of time with the conjunction *before.*

Grammar and Meaning

Punctuation Rules

In Chapter 1 you saw that the normal position of an adverbial is at the end of a sentence but that adverbials may be moved around in the sentence. An adverbial clause may therefore come at the end, in the middle, or at the beginning of a sentence.

The man finished the work *although he was tired.*   final—no comma
The man finished the work *before five o'clock.*

The man, *although he was tired,* finished the work.   medial—two commas
The man, *though tired,* finished the work.

Although he was tired, the man finished the work.   initial—one comma
Though tired, the man finished the work.

A final (at the end) adverbial clause or phrase is in its normal position; therefore, it is not usually separated from the rest of the sentence with a comma. However, a medial or initial clause or phrase usually is.

Now that you have learned the general punctuation rules for adverbials, see if you can add the commas where necessary in the passage about *Gone with the Wind,* a famous novel and movie.

Exercise 1   In the following passage, add commas to set off initial and medial adverbial phrases and clauses.

Gone with the Wind, Fifty Years Later

Fifty years ago Margaret Mitchell believed that if her publisher, the Macmillan Co., issued her novel, *Gone with the Wind,* for $3 per copy they would lose money because even the top-name authors were getting only $2.75 for their works. For the first novel of an unknown author no one would pay such an exorbitant amount, she thought.

Although some advance copies were printed in May 1936 the majority of the volumes were issued on June 30. From then through December of that Depression year the hefty novel by the tiny Atlanta writer sold a million copies.

To buy the book many people would pool their money, as little as 15 cents each, and pass it around among themselves, said Herb Bridges of Sharpburg, Georgia, a collector of *Gone with the Wind* memorabilia.

To commemorate the publication of the novel Bridges and the *Gone with the Wind* Fiftieth Anniversary Celebration, Inc., organized several events in June 1986. In Atlanta and other locations special exhibits, ceremonies, and tours marked the golden anniversary of one of America's best-loved novels.

Adverbial Clauses

Adverbial clauses may express many different interrelationships — for example, time, reason, cause, concession, or purpose. A discussion of the more commonly used conjunctions and conjunction phrases follows.

Time

In Chapter 4 you saw that certain time expressions require certain tenses. Conjunctions of time are also time expressions, so certain conjunctions require certain tenses. For example, the progressive may be used with conjunctions that express a specific point in time or a duration of time, and the perfect may be used with conjunctions that show sequence (for example, *before, after*) if the emphasis is on the result of the action.

The auxiliary *will* is not used in an adverbial clause of time.

Simultaneous Time

Introducing an event of short duration

When John came in, I was studying.
When John came in, I left the room.
The moment that John came in, I was studying.
The moment that John came in, I left the room.
As soon as John came in, I left the room.

Introducing an event of longer duration

When John was studying, I was reading.
While John was studying, I was reading.
As John was studying, I entered the room.
During the time that John was studying, I left the room.

Introducing a repeated event

Whenever I go to the movies, I buy some popcorn.
Every time that I call home, I get homesick.

Sequential Time

After I (had) finished studying, I watched TV.
After I have finished studying, I will watch TV.
After I finish studying, I will watch TV.

As soon as I finish studying, I will watch TV.   = immediately after
When I finish studying, I will watch TV.

Before I watched TV, I (had) finished studying.
Before I watch TV, I will have finished studying.
By the time that my favorite show starts, I will have finished my work.   = before
By the time that my favorite show started, I had finished my work.

I studied *until* my favorite TV show started.
I studied *till* my favorite TV show started.
I studied *up to the moment* that my favorite TV show started.
I will study *until* my favorite TV show starts.

Starting Time of a Continuing Event

I have studied English *since* I was twelve.
I have studied English *from the time that* I was twelve.

- -

Can you explain the use of tense and aspect in the examples? *Since* and *from the time that* indicate the point in time at which something started.

Note that the main clause after these conjunctions must be expressed in the perfect tense because the event is relevant to the present, because it is still going on in the present.

Exercise 2   With the conjunctions listed below, create English sentences based on the following situation. Use a separate piece of paper.

Situation: You didn't have any money. You had to buy school supplies. Your rent was due. The utility bill was due, and so on. You wrote to your parents. They sent you some money. You used it to pay your bills.

1. when
2. while
3. the moment that
4. as soon as
5. as
6. during the time that
7. after
8. before
9. until
10. up to the moment that
11. since
12. from the time that

Exercise 3   In a short composition, describe a trip that you have made (for example, your trip to the United States).

1. In your opening sentences, make clear how you feel about the trip. (For example, was it interesting, boring, tiring, frightening?)
2. Make sure that the composition supports your opening sentence.
3. Concentrate on one aspect of your trip: for example, the food, the people you met, or the confusion at the airport.
4. Try to use as many of the conjunctions of time as you can. Be consistent in your use of tense.

Place

- -

I will meet you *where* we met yesterday.
I will meet you *wherever* you want.

- -

The conjunctions *where* and *wherever* are not used very much to introduce an adverbial clause of place. Actually, these conjunctions (and the time conjunctions *when* and *whenever*) are often used to introduce noun clauses and adjective clauses. Example: *I can't remember where we met before* (noun clause); *I can't remember the place where we met before* (adjective clause).

Reason/Cause

- -

John stayed home *because* he was sick.

John stayed home *since* he had to study for a test. (reason)
John stayed home *as* he had a lot of work to do. (reason)

Now that John has a car, he drives to school.
Now that John has a car, he will not be late anymore.
Now that I have studied hard, I will do well on the test.

- -

Both *since* and *as* may express time as well as reason. Usually the context makes the meaning clear. Example: *I saw an accident as I was walking down the street* (time). *I cannot help you as I have a lot of work to do* (reason). The conjunctions *since* and *as* should be avoided if the meaning of the clause becomes unclear.

The conjunction *now that* means *because now;* it is used to refer to a present or a future situation.

Exercise 4   Using the conjunctions listed below, create English sentences based on the following situation.

Situation: You have to write a term paper. You need to do research in the library. You have a lot of work to do.

1. because

_____ .

2. since

_____ .

3. as

_____ .

4. now that

_____ .

Exercise 5   Look at the ad for vegetable oil on page 162. Assume that you are a dietitian. Give your patient five reasons for buying Puritan oil. Write in complete sentences.

Condition

- -

If you do not study, you will fail the course.   a definite possibility
If you did not study, you would fail the course.   a present contrary-to-fact situation
If you had not studied, you would have failed the course.   a past contrary-to-fact situation

- -

As you saw in Chapter 4, the past tense is sometimes used for a present contrary-to-fact situation, and the past perfect tense for a past contrary-

Down with cholesterol.

Bring high cholesterol down by using Puritan®Oil to prepare more chicken, fish and vegetables. It's cholesterol-free and lower in saturated fat than the leading oil. Proven in a university study to help reduce serum cholesterol in just three weeks.

Puritan helps your family cut cholesterol.

to-fact situation. Therefore, the tense and mood used in the *if*-clause and in the main clause determine the meaning of the sentence. (For more information on conditional sentences, see Chapter 8.) Other conjunctions that may be used with the subjunctive mood are *only if* and *unless*.

As long as you study, you will pass the course. = if
Not until you study *will you* pass the course. inversion in main clause
Only if you study *will you* pass the course. inversion in main clause

Even if you are tired, you should study.
Whether or not you want to, you must study. = It does not matter if

Unless you study, you will fail. = if not
If you do *not* study, you will fail.

In case you have trouble with these conjunctions, ask your instructor for further explanations.
In the event that you don't understand these sentences, you should ask your instructor.
Providing that you understand these conjunctions, we will go on to the exercises.
Provided that you understand these sentences, we will continue the lesson.

Note: The initial adverbial clause is not set off with a comma if the subject and verb are inverted. Example: *Not until he studies will he pass the course.*

Not until, which has a meaning similar to *only if,* has a positive meaning even though it starts with the word *not.* On the other hand, *unless,* which means *if not,* is negative in content.

EXAMPLE:

Not until you have enough money can you buy a car.

BUT:

Unless you have enough money, you cannot buy a car.

Exercise 6   Using the conjunctions listed below, create English sentences based on the following situation. Use a separate piece of paper.

Situation: You would like to travel around in the United States after you have finished your studies. This depends on whether or not you can afford it. It also depends on whether or not you have someone to travel with.

1. if
2. unless
3. provided that
4. whether or not
5. in the event that
6. as long as
7. not until

8. only if
9. even if
10. in case

Concession

- -

John came to school *although* he had a cold.
Even though John had a cold, he went to school.
Although he was feeling ill, he studied for his test.
He studied for his test, *although* he was feeling ill.

- -

Although, though, and *even though* express a meaning similar to *but, yet, however,* and *nevertheless.* (See Chapter 3.)
A final concessive clause may be preceded by a comma if it is felt to be loosely related to the main clause.

Exercise 7   Using the conjunctions mentioned, create English sentences based on the following situation.

Situation: You like the room or apartment in which you are living now. There are some minor problems, however. Give at least five sentences with *even though* or *although.*

Contrast

- -

John studied for the test *whereas* Mary didn't.
John studied for the test *while* Mary didn't.

- -

Whereas and *while* express a meaning similar to *on the contrary* and *on the other hand.* (See Chapter 3.)

Exercise 8   Using the conjunctions mentioned, create English sentences based on the following situation.

Situation: You like certain aspects of life in America. On the other hand, your friend doesn't. Give at least five sentences with *whereas* or *while.*

Result

- -

John was *so* lazy *that* he slept all day.   *so* + adjective + *that*
He walked *so* fast *that* I could not keep up with him.   *so* + adverb + *that*

There were *so* many people *that* we had to stand outside.　so + many + that
There was *so* much food *that* there was a lot left over.　so + much + that
There was *so* little food left *that* we gave it away.　so + little + that

John is *such* a good student *that* he passed the
  difficult examination.　such + noun phrase + that
There was *such* a big crowd *that* we had to stand
  outside.　such + noun phrase + that

POOR ENGLISH: She was *so* smart.　BETTER: She was *very* smart.
POOR ENGLISH: She was *such* a smart girl.　BETTER: She was a *very* smart girl.

- -

So...that is used with adjectives and adverbs and with *much* and
many. *Such...that* is used with noun phrases.

So...that and *such...that* should be used in complex sentences only
and not in simple sentences in written English. (In the spoken language
so and *such* are often used in simple sentences.)

Exercise 9　　Using the conjunctions mentioned, create English sentences based on the
following situation.

Situation: You did not hand in your writing assignment on time. Give
your instructor five excuses with *so...that* and five excuses with
such...that.

Anticipated Result

- -

John is studying very hard *so that* he can pass the test.
John is saving *in order that* he may buy a new car.
John was saving *in order that* he might buy a car.

PREFERRED: John is saving *to buy* a new car.

- -

The main clause after *so that* or *in order that* has a modal, usually
may, might, can, or *could.* In informal English, however, a *to*-infinitive
construction is usually preferred to express purpose. (See the section on
page 179 on *to*-infinitive phrases.)

Comparison

- -

Degree of similarity

John studies *as* hard *as* his sister does.　as + adverb + as
John studies *as* much *as* his sister does.　as + adverb + as
John is *as* tired *as* his sister is.　as + adjective + as
John has *as* many/few books *as* his sister has.　as + many/few + as
John has *as* much/little work *as* his sister has.　as + much/little + as

John studies *harder than* his sister does.	adverb-er + *than*
John is *happier than* his sister is.	adjective-er + *than*
John is *more* tired *than* his sister is.	*more* + adjective + *than*
John studies *more/less than* his sister does.	verb + *more/less* + *than*
John has *more* books *than* his sister has.	*more* + noun + *than*
John has *less* work *than* his sister has.	*less* + noun + *than*

INCORRECT: John studies more harder than his sister.

- -

A clause of comparison expresses the degree to which two persons or things are similar or different. When two persons or things are similar, the unchanged form of an adjective or adverb is used. If there is a degree of difference, the comparative form of the adjective or adverb is used.

To form the comparative an *-er* is added to (1) adjectives or adverbs that consists of one syllable (such as *tall/taller*) and (2) two-syllable adjectives or adverbs ending in *y* or silent *e* (such as *pretty/prettier; simple/simpler*). Other adjectives and adverbs form the comparative with the word *more* (for example, *beautiful/more beautiful*).

Note: Make sure that you avoid double comparisons. The suffix *-er* and the word *more* have the same meaning. It is therefore incorrect to say *more harder.*

Sometimes similarities and differences cannot be expressed with adverbial clauses of comparison. In those cases other expressions like *same, similar, alike, in common,* or *different* are used.

- -

These books are *the same.*	linking verb + *the same*
These books look *the same.*	linking verb + *the same*
He has *the same* book as I have.	*the same* + noun
He has a book (that is) *the same as* mine (is.)	noun + *the same as*
These books are *similar.*	linking verb + *similar*
These musical instruments sound *similar.*	linking verb + *similar*
These are *similar* books.	*similar* + noun
He has a book (that is) *similar to* mine.	noun + *similar to*
They behave *similarly.*	verb + *similarly*
These books are *different.*	linking verb + *different*
These papers seem *different.*	linking verb + *different*
Those are *different* dictionaries.	*different* + noun
Those dictionaries are *different from* mine.	*different from*
They talk *differently.*	verb + *differently*
These books are *alike.*	linking verb + *alike*
Those pies taste *alike.*	linking verb + *alike*
They talk *alike.*	verb + *alike*
These books *have* a lot *in common.*	*have... in common*
These books *have* many features *in common.*	*have... in common*
These books *have* nothing *in common.*	*have... in common*

- -

Sentences with *similar, alike,* and *different* may be modified by an adverbial clause beginning with *in that* explaining the respect in which the items are similar or different.

- -

They are alike *in that* they both are about geography.
They are similar *in that* they both are about geography.
They are different *in that* this book discusses world geography.

- -

Exercise 10   Using the words and expressions listed below, create English sentences based on the following situation.

Situation: Your roommate/friend/spouse and you have certain things in common. There are also some differences (for example, the kinds of foods you like, your study habits, your hobbies, the kinds of clothes you wear).

1. as . . . as
2. as much as
3. as many (   ) as
4. more than
5. the same
6. the same as
7. similar
8. similar to
9. alike
10. different
11. different from
12. similar/alike/different . . . in that

Exercise 11   Develop into a paragraph one of the sentences that you wrote in Exercise 10 (for example, sentence 4, 5, or 6). Give at least two specific examples to substantiate your topic sentence.

Manner

- -

Clause modifies complete sentence
─────────────────────────────────

You must do *as* you have been instructed (to do).
You must write *as* you have been shown (to write).
As I remember, we forgot to mail the letter.

Clause modifies verb
────────────────────

He looks *as if* he is sick.
He looks *as if* he were sick.   contrary-to-fact
He looks *as though* he were unhappy.   contrary-to-fact
He treats her *as if* she were a queen.   contrary-to-fact

- -

An adverbial clause of manner expresses how a person does something. Like conditional clauses, adverbial clauses of manner may have a subjunctive mood. Example: Your friend comes in. He has black circles under his eyes. He is very tired. You don't know why he looks like that, but you may say: *He looked as if he had not slept all night.* The past perfect tense is used for a past situation because the speaker is not at all sure that he did not sleep all night; in other words, it is not an established fact that he did not sleep at all. However, if the speaker has no doubt about the situation, the subjunctive is not used. Example: *You look as if you have a headache.* (The speaker believes strongly that you have a headache.)

Exercise 12   Create English sentences based on the following situation.

Situation: Your instructor doesn't seem very happy today. Guess what might be wrong with him or her. Give at least five sentences with *as if* or *as though*.

Exercise 13   Fill in the blank with an appropriate conjunction: *when, than, if, after, because, so...that, although, while, unless.*

1. _____ one spent at the rate of a dollar a minute, it would require approximately two thousand years to spend a billion dollars.

2. Reno, Nevada, is located farther west _____ Los Angeles, California.

3. No part of a snake's body leaves the ground _____ it is moving from place to place.

4. Mosquitoes dislike citronella _____ it irritates their feet.

5. There is a bird _____ strong _____ it can break a man's arm with its wing. It is the swan.

6. The nomination for president has never been turned down by any man _____ it has been made.

7. A beverage is not an alcoholic beverage _____ it contains more _____ half of one percent alcohol per volume.

8. The opossum, _____ it is slow and stupid, often feigns death _____ it is caught.

Exercise 14   On a separate piece of paper, combine each of the following sets of two sentences into one complex sentence containing an adverbial clause.

EXAMPLE:
Claire entered the room. Audrey was studying.
Claire entered the room while Audrey was studying.

OR:

Audrey was studying when Claire entered the room.

1. John's teacher had warned him about his mistakes. John was more careful.
2. I was shopping at the grocery store. I saw my friend Mary.
3. They came to the United States in 1979. They have been happy.
4. She studied very hard. She made a low grade.
5. I am not feeling well. I am going to class.
6. John studies very hard. Mary doesn't study at all.
7. His car was not very efficient. He decided to sell it.
8. The conditions in the contract have not been met. Our company will cancel the contract.
9. They had rehearsed many times. Their school play was successful.
10. He is a fast runner. I cannot keep up with him.
11. You must study hard. You want to do well in school.
12. My car breaks down. I will drive to Mexico.

Exercise 15   Read each sentence given. Then, on a separate piece of paper, create additional sentences that contain an adverbial clause with the conjunctions listed. Your sentences must be associated with the sentence given. The sentences must be meaningful by themselves and be a possible *description, result,* or *inference* of the situation given. (Make sure you use the correct tense.)

EXAMPLE:

I cashed a check at the bank yesterday.
because   *I cashed a check because I needed some cash.*
while   *I filled out a check while I was waiting in line.*
although   *I had to wait for ten minutes before the teller helped me,*
             although the bank was not very crowded.

1. I am going to the grocery store this afternoon.
   a. because
   b. when
   c. after
2. I went to the movies last night.
   a. before
   b. while
   c. although
3. I received a letter from my parents this morning.
   a. until
   b. the moment that
   c. not until
4. I call my parents once a month.
   a. when
   b. unless
   c. after

5. I have a test tomorrow.
   a. in spite of the fact that
   b. as soon as
   c. as

Exercise 16   Read the ad for a dictionary as many times as you need for a general understanding. Then rewrite the ad so that it applies to your own field of interest.

EXAMPLE:
Who helps engineers work on their orthography?

Your ad should contain at least five adverbial clauses.

Who helps bird-watchers work on their orthography?

How can you spot a whippoorwill when you don't know whether it has one p or two? Well, that's where orthography comes in. It's the art of writing words with the proper letters according to standard usage.

Webster's Ninth New Collegiate Dictionary, just published, can help. This new edition of America's best-selling dictionary has almost 160,000 entries including thousands of new ones, all defined clearly, concisely, and accurately. And at many of those problem words, you'll find authoritative essays on contemporary usage.

Webster's Ninth New Collegiate Dictionary. It's the one to turn to when you want to know about the language.

Take our word for it.

MERRIAM-WEBSTER®
More people take our word for it.

© MERRIAM-WEBSTER 1983

"Who Helps Bird-Watchers Work on Their Orthography?" By permission. Merriam-Webster Inc. © 1983 Advertisement. Publisher of the Merriam-Webster® Dictionaries.

Group assignment suggestion: Divide yourselves into small groups with similar interests, and together rewrite the ad as directed above. Each group writes its ad on the chalkboard.

Discussion:

1. Which ad is the most original?
2. Which ad has the funniest example?
3. Which ad has the best sentence structure?
4. Are there structural errors in any of the ads?
5. Has each ad used five adverbial clauses?

Reduced Adverbial Clauses

You have just studied ten different types of adverbial clauses (of time, reason, manner, and so on). Under certain circumstances, many of these clauses can be changed to such phrases as *-ing, to*-infinitive, and prepositional phrases, which are usually preferred in the English language. In this section we will examine the forms, meanings, and positions of these phrases.

Deletion or Substitution of Repeated Parts in Clauses of Comparison

In the English language repeated sentence parts (parts that are exactly the same) are usually substituted or, where possible, deleted.

- -

John swims fast. Peter swims fast.
(John swims as fast as Peter swims fast.)
(John swims as fast as Peter swims.)
John swims as fast as Peter does.   substitution
John swims as fast as Peter.   deletion

John swims fast. Peter swims faster.
(Peter swims faster than John swims fast.)
(Peter swims faster than John swims.)
Peter swims faster than John does.   substitution
Peter swims faster than John.   deletion

Mary can speak French well. Anne can speak French better.
(Anne can speak French better than Mary can speak French well.)
(Anne can speak French better than Mary can speak French.)
Anne can speak French better than Mary can.   deletion
Anne can speak French better than Mary.   deletion

CORRECT: The weather in New York is cooler than the weather in Miami.
INCORRECT: The weather in New York is cooler than Miami.
CORRECT: The weather in New York is cooler than Miami's.

- -

The repeated parts in a clause of comparison are either substituted with a form of the auxiliary *do* (if there is no other auxiliary in the clause) or deleted. When a clause is reduced, it is important to keep the comparison logical. Example: in the incorrect sentence *the weather* is compared to *Miami*. The possessive form makes it clear that it is Miami's weather, not Miami itself, that is compared to the weather in New York.

Exercise 17   Delete or substitute repeated parts where possible. Make sure the comparisons remain logical.

1. A man's heart beats eight to ten beats more per minute than a woman's heart beats per minute.

2. No fiber feels as good next to the skin as cotton feels next to the skin.

3. A dog is as old at twelve years as a man is old at eighty-four years.

4. A year on the planet Jupiter is twelve times longer than our year on earth is long.

5. For no apparent reason, men get appendicitis more often than women get appendicitis.

6. The diameter of the sun is 108 times longer than the diameter of the earth is long.

7. Frogs and flies can catch athlete's foot the same as people can catch athlete's foot.

Exercise 18   Develop the following topic sentence into a paragraph of about seventy-five words. Use at least three comparisons in your paragraph.

Although I enjoy traveling by car, I prefer to travel by plane.

Deletion of Subject and Be

You will see that in English the subject and the verb *be* — when *be* is not the finite verb in the main clause — are very often deleted. This deletion is also possible in many types of adverbial clauses like those of time, concession, condition, and manner.

- -

When *I am* tired in the afternoon, I take a nap.   time
When tired in the afternoon, I take a nap.

Although *he was* sick, he went to school.   concession
Although sick, he went to school.

	If *you are* unable to come, you should call me.	condition
	If unable to come, you should call me.	
	If *it is* necessary, you can ask for help.	*it + be*
	If necessary, you can ask for help.	
	They should leave as soon as *it is* possible.	*it + be*
	They should leave as soon as possible.	
	He acted as if *he were* unable to understand me.	manner
	He acted as if unable to understand me.	
INCORRECT:	When doing his homework, his radio is always on.	dangling modifier
CORRECT:	When doing his homework, he always listens to the radio.	
CORRECT:	When he is doing his homework, the radio is always on.	

- -

The subject and the verb *be* may be deleted from an adverbial clause if the subjects of the main clause and the adverbial clause are the same (Example: *I am tired; I take a nap.*) or if the subject is impersonal *it* (*If it is possible,...*)

However, if a clause is reduced when the subjects of the clauses are clearly different (Example: *He is doing his homework; his radio is always on.*) a serious error — *a dangling modifier* — results.

Exercise 19   Delete the subject and *be* from the adverbial clause if possible. (*Note:* The deletion is not possible in one sentence.)

1. When honey is swallowed, honey enters the bloodstream within a period of twenty minutes.

2. While a horse is trotting, a horse has all four feet off the ground part of the time.

3. A duck often swims while it is sleeping.

4. Snakes are often immune to their own poison when it is swallowed. (*Note: it* is not impersonal.)

5. When he was ten years old, Robert Earl Hughes of Fish Hook, Illinois, weighed 378 pounds.

Exercise 20   Identify the reduced clauses in the following sentences. Then tell what full clauses they were derived from.

1. John Keats and Robert Louis Stevenson wrote their greatest books while weakened by tuberculosis.

2. One cup of rice becomes three cups when cooked.

Reduced Adverbial Clauses   173

3. A rattlesnake holds its rattle above the water when swimming.

4. People chew gum when traveling by air because the working of the jaws tends to keep the air pressure equalized on both sides of the eardrums.

5. The opossum, although slow and stupid, often feigns death when caught.

Exercise 21   With the reduced adverbial clauses given below, create English sentences based on the following situation.

Situation: John is a very diligent, conscientious student. Describe his habits.

1. While studying, _____ .

2. When at the library, _____ .

3. Although sometimes bored, _____ .

4. _____ when finished.

5. _____ as if totally absorbed.

Final Participial Phrase to Express Means or Simultaneous Action

After a few verbs and after a few expressions, an *-ing* phrase often expresses a simultaneous action or attendant circumstances (*He sat in a chair [at the same time he was] staring at the ceiling*).

After a verb like *earn,* a final *-ing* phrase expresses means.

	Verb
He sat in a chair *staring at the wall.*	*sit*
He stood at the desk *waiting to be helped.*	*stand*
He lay on the beach *daydreaming.*	*lie*
He spends most of his time *studying.*	*spend*
He earns a living *(by means of) driving a truck.*	*earn*
He earns a living *driving a truck.*	
He earns a living *by driving a truck.*	
He ran into the room *screaming for help.*	*run*
He came *running into the room.*	*come*
He went home *wondering who would be there.*	*go*
He caught a cold *walking in the rain.*	*catch a cold*
He got tired *trying to catch up with us.*	*get tired*
We are busy *studying.*	*busy*

Exercise 22   Combine the following sets of two sentences by using a main clause and a final *-ing* phrase.

1. He lay awake all night long. He was thinking about his girlfriend.

2. He sits all day in that chair. He is watching TV.

3. John and Mary sat in the cafeteria. They were talking, and they were drinking a soft drink.

4. I spent the whole day. I was studying for my test.

5. The child stood by the window. He was watching his friends play.

Exercise 23   Use each of the verbs and expressions given in the chart above in an original sentence of your own.

Initial Participial Phrase to Express Reason

An *-ing* phrase at the beginning of the sentence set off with a comma expresses *why* or *when* something happened. In other words, an initial participial phrase may express *reason* or *time*.

- -

Because he was sick, John did not go to school.
Being sick, John did not go to school.

Because she had had an accident, Mary drove more carefully.
After she had had an accident, Mary drove more carefully.
Having had an accident, Mary drove more carefully.

INCORRECT:	Because having had an accident, she drove more carefully.
CORRECT:	After having had an accident, she drove more carefully.
CORRECT:	Having had an accident, she drove more carefully.
INCORRECT:	Not having much homework, the afternoon was pleasant. dangling modifier
CORRECT:	Not having much homework, we had a pleasant afternoon.
CORRECT:	Because we did not have much homework, the afternoon was pleasant.

- -

When an initial *-ing* phrase is derived from a clause with a past perfect tense, it has both a *because* and an *after* meaning, but unlike *after,* the conjunction *because* cannot occur before an *-ing* phrase: It must be deleted.

Also, just as with the reduced adverbial clauses mentioned just above, the subject of the reduced clause must be the same as the subject of the main clause; otherwise, a dangling modifier results.

As you can see in the diagram below, this type of reduced clause is very similar to the reduced clauses mentioned in the sections on deletion of subject and *be.* However, there are some important differences. First, the *-ing* phrase must be initial, and the conjunction *because* must be deleted.

Second, instead of deleting a finite verb, you must change the finite verb itself to an -*ing* form.

- -

Because	he	had	heard the bad news, he went to his room.
		Having	heard the bad news, he went to his room.
Although	he	was	very upset, he went on working.
Although			very upset, he went on working.

- -

Exercise 24   Combine the following sets of two sentences using a main clause and an initial present participle phrase.

1. He played tennis every day. He became a very good player.

2. They found no one at home. They left a note on the door.

3. They had run out of gas. They had to walk to the nearest gas station.

4. He opened his wallet. He found that a hundred dollars was missing.

Exercise 25   Complete the following sentences in your own words.

1. Having _____ , she became sad.

2. _____ , they were often hungry.

3. Not _____ , he failed his test.

4. After _____ , she ate breakfast.

5. _____ , we were late.

An initial -*ing* phrase of reason can sometimes be reduced even further. Examine the following examples.

Initial Adjective Phrase or Past Participle Phrase of Reason

- -

Conjunction	Subject	Finite verb	
Because	he	was	unable to attend the party, he sent some roses.
		Being	unable to attend the party, he sent some roses.
			Unable to attend the party, he sent some roses.
Because	he	was	depressed, he did not speak to anyone.
		Being	depressed, he did not speak to anyone.
			Depressed, he did not speak to anyone.

- -

If the present participle is *being,* it may be deleted. Note, however, that the resulting adjective phrase (*Unable to...*) and the resulting past participle phrase (*Depressed...*) still have a *because* meaning. This reduction is another example of the frequent omission of *be* when it is not the finite verb in the main clause.

Another variation of the initial participial phrase of reason is the so-called *nominative absolute.*

The Nominative Absolute

Conjunction	Subject	Finite verb	
Because	the train	was late,	we missed the plane.
	The train	being late,	we missed the plane.
Because	his test	was over,	he felt relieved.
	His test	being over,	he felt relieved.
	His test	over,	he felt relieved.

The absolute construction looks exactly like a sentence in that it has a subject and a predicate, but in an absolute construction, the finite verb is changed to an *-ing* form. When the present participle is *being,* it may be deleted from the phrase. Again, when the phrase is initial, it usually has a *because* meaning.

Because this type of construction is quite frequent in vivid narrative and descriptive writing, it is a structure that you should recognize in your reading and use judiciously in your writing.

Exercise 26 In a magazine or book find a short story or essay. Try to find at least three examples of a reduced clause of reason. Try to find at least one nominative absolute.

Initial Participial Phrase to Express Time

The conjunction *while* is sometimes deleted from a reduced adverbial clause of time.

While	I was	walking home, I found a dollar.
While		walking home, I found a dollar.
		Walking home, I found a dollar.

The initial reduced *while*-clause looks exactly like the reduced adverbial clause of reason, and only the context shows whether the initial participial phrase has a *while* or a *because* meaning. Sometimes the initial participial phrase can express both.

Walking, I found a dollar in the street.
(While I was walking, I . . .)

Finding no one at home, I left a note.
(Because I found no one at home, I . . .)

Walking home, I ran into my friend.
(While I was walking home, I . . .)
(Because I was walking home, I . . .)

Exercise 27   The following is an outline describing how knowledge greatly advanced in a single century in the city of Baghdad.

Use the information below to create a coherent passage. Use any of the conjunctive adverbs and conjunctions you have learned so far. Also use at least three reduced clauses as explained in the sections just above.

> EXAMPLES:
>
> *When (I am) tired, I take a nap.*
> *He sat on a chair (while he was) staring at the wall.*
> *Being sick, John stayed home.*

The city of Baghdad had been founded in 762. It became the seat of a rapidly growing empire. About forty years later, it became the capital of learning of the Western world. This was during the reign of Caliph Harun al-Rashid. In learning, Baghdad combined the best of both worlds, East and West.

Merchants and mathematicians from the East brought with them new number signs. They brought arithmetic from India.

Heretics had fled from the West. They brought copies of scientific work. This work had been written while the city of Alexandria was still in its prime. These copies included treatises on astronomy, geography, and geometry.

Muslim scholars translated such works into Arabic. This was ordered by the Caliph. The science and geometry of Greece became available throughout the Muslim world. The Muslim world was now equipped with an arithmetic far better than that the Greeks had ever known.

In the schools of Baghdad, trigonometry flourished. Muslim mathematicians had mastered the new arithmetic of India. They could make fuller use of the geometry of Euclid and of Archimedes.

The East made two other contributions to this growing body of knowledge. Chinese people were captured during a skirmish on the frontier. These prisoners taught Baghdad the art of paper making.

At the same time, Persian astrologers gave the caliph's court a keen interest in astronomy. Observatories were built by command of the caliph. These observatories enabled astronomers to advance the science of map making. These maps were much better than those that had been made in Alexandria.

The astronomer equipped the mariner with nautical almanacs for navigation by sun and stars. He also gave him improved instruments. These were designed in observatories. The geographer had new and better tools for land survey.

The knowledge of the East and West had met in Baghdad. Knowledge advanced very much in a single century. Never before had so much progress been made as between A.D. 800 and 900.

To-*Infinitive to Express Anticipated Result*

As was mentioned above under "Anticipated Result," a *so that* or *in order that* clause must contain a modal auxiliary in the clause. As you will see throughout this text, a clause containing a modal is often reduced to a *to*-infinitive construction.

The *to*-infinitive construction is usually preferred to the rather stilted *so that* or *in order that* clauses.

To form this type of construction, the conjunction, subject, and modal auxiliary are replaced by *in order to,* or just *to.*

- -

John is studying hard in order that he might pass the test.
John is studying hard (in order) *to pass* the test.

She stayed so that she might help.
She stayed (in order) *to help.*

- -

Exercise 28   Complete the following sentences in your own words with a *to*-infinitive to express purpose.

1. He bought the most expensive sports car _____

_____ .

2. He decided to learn English well _____

_____ .

3. I took my clothes to the laundromat _____

_____ .

4. He sat in the front row _____ .

5. I will write my parents today _____

_____ .

Exercise 29   Complete each of the following sentences with a main clause. The *to*-infinitive must express purpose.

1. _____ to buy a new shirt.

2. _____ to study.

3. _____ to become fluent in English.

4. _____ to mow the grass.

5. _____ to mail the letter.

A further reduction of the *to*-infinitive construction is possible when the infinitive is *to be*.

- -

He painted the house so that it would be green.	*push crack*
He painted the house to be green.	*cut wipe*
He painted the house green.	*wash freeze*
He was chosen so that he would be president.	*nominate*
He was chosen to be president.	*designate*
He was chosen as president.	*select*
He was chosen president.	
We call him John.	*call*
We named him Peter.	*name*
We made him president.	*make*

- -

Verbs that may occur in a pattern similar to the pattern with the verb *paint* are *push, cut, wash, crack, wipe,* and *freeze.*

Other verbs like *choose* are *nominate, designate, elect,* and *select.* The verbs *name, make,* and *call* occur in a similar pattern, but they are not followed by a clause or a *to*-infinitive.

Exercise 30   Fill in the blank with an appropriate word.

1. He _____ the house white.

2. We appointed _____ as treasurer.

3. He pushed _____ open.

4. We call him _____ .

5. We cut her hair _____ .

6. _____ designated it as their home base.

7. They _____ the clothes clean.

8. They elected him as _____ .

9. They cracked _____ open.

10. They _____ him the boss.

11. They _____ the chalkboard clean.

12. We nominated _____ secretary.

13. The _____ was frozen solid.

14. They selected _____ as their symbol.

Too ... To-Infinitive to Express Negative Result

- -

I am so tired that I cannot study.
I am *too* tired   *to*   *study.*

He is so poor that he cannot buy food.
He is *too* poor   *to*   *buy food.*

- -

A negative *so ... that* clause is often reduced to a *too ... to-infinitive* construction.

Exercise 31   On a separate piece of paper, create meaningful sentences containing the *too ... to*-infinitive construction.

1. tired/run a mile
2. sleepy/read a book
3. excited/sit down quietly
4. nervous/do well on the test
5. lazy/clean up their room

Exercise 32   Complete the following sentences in your own words.

1. He was _____ to work.

2. He was too upset _____ .

3. She was too busy _____ .

4. The child was too _____ .

5. The dog was too _____ .

Reduction is also possible when the subject of the main clause and the result clause are not the same. However, some changes are sometimes made.

- -

He is so young that he cannot go.   same subject
He is *too* young   *to go.*

This bag is so heavy that I cannot carry it.   different subject
This bag is *too* heavy   *for me to carry it.*   *for*-phrase + infinitive
This bag is *too* heavy   *to carry.*

This bag is so heavy that it cannot be carried.   passive construction
This bag is *too* heavy   *to be carried.*   passive infinitive

INCORRECT: This bag is too heavy to carry it.
 CORRECT: This bag is too heavy for me to carry it.
 CORRECT: This bag is too heavy to carry.

- -

If the subject of the main clause and the subject of the result clause are not the same, the subject of the *to*-infinitive may be expressed in a *for*-phrase. The *for*-phrase, in turn, may be deleted. *Note:* When the *for*-phrase is deleted, the object *it* must also be deleted.

Another possibility is to make the result clause passive. There is no difference in meaning between the active *too heavy to carry* and the passive *too heavy to be carried* phrases.

Exercise 33   Complete each of the following sentences with two infinitive constructions, an active one and a passive one.

EXAMPLE:

This bag is too heavy _____ .

to carry.
to be carried.

1. This book is too difficult to _____ .

2. The table was too wobbly to _____ .

3. The movie was too boring to _____ .

4. The house was too expensive to _____ .

5. The mouse was too fast to _____ .

Enough...To-Infinitive to Express Positive Result

- -

He studied so much that he passed the test.
He studied   *enough*   *to*   *pass* the test.   verb + enough

He studied so hard that he passed the test.
He studied *hard enough to pass* the test.   adverb + enough

He is so smart that he will pass the test.
He is   *smart enough   to   pass* the test.   adjective + enough

He has so much   money that he can buy a car.
He has   *enough money*   *to*   *buy* a car.   enough + noun

He has so many days off that he can go on vacation.
He has   *enough days off*   *to*   *go* on vacation.   enough + noun

- -

A *so...that* clause of positive result may be reduced to an *enough... to*-infinitive construction. *Enough* may be used with verbs, adverbs, adjectives, and nouns. It usually follows verbs, adverbs, and adjectives, but it precedes a noun.

Exercise 34   On a separate piece of paper, create meaningful sentences containing the *enough + to*-infinitive construction.

1. books/read
2. study/pass the course
3. rich/buy a house
4. time/go to the movies tonight
5. fast/catch up with John

Exercise 35   Use the information given below and rewrite it into a coherent passage. First, combine the sentences after each number into one complex sentence. (Try to use at least three *to*-infinitive constructions as explained in the sections above). Then, where necessary, connect your sentences with conjunctive adverbs such as *however, for example,* and so on, to make clear the meaningful relationships between the sentences.

Deceiving Looks

1. Some bodily characteristics are common to all insects.

2. Many species have special adaptations. These aid them. These insects can gain a livelihood and avoid their enemies.

3. Many insects are camouflaged very well. They can easily hide from their enemies or approach their victims.

4. Everyone has noticed how a katydid or a walking stick looks very similar to its background of leaves. It is undetected.

5. The color of a seashore grasshopper is very similar to the sand's. It is invisible on the sand.

6. In other instances, some insects resemble another insect very much. They may be protected in some special way.

7. The viceroy butterfly looks like a monarch. The monarch tastes very bad. Birds do not eat it.

8. Birds also avoid the viceroy.

9. Perhaps the viceroy's life is saved. It is mistaken for a monarch.

10. A robber fly is very similar to a bumblebee. It is avoided by other insects. These insects might otherwise prey on this robber.

11. Some insects are protected. They resemble other insects. This is a theory called *mimicry*. (Start with: *The theory that ...*)

12. Mimicry seems to account for the color and pattern of some insects. Many scientists do not accept the theory.

Prepositional Phrases

Prepositional phrases may express meanings similar to the meaning expressed by adverbial clauses. Example: *during his high school years* is similar to *while he was going to high school.*

- -

Because	he is very intelligent,	he makes straight As.
Because of	his intelligence,	he makes straight As.
Because	the weather is very bad,	we cannot go on a picnic.
Because of	the bad weather,	we cannot go on a picnic.
Owing to	the bad weather,	we cannot go on a picnic.

Although	he was very sick,	he went to school.
In spite of	his sickness,	he went to school.
In spite of	his being sick,	he went to school.

	He did not take	the red cup; he took the blue cup.
Instead of	(taking)	the red cup, he took the blue cup,

He became famous   while he was living.
He became famous   *during* his lifetime.

Before	he arrived,	he wrote us a letter.
Before	his arrival,	he wrote us a letter.
Prior to	his arrival,	he wrote us a letter.

After	he arrived,	he rented an apartment.
After	his arrival,	he rented an apartment.
Subsequent to	his arrival,	he rented an apartment.

He has been very happy since   he arrived.
He has been very happy *since*   his arrival.

I have taken all the required courses, but I have not taken   Math 113 yet.
I have taken all the required courses *except for*   Math 113.
I have taken all the required courses *but for*   Math 113.

- -

A preposition must be followed by a noun phrase. Unlike a clause, a noun phrase does not have a finite verb. The noun in a prepositional phrase is often an abstract noun, which is a noun made from a verb or an adjective (for example, *arrival,* made from *arrive*) or a gerund, which is an *-ing* form used as a noun (for example, *being*). (For more information on the formation of noun phrases see Chapter 10.)

Note: Some words have more than one function. Several conjunctions may also be used as prepositions (for example, *after, before,* and *until*).

Exercise 36   Using the list of prepositions below, create English sentences explaining why you are studying English and what your plans are when you finish with this course.

1. Because of _____ .

2. Since _____ .

3. Before _____ .

4. Subsequent to _____ .

5. Prior to _____ .

6. During _____ .

7. Instead of _____ .

8. In spite of _____ .

9. Owing to _____ .

Exercise 37   Change the italicized clauses to prepositional phrases. Make abstract nouns out of the underlined words.

1. *Because he was <u>able</u> to speak English,* he got a very good job.

2. *Because they <u>rejected</u> the offer,* the contract was canceled.

3. *While the children <u>napped</u>,* the mother relaxed and read a book.

4. *Although he is very old (use: <u>age</u>),* he is very energetic.

5. *I should have taken <u>Math 103</u>;* I took Math 105.

6. *I have not taken <u>Math 104</u> yet;* I have taken all other math courses.

7. *After he had <u>discussed</u> it with Mary,* he decided to have a party for the whole class.

8. *Before he had <u>decided</u> to change his major,* he was unhappy.

9. *Before he had <u>departed</u>,* he became ill.

10. *Although he wears <u>expensive clothes</u>,* he is not very wealthy.

Exercise 38   Summary exercise: Combine each of the following sets of two sentences into one sentence containing a reduced adverbial clause. (See pp. 171–186.)

1. Some students were sitting in the classroom. They were talking about the football game.

2. He is going to the United States. He wants to get a degree in pharmacy.

3. He believed that he was very sick. He was very unhappy.

4. She became very tired. She was trying to do too many things at the same time.

5. He backed out of his driveway. He hit the lamppost.

6. He earns a living. He drives a truck.

7. I will write you a letter. I will tell you all the news.

8. They selected him. He became the president.

9. I am very rested. I can study.

10. There is inflation. The price of gold has not gone up much.

Exercise 39   Change the italicized adverbial phrases to full adverbial clauses. Make sure each clause has a subject and a finite verb.

1. Hummingbirds lay only two eggs *during their entire lifetime.*

2. Spinach loses fifty percent of its vitamin C content within twenty-four hours *after being picked.*

3. *Having lungs instead of gills,* whales cannot breathe under water.

4. A Brahman bull purrs *when happy.*

5. American consumers spend a billion dollars a year *to buy cold relief preparations.*

6. *After having completely rusted,* one ton of iron weighs three tons.

7. *Because of the earth's rotation,* a golf shot can be thrown farther if it is thrown to the west.

8. The average American family spends more than three hours each day *reading newspapers.*

9. Thomas Jefferson is quoted more often and on more different subjects *than any other president of the United States.*

10. About seventy percent of hospital costs are used *to pay employees' salaries.*

Summary of Sentence Connectors

The following diagram summarizes the variety of structures that may be used to express the different relationships between ideas. The key words, such as *concession* and *contrast,* are explained in Chapter 3. Punctuation rules for coordinate conjunctions, correlative conjunctions, and conjunctive adverbs are also in Chapter 3. Subordinate conjunctions, prepositional phrases, and other structures are explained in this chapter. Note how limited the use of infinitive and present participle phrases is.

Coordinate correlative conjunctions	Conjunctive adverbs	Subordinate conjunctions and phrases	Prepositional phrases	Other structures
TIME				
and	next then later subsequently	when the moment (that) as soon as	during after until before	*Walking through the street,* he . . . *After seeing the accident,* he . . .

Coordinate correlative conjunctions	Conjunctive adverbs	Subordinate conjunctions and phrases	Prepositional phrases	Other structures
TIME				
	after that	when	up till	*Before leaving the*
	afterwards	while	since	*house,* he...
	before that	during the time	subsequent to	
	previously	(that)	prior to	
	formerly	after	previous to	
	meanwhile	before	following	
	during the same time	by the time (that)		
	at the same time	until		
	in the meantime	up to the moment (that)		
	first of all	since		
	in the first place	from the time (that)		
	secondly	once		
	at the end			
	finally			
PLACE				
		where		
		wherever		
CAUSE				
for		because	because of	*Having had an*
		since	owing to	*accident,* he...
		now that	in view of	*The train being*
		as	for the sake of	*late,* we....
		because of the fact that	(for lack of)	*(being) Unable to*
			inasmuch as	*come,* she...
CONDITION				
		if		
		on the condition that		
		as long as		
		not until		
		only if		
		even if		
		whether or not		
		in case		
		in the event that		
		provided that		
		providing that		

Coordinate correlative conjunctions	Conjunctive adverbs	Subordinate conjunctions and phrases	Prepositional phrases	Other structures
NEGATIVE CONDITION				
or or else	otherwise	unless		
CONCESSION				

but
yet
	however
	nevertheless
	nonetheless
	still
		although
		even though
		though
		in spite of the
		    fact that
		despite the fact
		regardless of
		    the fact that
			in spite of
			despite
			regardless of	

CONTRAST				
but	on the contrary in contrast on the other hand	whereas while	contrary to in contrast with	
EXAMPLE				
	for example for instance in other words		such as like	
RESULT				

so	therefore
	as a result
	consequently
	hence
	in consequence
		so...that
		such...that
				I am *too* tired
				    to study.
				I am tired *enough*
				    to go to sleep.

ANTICIPATED RESULT				

		so that
		in order that
			for the purpose of
			with a view to
			with the intention
			    of
			with the hope of
				He went there *to*
				    buy some rice.

COMPARISON				
but	similarly likewise	as...as more/*-er*...than	unlike like different from similar to	

Coordinate correlative conjunctions	Conjunctive adverbs	Subordinate conjunctions and phrases	Prepositional phrases	Other structures
MANNER				
		as if as though as		He sat on a chair *watching TV.*
RESPECT				
		in that	with respect to	
MEANS				
			by by means of	He earns a living *(by) driving a truck.*
CHOICE				
or nor either . . . or neither . . . nor				
SPECIFICATION				
	in fact actually specifically			
ADDITION				
and both . . . and not only . . . but also	moreover besides in addition furthermore next what's more		as well as in addition to next to besides	
EXCEPTION				
but		beyond that except (for the fact) that save (for the fact) that but for the fact that	beyond except for save for but for	

Solving Problems

Fragment

When a clause or a phrase is punctuated as if it were a sentence, it is called a *fragment*. A subordinate clause or phrase by itself is not a sentence but a part of a sentence.

INCORRECT: When I came to work.
  CORRECT: When I came to work, I started writing a report.
  CORRECT: I came to work.

INCORRECT: Being sick.
  CORRECT: Being sick, I stayed home.

Double Conjunction

A sentence must have *one* main clause. If two clauses are connected, only *one* conjunction is needed. If three clauses are connected, *two* conjunctions are needed, and so on. It is wrong to connect two clauses with two conjunctions. This is called a double conjunction error.

INCORRECT: Although I was tired, but I went to work.
  CORRECT: Although I was tired, I went to work.

INCORRECT: The boy who came when I wanted him to.
  CORRECT: The boy came when I wanted him to.

Exercise 40   In the passage below, many of the sentences (but not all of them) are wrong. They are (a) a fragment, (b) a fused sentence, (c) a comma splice, or (d) they contain a double conjunction error. Identify the errors and correct them.

Horseradish

Horseradish is a plant that is native to Europe. Although it is planted in gardens, but it also persists around old house sites, and sometimes it naturalizes in rich ground. It has large, rather crinkled roots they are somewhat similar to those of dock, but they are pungently flavored and odorous. In midsummer when flowers appear on high branched stalks. The deep, white, very pungent roots that are edible and they are supposed to be an excellent spring tonic. They were once used for dyspepsia, rheumatism, scurvy, and hoarseness. When it was made into a tea by putting one teaspoon of ground roots in one cup of boiling water. It is said that eating horseradish is a spur to digestion, it is also supposed to expel kidney stones.

Some people say the young leaves are edible; others say that they are not good to eat. Because they are extremely pungent and could probably only be used when they are very young and tender.

Illogical Comparison

INCORRECT: The climate in the South is warmer than the North.
CORRECT: The climate in the South is warmer than the climate in the North.
CORRECT: The climate in the South is warmer than the North's.

Double Comparison

INCORRECT: The climate in the South is more warmer than the climate in the North.
CORRECT: The climate in the South is warmer than the climate in the North.

Dangling Modifier

INCORRECT: While doing my homework, the telephone rang.
CORRECT: While doing my homework, I heard the telephone.
CORRECT: While I was doing my homework, I heard the telephone.

Confusion of Sentence Connectors

(See chart)

INCORRECT: During he was attending college, he worked.
CORRECT: While he was attending college, he worked.

INCORRECT: He studied, later he went to school.
CORRECT: After he studied, he went to school.

Illogical Use of a Reduced Clause

(See chart)

INCORRECT: Having a lot of homework, I went to the movies.
CORRECT: Having a lot of homework, I did not go to the movies.
CORRECT: In spite of having a lot of homework, I went to the movies.

INCORRECT:	He studied hard passing the test.
CORRECT:	He studied hard to pass the test.

Faulty Placement of a Reduced Clause

(See chart)

INCORRECT:	He stayed home having a fever.
CORRECT:	Having a fever, he stayed home.

INCORRECT:	Waiting for his friend, he spent three hours.
CORRECT:	He spent three hours waiting for his friend.

Faulty Use of Tense or Modal in a Subordinate Clause

INCORRECT:	As soon as he was entering the room, he saw me.
CORRECT:	As soon as he entered the room, he saw me.

INCORRECT:	He is studying hard so that he passes the test.
CORRECT:	He is studying hard so that he can pass the test.

Internal Punctuation Error

INCORRECT:	Although he is unhappy he is smiling.
CORRECT:	Although he is unhappy, he is smiling.

INCORRECT:	He is unhappy, because he failed his test.
CORRECT:	He is unhappy because he failed the test.

Exercise 41   Many (but not all) of the sentences in the following passage contain one of the errors mentioned above. Rewrite the passage correctly.

After the Spanish-American War officially has ended on August 12, 1898, a treaty of peace was signed on December 10, 1898, giving Cuba her complete independence. Yet conditions in Cuba were getting more worse, so American troops were required to remain on the island for some time. While many Cubans were without homes and thousands were starving disease, especially yellow fever, was spreading widely.

For years, yellow fever having been the most feared disease of warm countries. While the Spanish-American war, more American soldiers died of yellow fever than were killed by Spanish bullets. Since generally about fifty percent died of those who became sick with the disease, so in serious epidemics sometimes eighty-five out of a hundred died.

Because many of the American troops remaining in Cuba after the Spanish-American War continued to fall ill. Particularly, the year 1900 was worse than during the war. The whole island of Cuba seemed affected. Thousands of Cubans lay dead in the streets, completely unattended.

Then, on June 25, 1900, Major Walter Reed of the United States Army Medical Service arrived in Havana. Having just been named head of the Yellow Fever Board, the United States Government sent him to Cuba to study yellow fever and find its cause. Reed and his companions set to work at once.

They began experiments to test the theory that the disease was caused by the bite of a mosquito having established a kind of rough laboratory outside Havana. Because of the experiments were successful, the whole world soon applauded the men as great heroes. But, having taken some very great risks, some lives had even been lost in order that the experiments might go on. These brave men fought a dramatic fight to stamp out yellow fever.

Exercise 42 The following two exercises test your ability to relate structure to meaning. Read the passages carefully at least three times. Then answer the questions and complete the sentences with information from the passage. Your answers should be based on the passage and grammatically correct.

American books published in Great Britain are usually reset in type before publication, not because of American slang, which the British usually find quaint and even expressive, but because of certain differences in spelling.

For example, the English words *colour, honour,* and *labour* are spelled without a *u* in American English. The British spelling for *defense* and *offense* is *defence* and *offence.* The British spell *practice* with an *s* whereas Americans spell it with a *c.* The British use *-re* instead of *-er* in such words as *theater* and *center.* Some other differences are *tyre* versus *tire* and *checque* versus *check.* There are also some differences in word choices; for example, the British use certain adverbs (for example, *whilst*) that most Americans find old-fashioned.

1. American books published in Great Britain are usually reset in type before they _____ .

2. American books are usually reset in type because there _____

_____ .

3. As _____ the American slang is usually not changed.

4. Whereas the British spelling includes a *u* after an *o* in a word like *colour,* Americans _____ .

5. While Americans use *-er* in a word like *theater,* the British _____

_____ .

6. _____ , Americans do not use *whilst.*

Exercise 43

What Is Aberration of Light?

Aberration of light is what seems to be a change in the position of an object, not because the object is moving but because the observer is moving. In astronomy, the stars seem not to be in their true positions in the heavens because the earth moves in its orbit while the light is coming from a star to the the earth. The effect is that a star seems to move forward with the earth.

The rotation of the earth on its axis and the effect of the velocity of light on telescopic observation also contribute to the aberration. This was first explained and accurately measured by an English astronomer, James Bradley, in 1727. Using a star in the constellation Draco, he observed that in March, when the earth is traveling in the direction of the line joining the star to the sun, a telescope must be tilted toward the south to see the star; in September, when the earth is traveling away from this line, the telescope must be tilted toward the north.

1. Aberration of light is (a) an apparent change in the position of an object, (b) a moving object, or (c) a moving observer.
2. Aberration of light is caused by (a) a change in the position of an object or (b) a change in the position of the observer.
3. During the time that the light is traveling from the star to the earth,

the earth _____ ; therefore, the

star seems _____ and seems _____

_____ .

4. Moreover, the earth _____ and the

velocity of light _____ telescopic observation.
5. What did James Bradley measure and explain?
6. Why must a telescope be tilted toward the south to see a star in March?
7. Why must it be tilted toward the north in September?
8. How did Bradley observe this?
9. In your own words explain what aberration of light is.

Assignment for Writing

Reading

Look at the advertisement for a cruise trip from the United States to Europe. Read through the ad quickly to get a general idea about its content. Then answer the questions.

1. What is the key adjective used to describe the cruise trip?
2. Can you find some more adjectives to describe it?
3. What are some of the pleasant surprises aboard the ship?
4. Do you think different types of people would be entertained on the ship? Why? Where would you spend most of your time if you were traveling on that ship?
5. Name three advantages of traveling to Europe by ship.
6. Name three disadvantages of traveling by ship.
7. What is the Concorde? Do many people travel by Concorde? Why, or why not? What is the greatest advantage of flying by Concorde? Can you think of some disadvantages, too?
8. Would you prefer to travel to Europe by ship or by plane? Why? Give three main reasons.

Writing

You have just come back from Europe. You traveled to Europe by ship and you flew back on the Concorde. You are writing a letter to a friend who wants to make a similar trip, but your friend is not sure that he or she wants to go by ship. Help your friend make up his or her mind by describing the trips in detail. Compare the cruise with the flight. Describe the advantages and disadvantages of both. Convince your friend to go either by ship or by plane by giving enough examples, facts, and details.

Proofreading

After you have finished your rough drafts and you are happy with your organization and content, proofread it for the following errors:

EUROPE AND THE QE2:

ONE WAY IS FABULOUS.

THE OTHER IS FREE.

For the European vacation of a lifetime, spend five glorious days and nights on the one-and-only Queen Elizabeth 2—and fly the other way *free* economy-class on British Airways. QE2 is the ultimate travel experience, adding a whole new dimension to your European adventure.

Part palace, part playground.

QE2 has countless pleasant surprises aboard for you. She promises to be the most memorable part of your European vacation. Enjoy superb world-class restaurants. Nightclubs with smashing entertainment. Dancing under the stars at the lavish new Indoor/Outdoor Center. Gaming at the expanded Players Club. To stimulate your mind and body, a new computer learning center and the renowned "Golden Door" health program—with hydrocalisthenics, saunas, jogging deck. There are 25 QE2 transatlantic crossings from April into December; from as little as $1,250.*

Free BA 747 flights; Concorde at only $499—or even free!*

Your QE2 ticket entitles you to a free BA air ticket across the Atlantic to or from 57 cities. (Or, you can upgrade your free air ticket to Club Class, First Class or Concorde.) All QE2 passengers can save over $1,500 on specially reserved Concorde flights. Passengers sailing First Class on Oct. 27 or Nov. 9 fly Concorde free!

Big savings in Europe; book now!

All QE2 passengers get other great savings—Europe's top hotels, land tours—even the Orient Express! For details, see your travel agent or mail the coupon.

*Rate per person, double occupancy, subject to availability. Cunard reserves the right to cancel the Concorde program at any time. Free airfare based on lowest British Airways fare in effect as of 9/27/83. Length-of-stay restrictions apply.

QUEEN ELIZABETH 2
British Registry

(Q642)

FOR ONCE IN YOUR LIFE. LIVE.

CUNARD P.O. Box 999, Farmingdale, N.Y. 11737

NAME

ADDRESS

CITY   STATE   ZIP

MY TRAVEL AGENT   E30061

© 1984 Cunard

1. Is each sentence a sentence? (No fused sentences, fragments, double conjunctions, internal punctuation errors?)
2. Have you used tense consistently? Find the verb phrase in each sentence. Should it be progressive or perfect? Is the verb phrase in a main clause or a subordinate clause? Should the sequence-of-tense rule be applied? Does the sentence express a fact or a contrary-to-fact statement?
3. Have you used each verb form correctly?
4. Does each finite verb agree with its subject?
5. Does each pronoun refer to a specific antecedent?
6. Have you used enough transitions (conjunctive adverbs, coordinate conjunctions, correlative conjunctions, or adverbial clause conjunctions)?
7. Could you combine some sentences to form adverbial clauses or reduced adverbial clauses?
8. Check to make sure that you have used comparison expressions correctly.
9. Are there any spelling or article errors?

The Passive Voice

Review/Preview

In most of the English sentences you have studied thus far, the grammatical subject of the sentence is also the performer of the action mentioned by the verb. Example: *John is writing a letter. John* is the grammatical subject, and *John* performs the action of writing. This is called the *active voice*.

Sometimes the performer of the action is not the grammatical subject of the sentence. Example: *The letter was written by John. The letter* is the grammatical subject, but the performer of the action of writing is *John*. This is called the *passive voice*.

In an active sentence, the grammatical subject of the sentence performs the action expressed by the verb. In other words, the subject does something — he or she "acts."

In a passive sentence, the grammatical subject is not the performer of the action expressed by the verb. The subject does not act. In other words, the subject is *passive*. The performer of the action is expressed (or understood) in a *by*-phrase.

Not every kind of primary verb may be used in the passive voice. In Chapter 1 you saw that there are three kinds: *transitive, intransitive,* and *linking* verbs. Of these three, only transitive verbs may occur in the passive voice.

	Active sentence	Passive sentence
linking verb	John seems tired.	
intransitive verb	John runs fast.	
transitive verb	John is driving the car.	The car is being driven by John.

Grammar and Meaning

The Use of the Passive

There are several reasons that a passive voice may be used instead of an active voice, but one important reason is that the passive voice is used to make a passage more coherent. In English, it is common to first tell the listener or reader what we are talking about, and then give new information about that subject. Therefore, the subject position (at the beginning of a sentence) is very important in an English sentence.

Look at the following pairs of sentences.

1. I helped a little puppy yesterday. A car had hit it.
2. I helped a little puppy yesterday. It had been hit by a car.

They express the same meaning, but the second one "flows" better because the topic of conversation is a puppy, not a car. In other words, the passive voice is used here to put the *topic of conversation* at the beginning of the sentence. New information about the topic is given in the predicate.

Sometimes the passive voice is used because the performer of the action is unknown, unimportant, or unstressed.

This house was built in 1981.	The builder is unknown.
John and Mary were married last year.	The performer of the ceremony is not important.
The paintings were donated by a wealthy art collector.	The performer of the action is unstressed.

Exercise 1   The italicized verb phrases are in the passive voice. Explain why the passive voice is used: (a) to make the topic of conversation the subject

of the sentence or (b) because the performer of the action is unknown, unimportant, or unstressed.

Some metals are very sensitive to light. When light falls on them, the light knocks electrons out of the metal. This fact makes it possible to use these metals for changing light signals into electrical signals. The simplest device for doing this *is called* a phototube. A phototube is a special kind of diode. The cathode of this diode *is not heated.* Instead, it *is coated* with a metal that is sensitive to light. When light falls on the cathode, electrons *are released* into space near the cathode. If a voltage *is connected* between the cathode and the anode so that the anode *is made* positive, then the anode pulls these electrons, and a current flows through the tube. When no light falls on the cathode, no electrons *are released,* and no current flows. If the light falling on the cathode is weak, not many electrons *are released,* and the current through the tube is small. If the light falling on the cathode is strong, many electrons *are released,* and the current is somewhat larger.

Exercise 2 In the following passage, all sentences are active. However, to make the passage more coherent a few sentences should be made passive. Which sentences should be made passive to make the passage more coherent?

The Phototube Thermometer

1. A metal begins to glow when someone heats it. 2. As the temperature of the metal rises, the heat changes the color of the glow. 3. First, the heat changes the color to red, then orange and yellow, and, finally, white. 4. At the same time that the color of the glow is changed, the heat also changes the amount of light. 5. The higher the temperature becomes, the more light it sends out. 6. So someone can measure the temperature of a glowing metal by means of the light that comes from it. 7. Someone allows the light to fall on the cathode of a phototube. 8. Someone then feeds the current that flows through the tube onto an electric meter, where it makes a pointer turn. 9. The pointer shows the temperature directly on the dial of the meter.

The Formation of the Passive Voice

To make an active sentence passive, three changes are necessary.

1. The Original Object Becomes the Subject

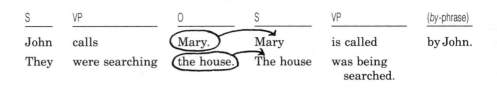

S	VP	O	S	VP	(by-phrase)
John	calls	Mary.	Mary	is called	by John.
They	were searching	the house.	The house	was being searched.	

First of all, the object of an active sentence becomes the subject of the passive sentence, and the finite verb must agree with it.

2. The Helping Verb *Be* Is Added, Followed by a Past Participle

John	*calls*	Mary.	Mary	*is called*	by John.
The police	*will have searched*	the house tonight.	The house	*will have been searched*	tonight.
The teacher	*punished*	John yesterday.	John	*got punished*	yesterday.

Second, a helping verb is added. In a passive verb phrase, the helping verb *be* or *get* is used, followed by the past participle form of the verb. *Be* is the main auxiliary of the passive voice, but in speaking, the verb *get* is also often used. *Get* seems to emphasize the action rather than the state.

Note: There may also be other auxiliaries in the passive verb phrase, such as a modal, *have,* or progressive *be.*

3. The Original Subject Becomes a Prepositional Phrase, or It Is Left Out

John called Mary.	Mary was called *by John.*
I threw away the paper.	The paper was thrown away.
The movie interests me.	I am interested *in the movie.*
The movie bores me.	I am bored *with the movie.*

In a passive sentence the performer of the action (the original subject) may be expressed in a prepositional phrase or left out. The preposition is usually *by,* but there are also many expressions with different prepositions. This prepositional phrase is called an *adverbial of agent.*

Exercise 3   The following sentences are all active. Identify those sentences that may be changed to the passive voice, and change them to passive sentences on a separate piece of paper.

    1. The class is studying the passive voice.
    2. Mary is walking in the street.
    3. John connected the electrical wires.
    4. John hasn't washed the dishes yet.
    5. Did Audrey clean up her room?
    6. The children are playing outside.
    7. The car is going fast.
    8. He rode a horse into town.

Tense, Aspect, and Mood in the Passive Voice

Like an active verb phrase, a passive verb phrase may be used in simple, perfect, and progressive tenses. It may also be used in the subjunctive mood and with modals. (See Chapter 8).

NON-PROGRESSIVE	ACTIVE	PASSIVE
PRESENT	John reads a book.	The book *is read* by John.
PRESENT PERFECT	John has read a book.	The book *has been read* by John.
PAST	John read a book.	The book *was read* by John.
PAST PERFECT	John had read a book.	The book *had been read* by John.
FUTURE	John will read a book.	The book *will be read* by John.
FUTURE PERFECT	John will have read a book.	The book *will have been read* by John.

PROGRESSIVE	ACTIVE	PASSIVE
PRESENT	John is reading a book.	The book *is being read* by John.
PRESENT PERFECT	John has been reading a book.	(The book *has been being read* by John.)
PAST	John was reading a book.	The book *was being read* by John.
PAST PERFECT	John had been reading a book.	(The book *had been being read* by John.)
FUTURE	John will be reading a book.	(The book *will be being read* by John.)
FUTURE PERFECT	John will have been reading a book.	(The book *will have been being read* by John.)

The passive progressive is usually limited to the present and the past because the two *be* auxiliaries (*been being*) sound very awkward together.

As you saw in Chapter 2, the auxiliaries always occur in a certain order. The passive auxiliary is the one right before the primary verb, and the primary verb is the last verb in the verb phrase. They may be preceded by a modal, *have,* or progressive *be.*

Not only finite verb phrases but also infinitive and *-ing* phrases may be passive. Examine the following diagram. Why, do you think, are some forms left blank?

NON-PROGRESSIVE	ACTIVE	PASSIVE
INFINITIVE	to read	to *be* read
PERFECT INFINITIVE	to have read	to have *been* read
-ING PHRASE	reading	*being* read
PERFECT *-ING* PHRASE	having read	having *been* read

PROGRESSIVE		
INFINITIVE	to be reading	_____
PERFECT INFINITIVE	to have been reading	_____
-ING PHRASE	_____	_____
PERFECT *-ING* PHRASE	having been reading	_____

- -

Exercise 4 On a separate piece of paper, change the following active verb phrases to passive verb phrases.

1. has seen
2. to make
3. needed
4. will show
5. had bent
6. is bringing
7. would turn
8. will have passed
9. can control
10. to have moved
11. will have reached
12. was pulling
13. has used
14. had done
15. having attached
16. burning
17. to have completed
18. counts
19. is hitting
20. let switch

Exercise 5 Create English sentences with the following sentence parts. Use a passive verb phrase in an appropriate tense.

1. before Aaron/lift/onto the operating table/he/already/anesthesize

2. through the natural fissure at the back of the spinal cord, a delicate cut/make/into the only part of the cord that/can/touch/without catastrophic consequences

3. during the entire operation/progress/measure/in millimeters

4. last night/two Americans/arrest

5. after the police had boarded their ship/fifteen pounds of marijuana/find

6. eighteen ships/require/usually/for the anti-drug and illegal-immigrant patrols

7. for thirty days the vessels/restrict/to six days' sailing time each

8. the new schedule/put/into operation/at this moment

9. the film's use of violence/condemn/by the reviewer

10. parental discretion/advise/usually/by the networks

11. a tax increase/announce/by the governor/at the press conference tomorrow

12. the 13 British colonies/declare/independent/on July 4, 1776

Exercise 6 Change the verbs in parentheses to an appropriate form in the active voice or in the passive voice in any appropriate tense and aspect.

The more men (learn) about weather, the more fully they (realize) how complex it (be). A slight appreciation of its complexity (can/gain) from the meteorologists' estimates that 10,000 statistical varieties of weather (occur) at any given moment in the United States alone, and that throughout the world at least 45,000 thunderstorms (may/develop) in an average period of twenty-four hours.

Nevertheless, weather (consist) of four basic ingredients: temperature, pressure, humidity, and wind. The influences that (manipulate) them (can/describe), with drastic simplification, in a few sentences.

The sun (fuel) the global engine that (produce) weather. The earth, although intercepting only two-billionths of the sun's total radiant energy, (receive) enough of it every minute to match an entire year's output of all of our man-made power plants. Nearly half this solar energy (lose) in space, however, by being reflected from cloudtops, icefields, and snow. The rest (absorb) and then (reradiate) as heat from oceans —covering almost three-quarters of the planet — and from the land.

Water vapor, predominantly in the lower five to ten miles in the atmosphere, (absorb) this heat, (condense) to clouds, and (churn) the atmosphere with the energy born of heat transfer. The clouds (put) in motion by this energy, and their circulation (manipulate) by high-altitude, high-speed winds spawned by the earth's spinning. Atmospheric motion (modify) further by the uneven distribution from land and water, and by the presence of mountain ranges, shores, plains, valleys, and other surfaces.

Exercise 7   Look at the ad for a computer program. Read the ad as many times as you need for a general idea about its content. Then complete the following sentences meaningfully from the content of the advertisement.

1. A loan should be as easily understood as it _____
   _____ .

2. This loan amortization software package can be _____
   _____ .

Understanding a loan shouldn't be harder than getting one.

Imagine an easy to use loan amortization software package that handles multiple loan combinations, negative amortization, variable interest rates, balloon payments, and much more.

Discover AMORTIZER III™.

This convenient menu-driven software package effortlessly analyzes all loan arrangements, then prints the resulting amortization schedules in an easy to understand, professional looking format.

AMORTIZER III manages a wide range of payments intervals including annual, semi-annual, quarterly, monthly, bi-weeky, and weekly. It will also uncover an unknown variable when given three of four variables such as original amount, payment amount, interest rate, or number of payments. In addition, AMORTIZER III will accommodate newer "creative financing" loan arrangements.

So make interest simple again, and discover the breakthrough of AMORTIZER III.

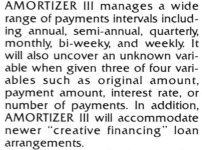

SOFTWARE CORP

Making dollars and sense out of information.

a division of the goodman group, inc. 12900 Preston Rd., Dallas, Tx. 75230 (214) 239-6085
Amortizer III — $79.00 suggested retail. Available on IBM PC and PC Compatibles. See your local dealer.

3. Multiple loan combinations are _____

_____ .

4. Negative amortizations _____

calculated.

5. Variable interest rates are easily _____

_____ .

6. Balloon notes _____ figured out.

7. All loan arrangements are effortlessly _____

_____ by _____ .

8. The resulting amortization schedules _____

_____ .

9. A wide range of payment intervals _____

_____ .

10. An unknown variable will _____ .

11. New "creative financing" loan arrangements will _____

_____ .

12. Dollars and sense are made out of information by _____

_____ .

Exercise 8   You are a loan processor at a mortgage company. You have been asked to find a good software package to help in calculating amortization schedules. Write a short report that explains which program you recommend and why you recommend it.

1. Include at least five passive sentences in your report.
2. Make sure your report is coherent. (Use the passive only when it serves to make the report more coherent. You should also include other transitions, such as conjunctive adverbs and adverbial clause conjunctions.)

Passive Constructions

Passive Constructions with Special Object Patterns

In Chapter 1 you learned that transitive verbs are verbs followed by objects. You also saw that objects may have different forms: for example, single words, phrases, clauses, or reduced clauses. There are many different types of object patterns. Chapter 10 will examine in detail which verbs take what kind of object, but this chapter will briefly examine how different types of objects are used in passive constructions.

An Indirect Object as Subject of a Passive Sentence

S	VP	IO	DO
John	gave	Mary	a book.

1. *A book* was given to Mary.   2. *Mary* was given a book.

Some transitive verbs have two objects: a direct object and an indirect object. Verbs like *give* may have two types of passive sentences: either the direct object or the indirect object may become the subject of the passive sentence.

The Object of a Two-Part Verb as Subject of a Passive Sentence

I must *hand in* my composition tomorrow.   My composition must be *handed in* tomorrow.
I *called* John *up*.   John was *called up*.
I *blame* the accident *on* John.   The accident is *blamed on* John.
I *blame* John *for* the accident.   John is *blamed for* the accident.

Some transitive verbs consist of a verb part and a preposition or adverb part. The objects of these verbs may also become subjects of passive sentences. *Note:* The prepositions or adverbs usually come immediately after the transitive verb in a passive construction.

That Clause as Subject of a Passive Sentence

They say that he is very rich.
    a. *It* is said that he is very rich.
    b. *He* is said to be very rich.

People believe that the legend is true.
    a. *It* is believed that the legend is true.
    b. *The legend* is believed to be true.

Someone requested that she leave.
    a. *It* was requested that she leave.
    b. *She* was requested to leave.

Some transitive verbs may be followed by *that*-clauses. The whole *that*-clause may become the subject of a passive sentence — usually with a temporary *it* construction.

Sometimes the subject of the *that*-clause becomes the subject of the passive verb phrase, which is followed by a *to*-infinitive construction.

The Noun Part of a Two-Part Object as Subject of a Passive Sentence

I saw John walking in the street.   *John* was seen walking in the street.
We caught him stealing an apple.   *He* was caught stealing an apple.

I let him go   *He* was let go.
I make him leave early.   *He* was made to leave early.

I am having someone paint my house.   I am having *my house* painted.
I got him to paint my house.   I got *my house* painted.

In Chapter 2, you studied the verbs *have, let, make,* and so on. These transitive verbs have a two-part object: a noun phrase followed by a plain infinitive or a present participle. The noun phrase may be made subject of a passive sentence.

Note: After *let* and *make,* the noun part of the object becomes the subject of a passive sentence, but after *have,* the object phrase itself becomes passive. In the spoken language, *got* is often used in a similar construction.

Exercise 9   Create good English sentences with the following sentence parts and based on the following situation.

Situation: John was kidnapped last week. Nobody knows where he is, but people are trying to guess where he could be. They also have some suggestions for the kidnappers and the police.

1. He is believed _____ .

2. He is thought _____ .

3. He is considered _____ .

4. The kidnappers are asked _____ .

5. The kidnapping is blamed on _____

   _____ .

6. The kidnappers are given _____ .

7. _____ have been notified of _____

   _____ .

8. The kidnappers are encouraged _____

   _____ .

9. Unfortunately, the kidnappers were not caught _____

_____ .

10. They should be made to _____ .

11. The police should have them _____

_____ .

12. We hope that John will be let _____

_____ .

Passive Constructions in Reduced Adjective Clauses

The passive is frequently used in adjective constructions because the passive voice often makes it possible to reduce an adjective clause. As you saw in Chapter 5, it is a general rule that a subject + *be* may be deleted from a subordinate clause, thus forming a reduced clause. In the following pairs of sentences you can see that if the adjective clause is active it cannot be reduced, but if it is passive, it can.

Object	Subject + *be*
I helped a puppy *that* a car had hit.	I helped a puppy *that had been* hit by a car.
	I helped a puppy hit by a car.
The man *whom* the police sought disappeared.	The man *who was* sought by the police disappeared.
	The man sought by the police disappeared.

The following chapter will discuss adjective clauses and reduced clauses in detail. For right now, it is important to realize that if a past participle is used as an adjective, it has a passive meaning. On the other hand, a present participle phrase used as an adjective has an active meaning.

PASSIVE CONSTRUCTION	ACTIVE CONSTRUCTION	
The books *used by the students* are blue.	The students *using the book* like it.	reduced adjective clause
that are used by the students	who are using the book	adjective clause
The books are used by the students.		passive sentence
The students use the books.	The students are using a book.	active sentence

Exercise 10   In the following passage, underline each passive verb phrase and each past participle used as an adjective.

Noisy Toys May Cause Hearing Loss

Any parent knows how annoying noisy toys can be. What they may not know is that those toys can damage their children's hearing.

According to researchers from the department of audiology at the University of Göteberg, in Sweden, many toys exceed the noise levels considered to cause hearing loss in adults. And there is evidence that children's hearing may be more vulnerable than adults' (*Pediatrics,* October 1985).

The researchers found that toy weapons and firecrackers had the most potential for harm. When used within twenty inches of a child's ear, the sound level produced by some toy weapons is comparable to the noise produced by jet engines at takeoff. "The sound levels are so high," say the researchers, "that in order to preserve normal hearing, ear protectors should be used!"

Even squeaking toys, such as those used by babies, are loud enough to cause hearing loss if the toy is used for a few minutes within four inches of the child's ear, they found.

The researchers suggest that manufacturers label noisy toys with a warning that they can cause hearing loss. Although manufacturers intend the toys to be used in a sensible way, "it is easy to imagine the situation of a [toy] pistol . . . pointed directly at or near the ear of a friend."

Prepositions in Passive Constructions

There are a few passive expressions followed by specific prepositions. Some of these passive expressions are used only in the passive and never in the active voice.

- -

The movie interests me.	I am *interested in* the movie.
The movie bores me.	I am *bored with* the movie.
The movie tires me.	I am *tired of* the movie.
He disappoints me.	I am *disappointed with* him.
	I am *disappointed in* him.
His grade satisfies him	He is *satisfied with* his grade.
The book disgusts me.	I am *disgusted with* the book.
The child worries me.	I am *worried about* the child.
The bad grade upsets me.	I am *upset about* the bad grade.
Tigers terrify him.	He is *terrified of* tigers.
Tigers scare him.	He is *scared of* tigers.
Tigers petrify him.	He is *petrified of* tigers.

Anne married him.
Janet divorced him.

He is *married to* Anne.
He is *divorced from* Janet.
We are *acquainted with* him.
He is *related to* her.

I am *accustomed to* the food.
I am *used to* the food.

He dedicates himself to his work.
He devotes himself to his work.
He commits himself to his work.
(He opposes himself to abortion.)

He is *dedicated to* his work.
He is *devoted to* his work.
He is *committed to* his work.
He is *opposed to* abortion.

She was *dressed in* black.

Chocolate covers his face.

His face was *covered with* chocolate.
Brazil is *located in* South America.

Ten units compose the book.

The book is *composed of* ten units.

International students often confuse the verbs *belong, consist, compose, locate, happen, occur,* and *situate.* The verbs *belong, occur, happen,* and *consist* are used only in the active voice. The verbs *compose, locate,* and *situate* are usually used in the passive voice.

Active expressions	Passive expressions
The book *belongs to* me.	The book *is composed of* ten units.
The book *consists of* ten units.	Malaysia *is located in* southeast Asia.
It *happened* that I saw you.	Malaysia *is situated in* southeast Asia.
The accident *occurred.*	

INCORRECT: The book is belonged to me.	INCORRECT: Malaysia located in southeast Asia.
INCORRECT: The book is consisted of ten units.	
INCORRECT: It was happened that I saw you.	
INCORRECT: The accident was occurred.	

Verbs like *allow, permit,* and *suppose* may also occur in a passive pattern followed by a *to*-infinitive. However, only transitive verbs that can be followed by *to*-infinitive objects can occur in this pattern.

I allow him to go.
I suppose that he will go.

He *is allowed* to go.
He *is supposed* to go.

As you saw in Chapter 1, a preposition can be followed by a gerund but not by an infinitive. Therefore, passive verb phrases that are followed by a preposition are followed by gerunds, not infinitives.

I am interested in *going* there.
I am used to *living* there.
I am upset about *getting* a low grade.

INCORRECT: I am interested to go there.

One expression in which infinitives and gerunds are often confused is *used to*. When *used to* is used by itself (without the helping verb *be*) it expresses a past habit and is followed by a *to*-infinitive. When *used to* is preceded by *be* it refers to being accustomed to something in the present, in which case it may be followed by a gerund.

I used to *live* there.   *Used to* is a semi-modal expressing a past habit.
I am used to *living* there.   *To be used to* is a passive expression meaning
                                 to be accustomed to.

INCORRECT: I am used to live there.
INCORRECT: I used to living there.

Exercise 11   Use the following situations and lists of verbs to create English sentences in the passive voice.

Situation: John is taking a very difficult chemistry course. The course confuses him, bores him, disgusts him, upsets him, and worries him.

EXAMPLE:

confuse *John is getting confused in the chemistry course.*

1. bore

2. disgust

3. upset

4. worry

5. tire

Situation: You need to give someone information about the United States of America.

1. consist

2. compose

3. belong

4. locate

Situation: John used to be Mary's husband. He will be Janet's husband. He knows Sylvia a little. He is good friends with Linda. He is Ruth's brother.

1. marry

2. engage

3. relate

4. acquaint

5. befriend

6. divorce

Situation: Many things scare John: spiders, snakes, mice, thunderstorms, and so on.

1. scare

2. terrify

3. petrify

Situation: John is a real family man. He loves his wife. He loves his children. He takes good care of his parents. He makes sure his grandparents are well, and so on.

1. devote

2. commit

3. oppose

4. interest

5. dedicate

Situation: At first John did not like studying at this university. Now he knows his way around, and he likes it very much. He has permission to go to another university, but he does not want to.

1. used

2. is used to

3. is allowed to

4. is supposed to

5. is willing to

6. is interested in

Solving Problems

Lack of Agreement

The finite verb must agree with the grammatical subject of the sentence, not the performer of the action.

INCORRECT: The house were painted by the people.
CORRECT: The house was painted by the people.

Unidiomatic Expressions

Some verbs are usually used in the passive voice (like *locate, compose, situate*); others are used only in the active voice (like *belong, consist, happen*).

INCORRECT: Malaysia located in Southeast Asia.
CORRECT: Malaysia is located in Southeast Asia.

INCORRECT: The book is consisted of 400 pages.
CORRECT: The book consists of 400 pages.

INCORRECT: The book composes of 400 pages.
CORRECT: The book is composed of 400 pages.

INCORRECT: The book is belonged to me.
CORRECT: The book belongs to me.

Certain prepositions have to be used in passive constructions.

INCORRECT: I am excited with my new bike.
CORRECT: I am excited about my new bike.

INCORRECT: I am interested swimming.
CORRECT: I am interested in swimming.

Do not confuse *used* + *to*-infinitive and *to be used to* + gerund.

INCORRECT: I used to living here.
CORRECT: I am used to living here. (accustomed to)
CORRECT: I used to live here. (past habit)

INCORRECT: I am used to work hard.
CORRECT: I am used to working hard. (present habit)
CORRECT: I used to work hard. (past habit)

Confusion of Passive and Active Adjectives

A past participle has a passive meaning, and a present participle has an active meaning.

INCORRECT: The book using by the students is blue.
CORRECT: The book used by the students is blue.

INCORRECT: The whole class fell asleep during the bored lecture.
CORRECT: The whole class fell asleep during the boring lecture.

Confusion of Passive and Progressive Verb Phrases

INCORRECT: I have been providing with a new car.
CORRECT: I have been provided with a new car.

Exercise 12   Many of the sentences in the following passage contain one of the errors just mentioned. Identify the errors and rewrite the passage correctly.

From Quill to Computer

Every advance in technology manages somehow to transform the creative process. A new vision of architecture's possibilities, for example, were stimulated by improved fabrication of steel forms. Also unimagining creative freedom and artistic control have been given to musicians by developments in electronics.

Now a relatively new technology, word processing, may be transformed the art of writing. It is too early to predict all the ways in which writing will change, but we can get some clues by looking at research in cognitive psychology and by studying the experiences of people used word processors.

If you are interested to buy a word processor, you will see that the market is consisted of many types of word processors. They vary in size from one small box weighed less than four pounds to a deskload of heavy equipment; their costs are similarly variable — from about $1,000 up to $20,000. But they all compose the same. They are electronic devices that allow you to type, store, modify, and print.

Exercise 13   The following exercise is to test your ability to relate structure to meaning. It is based on Exercise 10 earlier in this chapter. Read over the passage called "Noisy Toys May Cause Hearing Loss" again. Then complete the sentences below. Your answers should be true according to the information and grammatically correct.

Noisy Toys May Cause Hearing Loss

Many parents _____ that noisy toys can be very _____ What they may not know is that their children's hearing can _____ by those noisy toys.

Researchers from the department of audiology at the University of Göteberg, in Sweden, have _____ that the noise levels which are _____ to cause hearing loss in adults are _____ by many toys. And there is evidence that children's hearing may be more vulnerable than adults' (*Pediatrics,* October 1985).

The researchers found that toy weapons and firecrackers had the most potential for harm. When a child _____ a toy weapon within twenty inches of his or her ear, it may _____ a sound level which can be _____ to the noise that jet engines _____ at takeoff. According to the researchers, the sound levels are so high that in order to preserve normal hearing, the child _____ ear protectors!

Even squeaking toys, such as those that babies _____ , are loud enough to cause hearing loss if someone _____ the toy for a few minutes within four inches of the child's ear, they found.

The researchers suggest that noisy toys be _____ by manufacturers with a warning that they can cause hearing loss. Although manufacturers intend for children _____ the toys in a sensible way, children might _____ the toy directly at or near the ear of a friend.

Assignment for Writing

Before you read the ad on the following pages called "Electricity from the Atom," write down in a few sentences whether you are for or against nuclear energy, and briefly explain why.

ELECTRICITY FROM THE ATOM
Are we moving in the right direction?

1 **The value of nuclear power is being questioned these days mainly because of serious financial problems with some plants under construction. What's often overlooked is that with 80 plants operating, nuclear-generated electricity is already being used extensively, safely, and economically.**

2 Three hundred nuclear plants now generate electricity worldwide, and 200 more are being built. But in the U.S., recent plant cancellations and high construction costs have hampered the progress of nuclear power.

A decade of economic and energy upheavals

3 The energy crises of the 1970s jolted the whole world into a new eco-nomic era. America and many other industrialized countries fell into dam-aging recessions that we're only now coming out of.

4 The world of nuclear energy was transformed, too. The high interest rates and inflation of an oil-shocked economy, plus a massive updating of safety regulations, plus construc-tion slowdowns, made many of the nuclear plants now under construc-tion much more expensive than they were when originally planned.

5 Yet these plants will still be needed, because demand for electric-ity is growing. While the use of *non-electric* energy has declined, U.S. consumption of *electric* energy has increased by over 25 percent since the Arab oil embargo. In 1983, the hot summer, cold winter, and eco-nomic recovery caused more elec-tricity to be used in this country than ever before.

A growing economy needs more electricity

6 America is turning increasingly to electricity for its energy requirements.

7 Industry is shifting to manufactur-ing processes that use electricity for better energy efficiency. Electronic technology is improving productivity. Our heating and cooling needs in offices, factories, malls, and homes continue to boost electrical demand.

8 Every yearly increase in the U.S. Gross National Product has been accom-panied by a comparable increase in the use of electric power. Last year, for example, GNP grew by 3.3 percent, while electricity output grew by 3.6 percent.

9 Without a reliable supply of rea-sonably priced electricity, economic growth—and the social benefits that go with it—would suffer.

10 So the question raised in the past

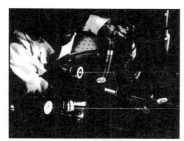

Laser technology is one of many industrial innovations that are totally dependent on electricity. U.S. demand for electric power has risen over 25 percent in the last decade.

few months boils down to this: Can nuclear power plants, fueled by uranium, produce reasonably priced electricity?

Uranium saves money and fuel

11 There are 80 nuclear plants now licensed to generate electricity in 28 states throughout the country.

12 The average cost of electricity from the 80 operating nuclear plants is less than half the cost of electricity from power plants that burn oil. And, in many regions of the country, nuclear-generated kilowatt-hours cost roughly the same as or somewhat less than coal-generated kilowatt-hours.

Over the past 4 years, 17 nuclear power plants have received operating licenses from the U.S. Nuclear Regulatory Commission. Twenty-eight states have nuclear-electric generating plants; 10 states get more than a third of their electricity from these plants.

13 If the electricity provided by nuclear plants between 1974 and 1982 had been provided instead by power plants burning fossil fuels, then consumers would have paid between $30 billion and $40 billion more for electricity, depending on the type of fuel substituted for uranium.

14 Most of the nuclear plants now operating were built before the years of double-digit inflation and persist-

ently high interest rates, which have been a huge factor in the higher cost of the plants now approaching completion. Even so, over their 30- to 40-year lifetimes, these new plants can provide economic benefits because of the lower cost of uranium fuel.

Renewing the nuclear promise

15 The lower cost of fuel is one big advantage of nuclear electricity. Another benefit is that nuclear power plants are environmentally clean. And they also have one of the best safety records of any major industrial enterprise.

16 Nuclear electricity helps balance the *mix* of fuels that keeps our lights on and our economy growing. We cannot afford to repeat past mistakes and become too dependent on any one energy source.

nuclear engineering staffs and strengthening their operator training programs.

20 At the same time, the Federal government is moving to reform the nuclear regulation process, which causes needless delays and often adds hundreds of millions of dollars in excessive construction and operating costs. Several regulatory reform bills that promote the standardization of nuclear plants are before Congress now.

21 But these steps alone are not enough. The full potential of nuclear power will be achieved only with a full public understanding of its benefits. Then, the development of America's nuclear-electric energy will continue to move in the right direction.

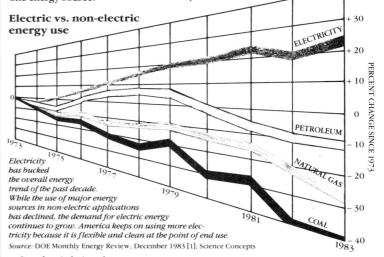

Electric vs. non-electric energy use

Electricity has bucked the overall energy trend of the past decade. While the use of major energy sources in non-electric applications has declined, the demand for electric energy continues to grow. America keeps on using more electricity because it is flexible and clean at the point of end use.

Source: DOE Monthly Energy Review, December 1983 [1]; Science Concepts

17 So what is being done to assure that nuclear power maintains its contribution to America's energy mix?

18 Utilities have learned that they must be realistic about what it takes to construct and run a nuclear generating station.

19 They have already taken a big step in this direction by forming the Institute of Nuclear Power Operations, which helps utilities improve construction quality as well as the overall safety of plant operations. Utilities have also been beefing up their

Information about energy America can count on today
U.S. COMMITTEE FOR ENERGY AWARENESS

Reading

Before you start answering the detailed questions below, read quickly through the ad for nuclear energy. Try to get a general understanding of the contents. Do not worry if you do not understand every word. Look up in a dictionary only words that are absolutely necessary for an understanding of the selection.

1. According to the author, what is the main reason that the value of nuclear energy is being questioned?

2. According to the author, nuclear energy is already being used

   _____ , _____ , and _____ . Which one of these three adverbs relates to *financial problems?*

3. In paragraph 2, the author states that although there are many nuclear plants all over the world, in the United States _____

   because of _____ and _____ .

4. In paragraph 3 the author explains that we are in a new economic era because of _____ .

5. In paragraph 4, the author explains that the world of nuclear energy was transformed, too. What were the three causes of this transformation? What was the result of this transformation?

6. The first word in paragraph 5, *yet,* expresses concession. Restate paragraphs 4 and 5 with one *although* sentence: Although nuclear plants now under construction are _____ , they are

   _____ because _____ .

7. In paragraph 5, the author states that although the consumption of non-electric energy is down, the consumption of electric energy is up. What does the author mean by non-electric energy?

8. Read over paragraphs 6–9 quickly again. Where is the main idea of these paragraphs stated? In paragraph 7 and 8 the author gives specific facts and details to support the thesis. List all the specific facts and details you can find.

9. Where do you find the conclusion of this section?

10. The conclusion in paragraph 9 leads to the question in paragraph 10, which in turn serves as the introduction to paragraphs

    _____ , _____ , _____ , and _____ .
    This paragraph serves to make a smooth transition between the two sections. Why is a smooth transition important?

11. Why does the author mention how many nuclear energy plants there are?

12. Of the three types of energy mentioned in paragraph 12, which one was the least expensive and which one the most expensive?

13. What is the author trying to prove in paragraph 13?

14. In paragraph 14, the author states that although the nuclear plants being built now are very _____ , these new plants can _____ .
15. Can you identify the transitional phrases used in the last part of paragraph 14 and the first part of paragraph 15?
16. Identify the four benefits of nuclear energy that the author mentions in paragraphs 15 and 16.
17. At the end of paragraph 16, the author mentions past mistakes. What mistakes is the author referring to? In what paragraph were these past mistakes alluded to? Why, in the author's opinion, is the *energy mix* so important?
18. In paragraph 18, what must the utility companies be realistic about: cost, safety, or both?
19. In paragraph 19, the author shows how _____ is being improved.
20. In paragraph 20, the author shows how _____ is being limited.
21. In paragraph 21, the author states that _____ is necessary if the development of America's nuclear energy is to continue to move in the right direction.
22. At the end of paragraph one, the author stated that nuclear energy was used *extensively, safely,* and *economically.* Which adverb has been supported the most? In which paragraph(s) has the author supported the adverb *extensively?* In which paragraph(s) has the author talked about *safely?*

Group Discussion

1. Does the ad called "Electricity from the Atom" support the use of nuclear energy? How do you know? Who wrote this ad? Why, do you believe, was it written?
2. Read the first paragraph again. According to the author, the value of nuclear energy has been questioned mainly because of financial problems. Do you agree with this statement, or do you think that there are other important reasons? What other reasons can you think of?
3. Do you agree or disagree with the main thesis of this ad? Do you believe that nuclear energy will help solve some of the world's energy problems? Can you think of some more arguments for nuclear energy? Can you think of some arguments against nuclear energy?
4. Name at least four other types of energy.
5. What are the main sources of energy in your country?
6. Name three advantages or three disadvantages of each source of energy mentioned in question 5.

Writing

1. Select one type of energy (for example, nuclear, fossil fuel, solar), and discuss it from a specific viewpoint (economic, technical, environmental, sociological). If, for example, you are a business student, discuss it from an economic point of view. If you are an engineering student, you may wish to discuss its efficiency or inefficiency from a technical point of view.
2. Decide whether you are mainly for or against this type of energy. Try to think of at least three advantages or disadvantages of this type of energy. Develop this information into an introduction.
3. Develop each advantage or disadvantage into a convincing paragraph by substantiating it with at least one specific example and/or fact.
4. Conclude your composition by offering a suggestion, a reservation, or a solution to the arguments presented in your theme.

Suggestions for Writing

Look back over the sentences you wrote before you read the ad. Has your opinion changed? Why, or why not?

This ad was basically an argumentative essay. An argument is a reasoned, logical way of demonstrating that your position, belief, or conclusion is valid so that you can persuade other people to agree with your position.

Let's look at some of the methods the author used to create this argumentative essay.

First of all, the author clearly took a stand for nuclear energy in general. However, rather than defending nuclear energy in general, the author clearly concentrated on one aspect: its financial benefits.

Second, the ad was written for a general audience. The author knew that it probably would be read by people who were educated but not necessarily experts in the field of energy and who were most probably against nuclear energy.

Third, the arguments are organized logically. First the author told readers about the financial problems, then explained why these financial problems occurred, then argued that although the cost was high, it was not as high as some other sources of energy. At the end the author clearly refutes the idea that nuclear energy is more expensive than other sources of energy. The writer of the ad helps the reader follow his or her thoughts by using clear transitions, instead of jumping from one topic to another without letting the reader see how these topics are logically related.

Finally, the author makes a convincing impression because many specific facts are used to support arguments: dates, statistics, amounts, numbers, and so on.

In your own writing, you should keep these points in mind:

1. Take a stand.
2. Write for a specific audience.
3. Limit your topic to one aspect of the problem.
4. Organize your points logically.
5. Use transitions to move between points.
6. Use plenty of specific facts and details to support your points.

Proofreading

1. Is each sentence a sentence (no fragments, fused sentences, comma splices, double conjunctions)?
2. Does each sentence contain a subject, verb phrase, object or complement, and adverbials when needed?
3. Does each finite verb agree with the subject?
4. Have you been consistent in your use of tense?
5. Have you been judicious in your use of the passive voice?
6. Are all verb forms correct? Have you used any participles as adjectives? Are they active or passive in meaning?
7. Have you been consistent in your use of pronouns?
8. Have you used appropriate transition words?
9. Could you combine some sentences to form adverbial clauses or reduced adverbial clauses?
10. Check for errors in punctuation and capitalization.
11. Check for errors in the use of articles and prepositions.
12. Check for errors in spelling.

7

The Adjective Clause

Review/Preview

What is an adjective? In Chapter 1, you saw that an adjective is a word, a phrase, or a clause that modifies a noun. Any noun in a sentence may be modified by an adjective.

Where is the adjective found in the sentence? If the adjective is a single word, it is usually found either before the noun or after a linking verb, but if the adjective is a phrase or a clause, it comes after the noun that it modifies.

Single-word adjective

I saw a *pretty* house.   before the noun
The house is *pretty*.   after a linking verb

Adjective clause or phrase

I saw a house *that was very pretty*.   after the noun
I saw a house *with red shutters*.   after the noun

In this chapter you will closely examine first the formation of an adjective clause and then the reduction rules that may apply to it.

Grammar and Meaning

The Terminology of Adjective Clauses

An adjective clause is also called a *relative* clause. The connecting words, *who, whom, whose, which,* and *that* are called *relative pronouns,* and the connecting words *where, when,* and *as* are *relative adverbs.* The noun that is modified by the adjective phrase or clause is called the *antecedent.*

Antecedent	ADJECTIVE CLAUSE relative pronoun or relative adverb	
The house	(which) *Mary bought*	is pretty.
John,	(who) *came here yesterday,*	is my friend.
Do you know the man	(who) *just left?*	
The room	(where) *we met*	was spacious.

Exercise 1

In the following sentences, underline the adjective clause <u>once</u>, underline the antecedent <u>twice</u>, and circle the relative pronoun.

EXAMPLE:

A "picture bride" is <u>a bride</u> (whom) the bridegroom has not met before the marriage.

1. On March 26, 1943, Elsie S. Scott, who was an army nurse, became the first woman to receive an air medal.

2. The pronghorn antelope, which is only found in North America, has no close relatives.

3. The oldest encyclopedia that is still in existence was compiled in the first century by a Roman writer by the name of Pliny.

4. An object that weighs five pounds on the earth would weigh two pounds on the planet Mercury.

5. Grover Cleveland was a bachelor at the time when he was elected president of the United States.

Punctuation Rules of Adjective Clauses

You have probably noticed that some adjective clauses require commas and that others don't. The use of commas depends on the identity of the antecedent.

Restrictive Clauses

When a clause limits the meaning of the antecedent — that is, when it is needed to identify the antecedent — it is called a *restrictive* adjective clause. When we leave off a restrictive adjective clause, the antecedent is unclear. Look at the following examples:

- -

The man who came by yesterday is my teacher.
The man is my teacher.   Which man?

The movie that I saw yesterday was fascinating.
The movie was fascinating.   Which movie?

The house that is on the corner belongs to him.
The house belongs to him.   Which house?

- -

Without the adjective clause, the reader would not know which man is my teacher, which movie is fascinating, or which house belongs to him. The antecedent by itself is too general for us to understand which one. The clause is necessary in order to identify the antecedent. If the clause is necessary, it is not set off by commas.

Non-Restrictive Adjective Clauses

When an antecedent by itself is specific enough so that the adjective clause is not really necessary to identify it, the clause is called *non-restrictive*. A non-restrictive clause is not really needed to identify the antecedent. Its function is to give more information about the antecedent, not to identify it. In other words, when we leave off the adjective clause, the antecedent is still clear, and the sentence does not really change in meaning. This type of clause must be set off with commas.

- -

John F. Kennedy, who was assasinated in 1964, was a popular president.
John F. Kennedy   was a popular president.

Solar energy, which is safe and clean, also has disadvantages.
Solar energy   also has disadvantages.

- -

In the following examples you can see what kinds of antecedents are usually followed by a non-restrictive clause.

Mr. Johnson, who is my Math teacher, is very kind.

Malaysia, which is located in Southeast Asia, is a multi-racial country.

Nasi goreng, which means fried rice, is a popular Indonesian dish.

BUT: He is not the Mr. Johnson *I used to know.*

I went to the movies last night.

The movie, which was about Gandhi, was fascinating.

Tennis, which is a popular sport, is not difficult to learn.

The highest mountain in the world, which is located in Asia, is Mount Everest.

The students, who studied hard, were praised by the teacher.

BUT: *The students* who studied hard were praised by the teacher.

Name of
a person,
a place,
a thing.

(more than one personality)

A noun is clear because
   it has been mentioned earlier,
   it is generally known,
   it is unique (only *one* is the highest), or
   it represents a class or a group as a whole.

(Only those who studied hard were praised by the teacher.)

Exercise 2   Punctuate the following sentences correctly. Explain why you put commas or why you did not.

1. Buenos Aires which is the capital of Argentina is the largest city south of the equator.

2. Pythagoras who was a Greek philosopher who lived in the sixth century B.C. was the first to conceive of the earth as a globe.

3. The city of New Orleans which was named in honor of the Duke of Orleans of France was founded August 25, 1718.

4. New Hampshire was the only one of the original thirteen colonies that was not invaded by the enemy during the American Revolution.

5. Abraham Lincoln who was six feet, four inches tall was the tallest president of the United States.

Exercise 3   Capitalize and punctuate correctly.

Australia which is the home of many unusual animals is the home of the kangaroo kangaroos are animals that have pockets or pouches in which they rear their tiny babies a kangaroo baby which is only about the size of a bumblebee when it is born lives in its mother's pouch until its back legs have grown long and strong kangaroos who have very strong legs can make long hops and give fierce kicks other animals that rear their babies in pouches are opossums wallabies wombats and koalas.

Formation and Position of Adjective Clauses

Like an adverbial clause, an adjective clause is made from a simple sentence. However, there are two main differences between an adjective clause and an adverbial clause. Look at the following examples.

- -

Adverbial clause

The student could not go to school. [He was sick.]
The student could not go to school *because he was sick*.　　no change in sentence 2
Because the student was sick, he could not go to school.　　different positions possible

Adjective clause

The student [He was sick.] could not go to school.
The student *who was sick* could not go to school.　　pronoun substitution
The student [You saw him yesterday.] was absent today.
The student *whom you saw yesterday* was absent today.　　only one position possible

- -

First of all, the position of an adjective clause is different. An adverbial clause may be placed in several positions — at the beginning, in the middle, or at the end of a sentence, but an adjective clause can occcur in only one position in the sentence — right after (or as close as possible to) the noun that it modifies.

Second, the formation of an adjective clause is different. Whereas an adverbial clause is formed simply by putting a conjunction in front of an unchanged sentence, an adjective clause is formed by substituting a noun in the sentence with a relative pronoun and moving the relative pronoun to the front of the clause. In other words, two steps are necessary in the formation of an adjective clause:

1. A noun is replaced by a relative pronoun.
2. The relative pronoun is moved to the beginning of the clause.

EXAMPLE:

The boy [you met (the boy)] is my roommate.

The boy whom you met is my roommate.

Exercise 4　　Change the sentences in brackets into adjective clauses.

1. One out of ten trucks [We meet the trucks on our highways.] carries explosives, flammables, or poisons.

2. Maine is the only state in the United States [The state adjoins only one other state.].

3. Three fourths of all sulphur [The sulphur is consumed in the United States.] goes into the manufacture of sulphuric acid.

4. It is an established fact that people [The people are married.] live longer than those people [The people are single.].

Functions of the Relative Pronouns

The pronouns *who, whom,* and *whose* are used for persons, *which* and ...*of which* for things.

The relative adverbs *when, where,* and *as* are occasionally used to refer to an expression of time, place, or manner.

The relative pronoun *that* may refer to either persons or things, but it can be used only in restrictive clauses as subject or object. *That* may also be deleted, but only if it functions as an object.

In the following sets of examples, each function of the relative pronoun is discussed separately, and the possible variations of the relative pronouns are illustrated. Each of the following sets of examples is divided into a restrictive and non-restrictive column.

Subject

Restrictive			Non-restrictive
The man *who came here yesterday* is my friend.			John, *who came here yesterday,* is my friend.
(The man *that came here yesterday* is my friend.)			
(A car	*which broke down*	caused a traffic jam.)	My car, *which broke down,* caused a traffic jam.
A car	*that broke down*	caused a traffic jam.	

INCORRECT: A car broke down caused a traffic jam.

The pronouns *who, which,* and *that* may function as the subject of an adjective clause. *That* cannot be deleted when it is the subject of the clause, and it may not function as the subject of a non-restrictive clause.

Note: When the antecedent is a person, the *who* construction is preferred, but when the antecedent is a thing, the *that* construction is preferred.

Exercise 5   Combine the following sentences. Use an appropriate relative pronoun as *subject* of the clause. Add commas where necessary.

1. The letter (The letter arrived today.) _____ contained good news.

2. This letter, (It was from my parents.) _____ , surprised me.

3. Yesterday I saw a movie. (It was about the Civil War.) _____ .

4. John (He was my neighbor.) _____ came to visit me yesterday.

5. The adjective clause test (It took me an hour to finish.) _____

was very difficult.

6. John paid for a collect call (It cost $12.00.) _____ .

Object

Restrictive	Non-restrictive
The man *whom you met yesterday* is my friend.	John, *whom you met yesterday,*
The man *that you met yesterday* is my friend.	is my friend.
The man *you met yesterday* is my friend.	
(A car *which someone hit* held up traffic.)	My car, *which someone hit,* held
A car *that someone hit* held up traffic.	up traffic.
A car *someone hit* held up traffic.	

INCORRECT: A car someone hit it held up traffic.

The relative pronouns *who(m)*, *which,* and *that* may function as the object of an adjective clause. The pronoun *that* is used only in a restrictive clause, and it may be deleted when it functions as object. Remember that a clause can have only one direct object.

Note: In spoken and in informal English, the relative pronoun *who* is frequently used as an object instead of *whom*.

Exercise 6 Complete each of the following sentences with a meaningful adjective clause in which the relative pronoun functions as the object.

EXAMPLE:

I need a suit _____ . (wear)
(I need a suit which I can wear to the wedding.)
I need a suit that I can wear to the wedding.
I need a suit I can wear to the wedding.

1. I want to buy a car _____ . (use)

2. I worked on my homework, _____ .

(assign)

3. I want to rent an apartment _____

_____ . (afford)

4. I want to find a housekeeper _____

_____ . (trust)

5. I want to find a painting _____ .

(put on the wall)

6. I want to visit my parents, _____ .

(not/see)

7. I wrote a letter to my friend, _____

_____ . (visit)

8. I want to find a roommate _____ .

(depend on)

9. I need to speak to John, _____ .

(ask a favor of)

10. I spoke to my brother, _____ .

(miss)

After a Preposition

Restrictive		Non-restrictive
The man *about whom we talked*	is my friend.	John, *about whom we talked*, is my friend.
The man *who(m) we talked about*	is my friend.	John, *who(m) we talked about,* is my friend.
The man *that we talked about*	is my friend.	
The man *we talked about*	is my friend.	
A car *with which someone collided* held up traffic.		My car, *with which someone collided,* held up traffic.
A car *which someone collided with* held up traffic.		
A car *that someone collided with* held up traffic.		My car, *which someone collided with,* held up traffic.
A car *someone collided with* held up traffic.		

Only the relative pronouns *whom* and *which* may occur directly after a preposition; the pronoun *that* may be used only if the preposition is at the end of a restrictive clause, in which case it may also be deleted. *Note:* The construction with a preposition at the end of a clause is usually preferred in informal English.

Exercise 7   Combine and/or complete the following sentences.

EXAMPLE:

The man (We talked about him.) _____ .
The man about whom we talked is not here.

1. The student (I borrowed a book from him.) _____ .

2. My car, (I traveled with it to New Mexico.) _____ .

3. The bank (I borrowed money from it.) _____ .

4. I like the movie *Star Wars,* (Han Solo gets his reward in this movie.) _____ .

5. He read a book (I told him about it.) _____

_____ .

6. I didn't like the TV program (I had heard so much.) _____

_____ .

7. I received a letter (I found good news in it.) _____ .

8. _____ (that) I told you about ____

_____ .

9. _____ (that) he was interested in

_____ .

10. _____ (that) she is tired of ____

_____ .

11. _____ , which the students are

bored with, _____ .

12. _____ , whom we asked about,

_____ .

After an Expression of Time, Place, and Manner

- -

This is the city *where* I was born.   (This is the city *in which* I was born.)
The day *when* I arrived, I lost my luggage.   (The day *on which* I arrived I lost my luggage).
The universe *as we know it* may have begun
  with a great explosion.   (The universe *in the manner that we know it...*)

INCORRECT: This is the city where I was born in.

- -

The relative adverbs *when, where,* and *as* function as a connecting word and as an adverbial at the same time. These relative adverbs are used in the place of a preposition plus *which* construction, so it is wrong to leave the preposition in the clause. The preposition plus *which* construction is not used often in spoken or informal English, but is is shown here to help you understand the underlying structures.

Exercise 8   Complete the following sentences in your own words.

1. Please, tell me the day when _____

_____ .

2. Please tell me the place where _____

_____ .

3. The bookstore where _____

_____ .

4. The place where _____ .

5. The time when _____ .

6. The problem as _____ .

7. I will see you on the day when _____

_____ .

8. The _____ where he lived was

_____ .

9. The _____ when I saw you was

_____ .

10. The _____ as we know it now will

_____ .

So far you have seen that the relative pronoun by itself can function as subject, object, or adverbial, but sometimes the relative pronoun can serve as a part of an object or subject. Instead of taking the place of a noun phrase, the relative pronoun may function as an adjective.

In *Of*-Expressions of Possession

- -

I bought *the man's car.*
The man *whose car* I bought is my friend.

> *The tires of the car* went flat.
> A car *the tires of which* went flat held up traffic.
>
> A car *whose tires* went flat held up traffic.
>
> PREFERRED: A car had a flat tire, and that held up traffic.

- -

Who has the adjective form *whose,* which precedes a noun, but *which* does not have a separate adjective form and must therefore follow the noun in an ... *of which* construction. Sometimes *whose* is used for a thing in order to avoid the awkward ... *of which* construction, but usually it is avoided altogether and phrased in a different manner.

Exercise 9   Combine and/or complete the following sentences.

> EXAMPLE:
>
> The student whose....
> *The student whose parents called is happy.*

1. The person (I found his hat.) _____ .
2. The neighbor (His dog barked all night.) _____ .
3. The car (The cushions of the car are blue.) _____

   _____ .

4. The chair the _____ of which is broken is _____

   _____ .

5. The bike the tire of _____ .
6. My friend, whose _____ .
7. I like the student whose _____ .
8. The chair the seats _____ are up-

   holstered is comfortable.

9. _____ the legs of which are metal

   is wobbly.

10. _____ the _____ of which

    is _____ .

In *Of*-Expressions of Quantity or Comparison

Expressions of quantity, such as *some of....., most of..., many of..., a part of..., much of..., two of..., the cutest of...,* may also occur in an *of*-construction with *whom* or *which.*

234   The Adjective Clause

(*Some of these tourists* are from abroad.)
New York has many tourists, *some of whom* are from abroad.

(*Most of the cake* had already been eaten.)
We brought him a delicious birthday cake, *most of which* had already been eaten.

(I skipped *a part of this book.*)
I finished reading the book, *a part of which* I skipped.

(I did not understand *much of the movie.*)
I did not enjoy that movie, much *of which* I did not understand.

(*Two of the boys* live on my street.)
I recognized the boys, *two of whom* live on my street.

(We picked *the cutest of the puppies.*)
The puppies, *the cutest of which* we picked, were adorable.

The following chart summarizes the forms and the functions of the relative pronouns. If necessary, refer to it for the next exercises.

Function of relative pronoun in the clause	RESTRICTIVE CLAUSES		NON-RESTRICTIVE CLAUSES	
	persons	things	persons	things
SUBJECT	*who* *(that)*	*(which)* *that*	*who*	*which*
OBJECT	*who(m)* *(that)* 0	*(which)* *that* 0	*who(m)*	*which*
AFTER PREPOSITION	*whom*	*which*	*whom*	*which*
AS ADVERBIAL AFTER AN EXPRESSION OF TIME, PLACE, OR MANNER		*when* *where* *as*		*when* *where* *as*
AS ADJECTIVE BEFORE OR AFTER A NOUN	*whose*	*...of which*	*whose*	*...of which*

Note again that the pronouns *who* and *whom* are preferred when we refer to persons, while *that* refers to things. Remember also that there are special rules for the pronoun *that.*

1. *That* is used in restrictive clauses only; therefore, an adjective clause beginning with *that* is not set off with commas.
2. *That* may be deleted (because it is understood) when it functions as direct object of the clause, but not when it functions as subject of the clause.
3. *That* cannot come directly after a preposition.

Exercise 10   Fill in the blanks with an appropriate relative pronoun. Use all possible variations. Explain your choices.

1. I saw the man _____ helped us.

2. Mary, _____ you met yesterday, is my cousin.

3. We ate the cake _____ Mary baked.

4. The grammar book _____ I am studying is boring.

5. The book, the most boring part _____ I skipped, was long.

6. The girl _____ friend called the school is sick.

7. The doctor _____ Mary went to yesterday was not in his office.

8. Dr. Jones, _____ Mary went to yesterday, is off today.

9. Her friends, three _____ I had met before, came to visit.

10. John, _____ car I borrowed, is in New York.

11. The man _____ I talked to is from Venezuela.

12. The book at _____ John was looking is on the desk.

13. At night, _____ I study, I go to the library.

14. At night, I go to the library, _____ I study.

15. I saw two movies, the latter one _____ I liked best.

Exercise 11   Complete each of the following sentences with a meaningful adjective clause.

1. The student who _____ is my friend.

2. John, whom _____ , is my friend.

3. The student from whom _____ is my friend.

4. Mary, whose _____ , is my friend.

5. The student that _____ is my friend.

6. The student (0) _____ is my friend.

7. The students many of whom _____
   are my friends.

8. This book, which _____ , is
   interesting.

9. The book that _____ is
   interesting.

10. This book, the _____ of which _____
    _____ is interesting.

11. The book (0) _____ is interesting.

12. This book, most of which _____ ,
    is interesting.

13. Last Saturday was the day when _____
    _____ .

14. This is the house where _____ .

Exercise 12   Combine the following sentences by making an adjective clause out of the *second* one. Make sure you move the clause after the noun.

1. Gypsum is a crystalline rock. The rock is made up of calcium and sulphur.

2. The albatross is an exceedingly large and strong seabird. The albatross' wingspread has been known to reach up to seventeen feet.

3. Anne Boleyn was deformed by the presence of an extra finger. She was the second wife of King Henry VII.

4. The Eiffel Tower is 984 feet high. It is in France.

5. Mozart began to compose at the age of five. He was the noted Austrian composer.

6. Harry S. Truman was the first president. This president vetoed a tax reduction bill.

7. The spot is Mount Katahdin in the state of Maine. On this spot the sun shines first in the United States.

8. More than twenty thousand men were killed, wounded, or missing in action in the Battle of Antietam of September 17, 1862. The bloodiest one-day fight during the Civil War took place on this day.

9. The completion of the railroads contributed greatly to the decline of the canals. These canals were built during the nineteenth century.

10. Assembly line production was adopted by Henry Ford in his Detroit auto factory. It became effective on June 6, 1913 in this factory.

Exercise 13   The following passage contains choppy sentences. Rewrite it to make it smoother and more coherent. Include adjective clauses where possible.

If the earth were a perfect sphere, which had its mass spread out evenly in all directions, the pull of gravity would be the same in all directions. But the earth is not a perfect sphere. It is flattened slightly at the poles. It bulges out at the equator. It is like a man with a big roll of fat on his belly. Its surface is irregular. It has continents and oceans, mountains, valleys, and plains. Its mass is not spread out evenly. In fact, the rocks in some places are heavier than the rocks in others. As a result, the pull of gravity is not the same in all directions. When an earth satellite passes over different regions of the earth, it receives a different pull. This has an effect on the way it moves. Its orbit is disturbed. Astronomers call the effects of such disturbances "aberrations." By studying these aberrations, they get information about the shape of the earth.

Exercise 14   Write a paragraph of about fifty words describing the ice chest in the ad for the Gott cooler. Your topic sentence should contain a word that expresses one of its excellent qualities (for example, strong, convenient, handy, ingenious). Then make sure that all the sentences in the paragraph support the opening statement. Try to use at least four adjective clauses in your paragraph.

Reduced Adjective Clauses

As you saw in Chapter 5, several types of adverbial clauses may be reduced. These reduced clauses are very common in English, and they are often preferred to complete clauses. Many adjective clauses may be reduced in a similar manner.

The reduction rule that accounts for the majority of the reduced adjective clauses is the deletion of subject and *be*.

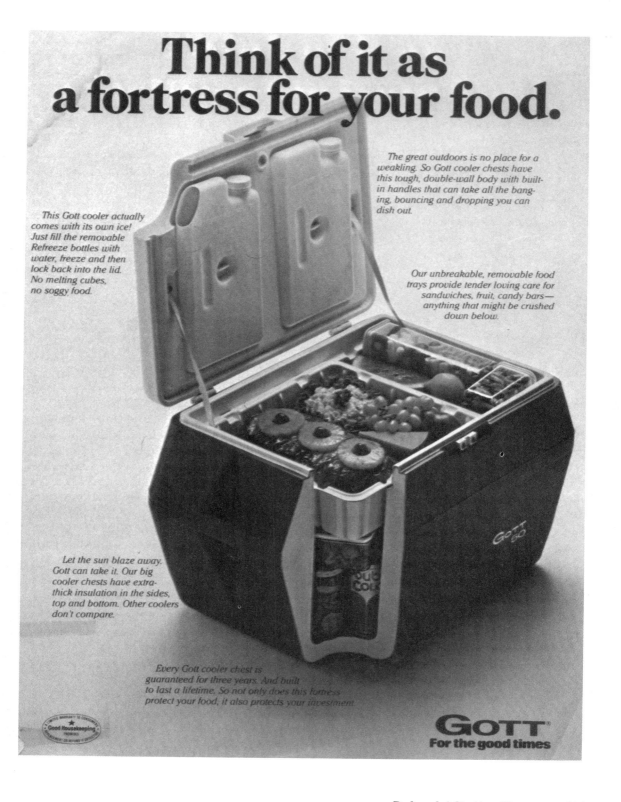

Think of it as a fortress for your food.

The great outdoors is no place for a weakling. So Gott cooler chests have this tough, double-wall body with built-in handles that can take all the banging, bouncing and dropping you can dish out.

This Gott cooler actually comes with its own ice! Just fill the removable Refreeze bottles with water, freeze and then lock back into the lid. No melting cubes, no soggy food.

Our unbreakable, removable food trays provide tender loving care for sandwiches, fruit, candy bars—anything that might be crushed down below.

Let the sun blaze away. Gott can take it. Our big cooler chests have extra-thick insulation in the sides, top and bottom. Other coolers don't compare.

Every Gott cooler chest is guaranteed for three years. And built to last a lifetime. So not only does this fortress protect your food, it also protects your investment.

GOTT
For the good times

Deletion of Subject and Be

$$\overset{S\quad be}{}$$

	S — be	
Where is Dr. Johnson, who is	the head of the English Department?	
Where is Dr. Johnson,	*the head of the English Department?*	noun phrase (appositive)

Dr. Johnson, who is   unable to attend the meeting, will be here later.
Dr. Johnson,   *unable to attend the meeting,* will be here later.   adjective phrase

I don't know the people who are   in this room.
I don't know the people   *in this room.*   prepositional phrase of place

The boy who is   sitting next to me is from Taiwan.
The boy   *sitting next to me* is from Taiwan.   present participle phrase

The vet treated the puppy that was   hit by a car.
The vet treated the puppy   *hit by a car.*   past participle phrase

The first person who was   to fly to the moon was Neil Armstrong.
The first person   *to fly to the moon* was Neil Armstrong.   to-infinitive phrase

----

If the relative pronoun is the subject of the clause and if it is followed by a form of *be,* both may be deleted. *Note:* This rule is basically the same as the rule discussed in Chapter 5: *When (I am) in New York, I like to go shopping. Although (he was) sick, he went to school.*

As you can see, the reduced clause may have one of several forms: It may be a noun phrase, an adjective phrase, a prepositional phrase of place, a present participle phrase, a past participle phrase, or a *to*-infinitive phrase. All these forms are possible because the verb *be,* as you saw in Chapter 2, has several functions: *Be* may be a linking verb, an intransitive verb, or an auxiliary verb to form the progressive, the passive, or the future.

Exercise 15   Reduce the adjective clauses in the following sentences, and identify each phrase as a noun, an adjective, or as a prepositional, a present participle, a past participle, or an infinitive phrase.

1. A person who is swimming in the Dead Sea cannot sink or completely submerge himself.

2. Warren G. Harding, in June 21, 1923, became the first president who was to speak over the radio.

3. Two nails that are driven into a tree trunk, one above the other, will remain the same distance apart as the tree grows.

4. The American moose, which is a native of North America, is the largest member of the deer family.

5. "Breach of promise" means the failure, which is deliberate or intentional, to do any lawful thing that one has bound oneself by contract to do.

6. The yellow stain from cigarettes is caused by the tar oil that is in cigarette smoke.

Changing of a Relative Pronoun that is a Subject and Finite Verb to a Present Participle Phrase

$$\overline{\text{The boy } \overset{\text{S}}{who} \overset{\text{f.v.}}{works \; here} \text{ is my friend.}}$$

The boy *who works here* is my friend.
The boy *working   here* is my friend.

I can't find the book *that belongs to you.*
I can't find the book *belonging   to you.*

NOTE:	I don't know the boy *who has the bike.*	verb expressing possession
	I don't know the boy *with the bike.*	*with*-phrase of possession
INCORRECT:	I don't know the boy *having the bike.*	
	Do you know Mr. Jones, *who works at Sears?*	
INCORRECT:	Do you know Mr. Jones, *working at Sears?*	non-restrictive clause
CORRECT:	Mr. Jones, *working at Sears,* meets a lot of people.	non-restrictive phrase of reason
CORRECT:	*Working at Sears,* Mr. Jones meets a lot of people.	adverbial phrase of reason

Another reduction rule in adjective clauses is the changing of the subject + finite verb to a present participle phrase. *Note:* This reduction is also similar to a reduction rule in adverbial clauses: *Feeling tired, he wanted to take a nap.*

However, it is not always possible to change an adjective clause to a present participle phrase. First of all, verbs of possession are usually reduced to *with*-phrases, not to present participle phrases. Also, the adjective clause has to be restrictive. Non-restrictive relative clauses may be reduced to present participle phrases only if they express reason. These phrases may come either after the noun or at the beginning of the sentence, in which case the present participle phrase is usually considered an adverbial phrase of reason. (See Chapter 5).

Exercise 16   In the following passage change the reduced adjective phrases, which are in italics, to adjective clauses.

In the summer of 1859, a French acrobat *called Blondin* strung a rope across the gorge *just below Niagara Falls.* On June 30, he was ready to walk from the United States to Canada across that rope, *more than 150 feet above Niagara's violent waters.*

Blondin, *sitting down on the rope halfway across,* scared the crowd as he lowered a string to a boat *below,* pulled up a bottle, and took a drink. Then he continued his terrifying walk. Eighteen minutes after he began his stroll, he was greeted by a crowd *cheering tremendously* as he stepped onto the Canadian side. In less than seven minutes he completed his trip back to the United States.

People *coming to the Falls that summer to see what the acrobat would do next* were never disappointed by Blondin, who always thought of different tricks. He walked across with a sack *over his head!* He held out his hat *for a marksman to shoot from below!* He pushed a wheelbarrow across! He did a headstand on the rope!

Somehow he convinced his manager, *Harry Colcord,* to ride across on his back; however, he did not try that stunt, *a near disaster,* again. A support wire snapped and jerked the main rope sideways. Finally, Blondin, *managing to keep himself and his manager from falling,* was able to land safely on the other side after forty-five agonizing minutes.

Once Blondin, *ready for a snack,* even took a table, chair, and stove with him to the middle of the rope and fixed an omelet! It is no wonder that Blondin became the most famous daredevil of his time.

Changing of a Modal Construction to a To-Infinitive Phrase

- -

I need a bag that I can carry with me on the plane.
I need a bag   *to carry with me on the plane.*

Mr. Johnson is the man whom you should ask that question.
Mr. Johnson is the man   *to ask that question.*

The city that you should visit is New Orleans.
The city _____ *to visit is New Orleans.*

Note: This construction is also similar to an adverbial clause reduction: *This bag is too heavy for me to carry,* or *This bag is too heavy to carry.*

Solving Problems

This unit has presented some of the most troublesome structures in the English language. However, if you are aware of the trouble spots, it is easier to avoid them.

First of all, it is important to see that the clause is complete — if there is a subject, there has to be a finite verb, and vice versa. In addition, a clause can have only one object. Do not forget that an understood *that* may function as object of the clause.

No Subject in the Adjective Clause

INCORRECT:	The boy is walking there is my friend.
CORRECT:	The boy who is walking there is my friend.
CORRECT:	The boy walking there is my friend.

INCORRECT:	I don't like a place where is cold.
CORRECT:	I don't like a place where it is cold.
CORRECT:	I don't like a place that is cold.

No Finite Verb in the Adjective Clause

INCORRECT:	The boy who walking there is my friend.
CORRECT:	The boy who is walking there is my friend.
CORRECT:	The boy walking there is my friend.

Two Objects in the Adjective Clause

INCORRECT:	The boy you see him is my friend.
INCORRECT:	The boy (that) you see him is my friend.
CORRECT:	The boy that you see is my friend.
CORRECT:	The boy you see is my friend.

INCORRECT:	The movie I like it is about a soccer player.
INCORRECT:	The movie (that) I like it is about a soccer player.
CORRECT:	The movie that I like is about a soccer player.
CORRECT:	The movie I like is about a soccer player.

Fragment — No Main Clause

INCORRECT: The man who was sick because he had gone out in the
cold weather.

CORRECT: The man was sick because he had gone out in the cold weather.

CORRECT: The man who was sick had gone out in the cold weather.

Exercise 17   Many of the sentences in the following passages contain one of the errors
mentioned above in the formation of an adjective clause. Identify the
errors and rewrite the passages correctly.

Passage A

Even when he was a small boy, Dr. Robert Goddard was fascinated
with rockets that people could send them into space, even though most
people considered such travel impossible. Signal flares and fireworks
were the only rockets had ever flown, and they had traveled into the air
only a few hundred feet.

Many people laughed at him, but he paid no attention. In 1914,
he patented some basic principles of modern rocketry which including
a multi-stage design. This design, in which each stage drops away
when its fuel supply is used up, is still in use today. So are many of his
other ideas.

Goddard, even invented the first liquid-fueled rocket, began design-
ing and building his own rockets. None of Goddard's rockets ever made
it into space. However, every modern space flight owes much of its success to the experiments which done by him in his pioneering days.

Passage B

Engineer Othmar H. Amman, was one of the world's greatest bridge
designers, designed the George Washington Bridge. The bridge that
crossing the Hudson River between New York City and New Jersey
was by far the longest suspension bridge ever built when it was opened
in 1931.

Amman worked on many bridges after that. But his greatest achievement was the 6,690 foot Verrazano-Narrows Bridge, where stretches
between Brooklyn and Staten Island in New York City.

The roadway is supported by cables which made up of more than 145,000 miles of wire. That's enough wire to go around the world nearly five times!

Each of the 690-foot-tall main towers is made of pieces of steel, which more than 4,000,000 bolts and rivets hold them together.

The Verrazano Bridge is so long that the two main towers are more than an inch and a half further apart at the top than at the bottom — to allow for the curvature of the earth. When the bridge opened in November 1964, its center span which was the longest of any suspension bridge on earth.

Incorrect Position of the Adjective Clause or Phrase

An adjective clause or phrase must come immediately after the noun that it modifies. Sometimes there are several adjectivals in a row, but it is not possible to have another part of the sentence between a noun and its adjectivals.

INCORRECT: Students usually accomplish much who have great expectations.
CORRECT: Students who have great expectations usually accomplish much.

Punctuation Errors

Only a non-restrictive adjective clause or phrase is set off with commas. Note that a non-restrictive element must be punctuated before and after it.

INCORRECT: John, who came over yesterday told me about the accident.
CORRECT: John, who came over yesterday, told me about the accident.

INCORRECT: John unable to attend the meeting did not hear the news.
CORRECT: John, unable to attend the meeting, did not hear the news.

INCORRECT: Anyone, who lives in this area, should register to vote.
CORRECT: Anyone who lives in this area should register to vote.

The verb in the adjective clause or phrase may also cause several errors.

Lack of Agreement in Adjective Clauses

INCORRECT: One of the boys who lives here is my friend.
CORRECT: One of the boys who live here is my friend.
(One boy is my friend; several boys live here.)
BUT: He is the only of the boys who lives here. (Only one boy lives here.)

Inconsistency in the Use of Tenses

Make sure the tenses are sequenced logically.

INCORRECT: The police caught the thief who escaped.
CORRECT: The police caught the thief who had escaped.

INCORRECT: A person who ate a large meal should wait an hour before going swimming.
CORRECT: A person who has eaten a large meal should wait an hour before going swimming.

Faulty Verb Form in a Reduced Clause (Confusion of Present Participle, Past Participle, and *To*-Infinitive)

INCORRECT: The boy interesting in electronics asked a question.
CORRECT: The boy interested in electronics asked a question.

INCORRECT: The boy called his dog is my friend.
CORRECT: The boy calling his dog is my friend.

INCORRECT: The first man living on the moon will be famous.
CORRECT: The first man to live on the moon will be famous.

Inappropriate Reduction of an Adjective Clause

A non-restrictive clause can be reduced to a present participle phrase only if it expresses reason. Clauses containing verbs of possession are usually reduced to *with*-phrases.

INCORRECT: John, talking to Mr. Jeffrey, is a student.
INCORRECT: Talking to Mr. Jeffrey, John is a student.
CORRECT: John, who is talking to Mr. Jeffrey, is a student.

INCORRECT: The young man having the sports car is rich.
CORRECT: The young man with the sports car is rich.

Inappropriate Use of *that*

That cannot come after a preposition, and it cannot introduce a non-restrictive clause. Note that a non-restrictive clause must have a relative pronoun because only *that* can be deleted from a clause.

INCORRECT: The man about that you talked is Mr. Johnson.
CORRECT: The man about whom you talked is Mr. Johnson.
CORRECT: The man that you talked about is Mr. Johnson.

INCORRECT: Mr. Johnson, that you met yesterday, is my teacher.

INCORRECT: Mr. Johnson, you met yesterday, is my teacher.

CORRECT: Mr. Johnson, whom you met yesterday, is my teacher.

Exercise 18 The following passage describes the house pictured above the words, "Visit Georgia's Architectural Puzzle." Many of the sentences marked in the passage contain one of the errors named above. Identify the errors and correct them.

Georgia's Architectural Puzzle

Amid rolling farmland and plantation style homes, the Rock House in Thomson, Georgia, seems out of place. The house, looking like someone picked it up from the Delaware Valley in the eighteenth century, is located in eastern Georgia. The three-story fieldstone construction is unique for Georgia is surprisingly the oldest dwelling in the state.

Photographs:
Bruce Roberts

*Due to its amazing construction, the Rock House (**left**) in Thomson, Georgia, is the only known surviving stone house from a period when other building materials were more common.*

Visit Georgia's Architectural Puzzle

The house, built by Thomas Ansley, is the last remaining dwelling associated with the village of Wrightboro a Quaker settlement begun in 1768. When Ansley and his family moved from New Jersey to North Carolina, where they joined a group of Quakers moving south. Although the Ansleys probably weren't Quakers, they were awarded land in the Quaker settlement.

When Ansley built his house in the early 1780s, he chose a style he was familiar with it from New Jersey. Fieldstone which was cut from the nearby granite outcroppings for the exterior. The stone construction is one of the reasons it was chosen in 1970 for the National Register of Historic Places which was unusual. However, the fieldstone has an unusual physical property. The stone, which crumble when it gets wet, hardens when it dries.

Decades later, the house, the mortar of that began to give way, was covered with a shell of concrete, and its roof of remaining oak shingles was covered with tin. This was fortunate because the concrete saved the house that looked then totally different from when it was built, from crumbling into pieces.

Since then, the interior has been restored to its original state and the concrete removed to reveal the original stonework, repairing with new mortar. Now you can appreciate the craft that gone into this house. It is believed that Ansley, who has even made the molding by hand, used no more than five tools to do the detailing.

Exercise 19   Read the following passage, and then complete the sentences. Your sentences should be grammatically correct and based on the reading selection.

Cells: The Building Blocks of Life

The work of Mendel and Darwin told the world much about the science of heredity and the variations and changes in plants and animals. But, without an understanding of the tiny cells that make up all living organisms, we would be unable to know exactly how heredity works.

In 1655, The Englishman Robert Hooke, an inventor and scientist, designed his own microscope, so that he would have a workable tool with which to magnify small objects.

One day, when he was experimenting with his new invention, he picked up a small piece of cork, sliced a thin portion of it, and placed it under the microscope's magnifying glass. It surprised him that the cork was made up of a series of tiny compartments. He called these compartments cells because they resembled the cells of a honeycomb.

It wasn't until two centuries later, however, that scientists, using an improved microscope to study the structures of plants and animals, realized how important Hooke's discovery was. The credit for this goes to two German scientists, Matthias Schleiden, a botanist, and Theodor Schwann, a zoologist.

Independently of each other and at about the same time, Schleiden discovered that all plants are made up of a series of tiny cells, and Schwann reported that the same thing was true of animals.

That same year, 1883, the two men met for the first time and compared notes. When Schwann took Schleiden to his laboratory to examine a section of animal tissue he had been working on, Schleiden was amazed that plant and animal cells were very similar.

The work of these two men led to the cell theory, now accepted as fact, which states that all living organisms, plant and animal, are made up of similar tiny structures, called cells, which are the building blocks of life.

1. The work of Mendel and Darwin, which _____

_____ , would not have been possible if they had not under-

stood that _____ .

2. Because they had an understanding of the tiny cells that

_____ they were able to find out

_____ .

3. A microscope is a tool with which _____

_____ .

4. One day, the inventor and scientist Robert Hooke, who _____

_____ , picked up a small piece of cork, a

small slice of _____ he placed under _____

_____ .

5. He discovered that a series of _____

_____ .

6. He called these compartments cells because _____

_____ .

7. Two centuries later, scientists who _____

_____ began to realize the importance of _____

_____ .

8. Two German scientists, Matthias Schleiden and Theodor Schwann,

should _____ .

9. Independently of each other and at about the same time, both

Schleiden and _____ .

10. Not only were plants _____ .

11. That same year, 1883, when the two men met for the first time, they

_____ .

12. Schwann, who _____ took Schleiden

to his laboratory because _____ .

13. The similarity between plant and animal cells _____

_____ .

14. It was the work of these two men that _____

_____ .

15. Cells, the building blocks of life, are _____

_____ .

Assignment for Writing

The following passage about the Taj Mahal contains many choppy sentences. Rewrite the passage to make it smoother and more coherent. Include adjective clauses and reduced adjective clauses where possible. Try to include at least five reduced adjective clauses.

The Taj Mahal

(1) The Taj Mahal is one of the world's most breathtaking spectacles. Its construction took 22,000 men and women 24 hours a day for 22 years. The full story behind the wondrous creation is little known beyond India. This creation rises out of the dusty plains of Agra,

125 miles southeast of Delhi. The Taj is the enduring legacy of a great love. Emperor Shah Jahan loved his wife of 19 years, Mumtaz Mahal, very deeply. She died while bearing their fourteenth child.

(2) Shah Jahan was the fifth emperor of India from the Mughal dynasty. People believed that he was descended from Tamerlane and Genghis Khan. Tamerlane was the conqueror. Genghis Khan was the famed Mongol warrior. Shah Jahan went south to make war upon rebel forces in 1631. His beautiful, dark-eyed queen was at his side, as usual. She was pregnant. Tragedy struck on this journey. Mumtaz Mahal died in childbirth. She was in an encampment at Burhanpur.

(3) This event devastated Shah Jahan. He left his wife's deathbed. He went straight to his quarters. He locked the doors behind him. He remained there for eight days. He took no food or drink. The only evidence of life was a low continual moan. On the ninth day he reappeared. His raven-black hair had turned completely white.

(4) The emperor returned to his palace in Agra. He chose a site along the Jumna River as the location of his wife's tomb. This site was within easy view of his windows. Workmen used twenty-eight types of gems for inlay all through the building. These gems included agate, jade, and garnet. When the tomb was complete, a sheet of pearls was spread over the coffin. Doors opened onto the tomb. The workmen had made these doors of solid silver. A balustrade of solid gold surrounded the cenotaph. These things are all gone now. Soldiers plundered these things during attacks on the Mughal empire in the eighteenth century. The essence and the enduring beauty of the tomb remains.

(5) Shah Jahan had planned a mirror image of the Taj as his own tomb. This mirror image was in black marble. It was not to be. His own son took him prisoner. His son usurped the throne in 1658. His son confined Shah Jahan to his own palace. The Shah lived there for eight years. He was only able to gaze out on the Jumna River toward his beloved wife's resting place.

(6) His guards found Shah Jahan dead at the age of 74. His eyes were still open. His eyes were fixed upon the shimmering jewel of the Taj Mahal.

Group Discussion

Quickly read over "The Taj Mahal" again, preferably the rewritten version. Answer the following questions.

1. In the introduction (paragraph 1), what adjective did the author use to describe the Taj Mahal?
2. A little further in paragraph 1, what noun phrase did the author use to describe the Taj Mahal?
3. From the introduction we learn several facts. What do the following sentences tell us about?

a. To build the Taj Mahal, 22,000 men and women labored 24 hours a day for 22 years. (*its construction*)

b. This creation rises out of the dusty plains of Agra, 125 miles southest of Delhi. (its _____)'

c. The Taj is the enduring legacy of the great love that Emperor Shah Jahan had for his wife of 19 years. (its _____)

4. From the introduction we know that the reading selection is going to discuss the Taj Mahal's construction, its _____ , and its _____ .

5. The first developmental paragraphs (2 and 3) deal mainly with its _____ .

6. The third developmental paragraph (4) deals both with its _____ and _____ .

7. The fourth developmental paragraph (5) deals again with its _____ .

8. What do the following words in the conclusion tell us about: history, location, or construction?

a. Shah Jahan died at the age of 74.

b. His eyes were fixed upon the shimmering jewel of the Taj Mahal.

9. Which is emphasized the most in this reading selection: its construction, its location, or its history?

10. The reading selection is interesting because the author gives us many specific facts and details. We can see that the author is very familiar with the topic, and we learn a lot of new information from the selection.

a. What specific facts do we know about the Emperor? Name at least 15.

b. What specific facts do we know about his wife? Name at least 3.

c. What specific facts do we know about the location of the Taj Mahal? Name at least 5.

d. What specific facts do we know about the construction of the Taj Mahal? Name at least 5.

Writing Assignment

Describe an interesting place. Make sure that you include enough specific facts and details in each paragraph to be of interest to your reader. Your reader does not want to read something he or she already knows. Readers want to learn something!

Before you start on your theme, brainstorm. Ask yourself the following questions.

1. Which place (geographical area, city, town, village, building, structure, or house) do you know a lot about?

2. Make a list of at least 20 facts and details that you know about the place.
3. Group details and facts into categories.
4. What aspects do most of the facts describe: its history, location, attractive features, design, technical innovations, financial history (Who built it? Why?), financial status now (does it make money for the builders, owners, or inhabitants?)?
5. What aspect do you want to emphasize?
6. Where can you find out more about the place? Do your friends have information that might be helpful? Is there information in the library?

Suggestions for Writing

There are two ways to describe a place or a thing. One can describe it very objectively by giving only facts and specific details, or one can describe it subjectively by creating a mood.

In most technical writing, the former is preferred, but in creative writing, the purpose is to give the reader a feeling for the place. If you are writing a creative essay, remember that you have five senses: sight, sound, smell, taste, and touch. Try to include at least three of these to make your essay more interesting.

In both technical and creative description, it is important to use specific words. For example, *large* can mean anything from the size of a book to the size of a mountain. Specific measurements or more specific words like *humongous* or *enormous* give the reader a more accurate picture. You may want to look up words in a thesaurus or dictionary to give you ideas. Just make sure that you really understand the word before you use it.

When you describe a place, you must put your descriptions in a logical order — one that your reader can follow. For example, if you describe a building, you might want to start with its exterior (from top to bottom or vice versa) and then go to its interior (from the first area you enter to the ones that are adjacent to it).

There are many ways to order your material, but you must make sure that the order is clear and logical so that your reader can understand your descriptions.

Go back over "The Taj Mahal" and "Georgia's Architectural Puzzle" again. Are they mostly subjective, or mostly objective descriptions? What kinds of specific words and phrases can you find? Can you find any subjective phrases? What kind of spatial order was used in paragraph 4 of "The Taj Mahal"?

Proofreading

After you have finished writing and you have made sure that you have limited your topic, included lots of facts and details, used vivid language, and ordered your materials logically, it is time to proofread for errors in grammar and mechanics.

1. Read through each paragraph. Is it coherent? Have you used enough transitions (conjunctions, adverbs, reduced clauses, passive constructions) to make logical connections between the sentences?
2. Have you used tense consistently throughout the paragraph? Have you used pronouns consistently throughout the paragraph?
3. Look at each sentence separately. Is it a complete sentence (no fused sentences, fragments: each has a subject, finite verb, object)?
4. Could you combine sentences with adjective clauses or reduced clauses?
5. Look at each clause in each sentence. Is it a complete clause (conjunction, double conjunction, position, subject, finite verb)?
6. Look at each reduced clause in each sentence. Is the verb form correct (active, passive, future)?
7. Look at each verb phrase in each sentence and clause. Check subject/verb agreement, tense, aspect, voice.
8. Look at each word in the sentence. Spelling? Singular/plural? Article? Right preposition?

Once you are satisfied with the content, organization, and grammar, rewrite the composition to your instructor's specification.

Mood

Review/Preview

In the preceding chapters about verbs you have learned three factors that affect verb phrases: tense, aspect, and voice. In this chapter, the fourth and the last factor, *mood,* is discussed. Mood refers to the way the speaker or writer regards a sentence — factual or non-factual. Is the speaker describing a reality? Is the speaker or writer expressing a request or command? Or does the writer's statement express a non-factual situation like a supposition, a hypothesis, a recommendation, or a condition that is contrary to fact?

The three moods that may express these are the *indicative,* the *imperative,* and the *subjunctive* moods.

- -

I have studied very hard.	indicative
Study hard!	imperative
It is necessary that he study hard.	subjunctive
If he studied harder, he would pass the course.	subjunctive

- -

Grammar and Meaning

The Indicative

The indicative, which expresses statements perceived as a fact or as describing a reality, is the most widely used mood. In fact, most sentences that you have studied so far have been in the indicative mood. It can be used in all tenses, both aspects, and both voices.

Stephanie went to the store yesterday.	all tenses
Jennifer goes to the library every day.	
Jim will leave tomorrow.	
Charles is studying.	progressive aspect
Trent has played with the computer for an hour.	perfect aspect
The movie was filmed in Hawaii.	passive voice
They elected Beth class president.	active voice

The Imperative

The imperative mood expresses requests and commands. Although it is not much used in writing, it is quite commonly used in the spoken language (especially by a teacher to his or her students!).

The imperative, which has only one form, is formed by the base of the verb. The subject *you* is implied.

Open your books to page 256.
Read sentence three.
Write sentence six on the board.
Close the door, please!

Exercise 1   Pretend that you are a policeman. Write ten orders that you might give.

1. *Stop at the stop sign.*

2. _____ .

3. _____ .

4. _____ .

5. _____ .

6. _____ .

7. _____ .

8. _____ .

9. _____ .

10. _____ .

Note: A structure like *Let's go now* (Let us. . .) is not really an imperative but a subjunctive expressing a suggestion; however, for practical purposes we will group it with the imperative. The verb form after *let* is the infinitive form without *to*.

- -

Let's leave now.   I suggest that we leave now.
Let's go to the party.   I suggest that we go to the party.

- -

Exercise 2   You and your friend are trying to decide what to do this weekend. Make some suggestions.

1. *Let's go to the movies.*

2. _____ .

3. _____ .

4. _____ .

5. _____ .

6. _____ .

7. _____ .

8. _____ .

9. _____ .

10. _____ .

The Wish-and-Demand Subjunctive

The wish-and-demand subjunctive is mainly used in very formal or old-fashioned spoken and written English to express wishes that can be fulfilled or to express demands, suggestions, and requests. It is formed with the unchanged form of the verb and does not take an *-s* ending in the third person singular.

To Express Wishes that Can Be Fulfilled

The wish-and-demand subjunctive is used to express a wish that can be fulfilled by divine power. It occurs only in old standard expressions and in prayers. Note the word order and the verb form. The subject follows the verb, if the sentence starts with an adverb, object, or complement. The verb does not get an -s ending.

Long *live* the Queen!	I hope that the queen will live long.
Be that as it may.	If that is the way it is,...
Our Father, who art in Heaven, hallowed *be* thy name.	I hope that Your name will be hallowed.
Thy kingdom *come;*	I hope that Your kingdom will come.
Thy will *be* done on Earth as it is in Heaven.	I hope that Your will will be done.

To Express Demands, Suggestions, and Requests

The wish-and-demand subjunctive is required in noun clauses (subject, direct object, or complement clauses) to express a demand, a suggestion, or advice. This use of the subjunctive is much more common than the preceding one, but people often avoid it by using a *to*-infinitive construction instead. Note that the finite verb in the noun clause is the unchanged form of the verb. It does not take an -s ending and cannot change tense.

He demanded that he *be* given more pay.
His demand was that he *be* given more pay.
It is imperative that he *be* given more pay.
OR: He demanded to be given more pay.

I suggested that he *work* harder.
My suggestion was that he *work* harder.
It is important that he *work* harder.
OR: I told him to work harder.

My advisor requested that I *fill* out this form.
Her request was that I *fill* out this form.
It is necessary that she *fill* out this form.
OR: She asked me to fill out this form.

INCORRECT: I demand that he is given more pay.
INCORRECT: I suggest that he works harder.

The following verbs and their noun equivalents require the use of the subjunctive mood in the *that* clause:

demand, command, order, require, stipulate, insist, forbid, suggest, advise, recommend, urge, propose, move, request, desire, prefer, beg, ask

Adjectives that express a necessity or a suggestion are also used with the subjunctive mood:

important, necessary, imperative, essential, advisable, preferable, desirable

Exercise 3   Complete the following sentences in your own words.

1. My advisor suggested that I _____

   _____ .

2. Before I came here, my father's advice was that I _____

   _____ .

3. Our program director insists that we _____

   _____ .

4. It is preferable that _____ .

5. Our instructor urges that we _____

   _____ .

6. My request was that he _____ .

7. It is necessary that _____ .

8. The stipulation in our apartment lease is that the apartment ____

   _____ .

9. The general commanded that the soldiers _____

   _____ .

10. The law forbids that _____ .

11. My roommate thinks that it is important that _____

    _____ .

12. My proposal is that the instructor _____

    _____ .

The Contrary-to-Fact Subjunctive

The contrary-to-fact subjunctive, which is quite common, expresses wishes that cannot be fulfilled or wishes that are unlikely to be fulfilled. It also expresses hypotheses and statements that are known to be untrue.

- -

I wish I *had* a Rolls Royce.   a wish that is unlikely to be fulfilled
I wish I *had* green eyes.   a wish that cannot be fulfilled

If I *were* you, I would study harder. a hypothetical statement; untrue

If we *had studied* harder, we would have made *A*'s. a hypothetical statement; untrue

He acts as though he *were* sick. a hypothetical statement; uncertain

- -

In the contrary-to-fact subjunctive there are only two time distinctions: *present/future* and *past*. The past tense of the verb is used for a "now" situation, and the past perfect for a "before" situation.

Note: The verb *be* is the only verb in the English language that still has a special form for the subjunctive mood. Example: *I was in New York last week.* (Indicative) *I wish I were in New York right now.* (Subjunctive)

INDICATIVE		SUBJUNCTIVE	
I	was	I	were
you	were	you	were
he	was	he	were
we	were	we	were
you	were	you	were
they	were	they	were

- -

VERB TENSE		TIME
past	I wish I *had* a lot of money.	present/future
past	If he *were* here, he would help me.	present
past	I wish we *didn't* have a test tomorrow.	future
past perfect	I wish he *had been* here to help me.	past
past perfect	If he *had been* here yesterday, he would have helped me.	past
past perfect	I wish I *had started* college last year.	past

- -

Exercise 4 Identify the mood in the following sentences. (1) Indicative; (2) Imperative; (3) Subjunctive a. Wish-and-Demand b. Contrary-to-Fact

1. _____ Be quiet!

2. _____ You are not quiet.

3. _____ The teacher demands that we be quiet.

4. _____ He wished we were quiet.

5. _____ If we had been more quiet, we would have understood the problem.

6. _____ Quiet be the students!

To Refer to Present Time

In hypothetical statements, which are known not to be factual, or in wishes that are unlikely to be fulfilled or that cannot be fulfilled, the past tense is used for a present or future situation. In other words, the past tense refers to something that is not happening now or will not happen in the near future.

Note: In a hypothetical statement, the *if* clause is in the past (or past perfect) tense, and the main clause has a modal auxiliary like *would, could* or *might*. In addition, the noun clause after *wish* is in the past (or past perfect) tense. The verb *wish* itself may be used either in the present or past tense.

- -

If I *had* a car, I *could travel* around the states.
If she *were* here, she *would help* us.
If we *laughed* at him, he *would get* mad at us.

I wish that I *had* a large house.
I wished that we *didn't have* so much work.

- -

Exercise 5 Change each of the verbs in parentheses to the appropriate form to express a present, contrary-to-fact situation.

1. If he (have) money, he (buy) a car.

2. If he (buy) a car, he (travel) around a lot.

3. If he (travel) around a lot, he (visit) many interesting places.

4. If he (visit) many interesting places, he (tell) us about them.

5. If he (tell) us about them, he (not be) so boring!

Exercise 6 Change each of the verbs in parentheses to the appropriate form to express a present, contrary-to-fact situation.

1. A man whose normal weight is 150 pounds (weigh) 50 pounds if all the water in his system (be) dried up.

2. If you (drop) a pint of oil in a lake or sea, it (cover) the surface of an acre of water.

3. If the sun (stop) shining suddenly, it (take) eight minutes for people on earth to become aware of that fact.

4. If a child (eat) as much, comparatively, as a growing bird, he (eat) three lambs and one calf in a single day.

5. If one (spend) at the rate of one dollar per minute, it (require) approximately two thousand years to spend a billion dollars.

Exercise 7   Pretend that you have a business and that you would like to have a Commodore Computer. Start your paragraph with the following sentence and rewrite the ad for Commodore computers. Make sure that you add *would* or *could* when appropriate.

I wish I had a Commodore Computer. If I had one, I would be able to get organized. If I had the Manager, I . . . .

To Refer to Past Time

For a past situation in contrary-to-fact statements, the past perfect tense is used in the *if* or *that* clause, and *would/could/might have* + past participle in the main clause.

- -

If he *had studied* harder last semester, he *could have made* an A in the course.
If we *had eaten* breakfast faster, we *would not have been* late for class.
If we *had been* there on time, we *might have been* able to save him.

I wish he *had studied* harder last semester.
We wish we *had eaten* breakfast earlier.
We wish we *had been* there on time.

- -

Exercise 8   Change each verb in parentheses to the appropriate form. Base your sentences on the following fact: Last year John did not study hard.

1. If John (study) harder last year, he (pass) the course.
2. If he (pass) the course, he (not, need) to take it over again.
3. If he (not, need) to take it over again, he (not, be) so unhappy all semester long.
4. If he (not, be) so unhappy all semester long, he (not, make) the instructor so miserable.
5. I am sure that the instructor wishes that John (be) more diligent last year.

Exercise 9   Complete the following sentences in your own words.

1. If I had studied less last semester, _____

_____ .

2. If I had gone to the movies last night, _____

_____ .

3. If the wind had blown any harder, _____

_____ .

4. If I had been president of my country last year, _____

_____ .

5. If _____ , I would have seen a kangaroo.

6. If _____ , I would have been furious.

7. If _____ , I would have been very happy.

8. If _____ , I would have gone to the party.

9. I wish that _____ last year.

10. I wish that _____ a few minutes ago.

Exercise 10

Pretend that you went on vacation last summer and that you took many pictures. However, the pictures were very bad. Now you wish that you had had a Minolta X–700 so that you could have taken good pictures. Read the ad about the Minolta. Write a paragraph starting with the following sentences:

I wish I had bought a Minolta before I went on vacation last year. If I had had a Minolta, I would have been able to take some very good pictures. The camera could have taken me from full program automation to total manual control with the turn of a dial.

Note: Often you will find sentences that have mixed tenses if, for example, something happened in the past that affects the present.

PAST EVENT	PRESENT SITUATION
If I *had worn* a raincoat yesterday,	I *would* not *have* a cold today.
If you *had saved* your money,	you *could buy* a car now.

Are you ready for high-performance photography?

The Minolta Program System X-700 will put you into high-performance photography!

Voted "Camera of the Year" on two continents, it can take you from full program automation to total manual control with the turn of a dial.

In the program mode, all you do is focus and shoot. Its computer balances the light for startling results. It shoots "faster" than other program cameras, so you can stop the action even in fading light.

In program Autoflash mode, you get flash performance simply unavailable in any other camera system. You literally set nothing. Minolta's advanced off-the-film-plane system accurately measures the light and controls the flash for perfect exposures.

In aperture-priority "A" mode, you select the lens opening, the computer selects the shutter speed.

And in metered-manual mode, it's total creative freedom. You tune the light to your own inner vision.

You can also expand the performance of the X-700: fire off 3.5 frames a second with the optional Minolta Motor Drive. Add the micro-computer Multi-Function Back to chronicle your life and times. And choose from more than 50 Minolta lenses and other accessories.

You get all this plus the protection of Minolta's 2-year camera/5-year lens limited U.S.A. warranty.

See the X-700 at your high-performance Minolta dealer. Take your photography into the fast lane.

MINOLTA

X-700

MPS

© 1983 Minolta Corporation

Minolta X-700 shown with optional Motor Drive 1 and 50mm 1.4 Minolta MD lens.

X700
ONLY FROM THE MIND OF MINOLTA

If-Clause Reductions

Some types of *if*-clauses may be reduced. Although these structures are not very common in writing, they are common in the spoken language; moreover, they occur frequently on standardized tests like the Test of English as a Foreign Language (TOEFL) and the Michigan Test.

1. *If*-clauses that express a real possibility in the present or future (not in the subjunctive mood) may be reduced to an inverted *should* clause.
2. *If*-clauses and wishes that express a past contrary-to-fact situation (in the subjunctive mood — with the verb in the past perfect tense) may be reduced to an inverted *had* clause.

- -

Should he go to the store, ask him to bring some rice.   present
(If he goes to the store, . . .)   real possibility

Had he studied, he would have passed the course.   past
(If he had studied, . . .)   contrary-to-fact

Had he only been here on time!   past
(I wish he had been here on time.)   contrary-to-fact

- -

Exercise 11   Fill in each blank with an appropriate verb in the right form.

1. If John _____ in the library, ask him to see his advisor.

2. _____ John be in the library, please _____ him to see his advisor.

3. If he had been in the library, I _____ _____ asked him to see his advisor.

4. _____ he been in the library, I would _____ _____ him to see his advisor.

5. Should he _____ in the library, tell him to call me.

6. _____ he _____ somewhere else, I _____ him later.

7. If he _____ gone somewhere else, I will see him later.

8. Should he _____ somewhere else, I _____ him later.

The Auxiliaries of Mood

There are nine true auxiliaries of mood, also called *modals: can, could, may, might, shall, should, will, would,* and *must.* There are also some verbs with similar meanings and functions to these auxiliaries, which we call *semi-modals: to be able to, to be allowed to, to be permitted to, to have to, ought to, used to,* and *had better.*

The modals are a special group in the English language because they are very different from other verbs.

First of all, they have only one form: the finite form. The infinitive, past participle, and present participle forms have disappeared from the language. (This is not really surprising because they can occur only at the beginning of the verb phrase; they are therefore used only in the finite form.)

Second, they are different because they never take an *-s* ending in the third person singular.

The last and most important difference is that their past tense forms usually have present or future meanings. Example: *I might go home next year.*

Modals are followed by infinitives without *to;* most semi-modals are followed by *to*-infinitives.

You are probably familiar with most of the meanings and uses of the modals; we will therefore concentrate on the meanings and uses that are problematic to the non-native writer:

1. Expressing ability, permission, and necessity in past situations, and
2. The meanings of modals + *have.*

Note: Only the uses of the modals in direct speech are discussed in this chapter. For verb tenses used in noun clauses after a past tense main verb, see Chapter 4.

Permission

TIME		MEANING
present/future	I *may borrow* my father's car now/tomorrow.	permission
	I *can borrow* my father's car today/tomorrow.	permission (informal)
	I *am allowed to borrow* my father's car today.	
	I *am permitted to drive* his car.	
	John, *could* I please *borrow* your car?	permission (polite request)

TENSE		
past	I *was allowed to drive* my father's car yesterday.	
past perfect	Before the accident, I *had been allowed to drive* his car.	
present perfect	I *have been allowed to drive* his car for two years.	
INCORRECT:	I might borrow his car yesterday.	
INCORRECT:	I could borrow his car yesterday.	

Permission may be expressed by *may, can, could, to be permitted to,* and *to be allowed to.*

Both *may* and *can* express permission in the present and future, but *can* is a little less formal. *Could* expresses permission in polite requests.

Note: The modals may be used only for present and future situations; in other words, there is no modal that can express permission for a past situation. The semi-modals must be used to express permission in other tenses like the past, the present perfect, and the past perfect.

Exercise 12   Pretend that you are in charge of a dormitory. List eight general rules for the dormitory residents with *may* or *can*.

1. Residents may not have refrigerators in their rooms.

2. _____ .

3. _____ .

4. _____ .

5. _____ .

6. _____ .

7. _____ .

8. _____ .

Exercise 13   Finish the following sentences to express what you were or were not permitted to do in the past.

EXAMPLE:

When I was a young child, I was not allowed to walk in the street.

1. When I was in elementary school, _____

_____ .

2. When I was in high school, _____ .

3. When I was eighteen, _____ .

4. Before I came to the States, _____ .

Ability and Opportunity

TIME		MEANING
present	I *can talk*.	ability
present	I *am able to speak* English.	ability
present	Computers *can calculate* fast.	ability
present/future	I *can give* a speech now.	opportunity
INCORRECT:	I *can speak* English tomorrow.	ability

past	I *could* not *walk* when I was a baby...	ability
past	I *was* not *able to speak* English five years ago.	ability
past	The first computer *could calculate* fast.	ability
present perfect	I *have been able to speak* English for two years.	ability
past perfect	I *had been able to speak* English before I came.	ability
past	I *was able to give* a speech yesterday.	opportunity
INCORRECT:	I could give a speech yesterday.	opportunity

- -

The meaning of *ability* is closely related to, but not exactly the same as, the meaning of *opportunity*. The former expresses a natural, innate ability, whereas the latter expresses favorable circumstances or a chance.

The modals *can/could* can express both, but when they express ability, they can be used for present and past situations only. When they express opportunity they may also refer to future situations. On the other hand, *could* cannot express past opportunity.

Note: The use of *could* to express past ability is the only past tense modal used for a past situation. No other modal can express past tense by itself (except in indirect speech). As you will see in the following sections, all other modals are combined with *have* to express a past situation.

Exercise 14

With each of the following words, write a sentence on a separate piece of paper to explain what animals can or cannot do.

1. *Fish can swim.*
2. frogs
3. elephants
4. cows
5. whales
6. snakes
7. dolphins
8. camels

Exercise 15

On a separate piece of paper, give your predictions of the future. What do you think the following things will be able to do twenty years from now?

1. *I believe computers can/will be able to translate languages.*
2. rockets
3. telephones
4. televisions
5. airplanes
6. refrigerators
7. robots
8. microwave ovens

Exercise 16   Pretend you are on vacation at The Grand, the hotel described in the ad. Write a letter (of at least 100 words) to a friend about the wonderful time you are having. Tell him or her about all the things you *can* do at The Grand.

Necessity

TIME		MEANING
present/future	I *must study* now/tomorrow.	necessary (strong)
	I *have to study* now/tomorrow.	
	I *have got* to study.	(informal)
	I *need to study* now/tomorrow.	necessary (weak)

TENSE		
past	I *had to study* yesterday.	
	I *needed to study* yesterday.	
present perfect	I *have had to study* for two hours.	
INCORRECT:	I must study yesterday.	
	He *doesn't have to come* to class.	not necessary
	He *doesn't need to come* to class.	not necessary
BUT:	He *mustn't come* to class.	not advisable
BUT:	He *shouldn't come* to class.	not advisable

Necessity, which expresses the meaning that something is necessary and that there is no choice, may be expressed by *must, to have to, to have got to,* and *to need to.*

Note: The use of *must* to express necessity is very limited. It can be used only in present and future situations that are positive. In other words, *must* cannot be used with a past meaning, and it does not express necessity when it is negative.

Exercise 17   On a separate piece of paper, explain what a person *must* do to stay alive or healthy. Provide additional ideas in numbers 7 and 8.

1. (water) *A person must drink water.*
2. oxygen
3. vitamins
4. protein
5. exercise
6. sleep
7. _____
8. _____

This year, you've earned The Grand.

Marriott's Grand hotel

POINT CLEAR·ALABAMA

For more information and a free, full color brochure call **800-228-9290** toll-free, 205-928-9201 direct, or your travel agent.

For nearly 140 years, families have come to relax and enjoy the special quality of life that's uniquely The Grand.

Here you'll find people who cherish the opportunity to make your vacation a memorable experience. While the children are off having the time of their lives in our Junior Hostess program, you can tee off at your leisure for a round of golf on 27 championship holes. Or perfect your backhand on uncrowded tennis courts. Board our lavishly out-fitted 53' Hatteras and match wits with trophy sized game fish. Cool off in one of the world's largest resort swimming pools.

There's dancing every night, and on Wednesdays, a 14-piece orchestra under the stars at Julep Point.

Vacation at The Grand. It'll make the rest of the year seem worthwhile.

A gentle era whose time has come. Again.

Exercise 18 On a separate piece of paper, explain what is not necessary for you to do when you live at home. Provide additional ideas in numbers 7 and 8.

1. (laundry) *I don't have to do my own laundry.*
2. cook
3. make my bed
4. wash the dishes
5. vacuum clean
6. iron my own shirts
7. _____
8. _____

You have just seen that *may* and *could* express permission, that *can* and *could* express ability and opportunity, and that *must* expresses necessity in the present. You have also seen that in a past situation semi-modals are usually needed to express permission, ability, opportunity, or necessity.

However, most of the modals also occur with the helping verb *have* (for example, *may have, could have, must have*), which give the whole phrase a past meaning. What do they mean? Actually, when a modal is followed by *have* it can have only one of two meanings: either a past possibility or a past contrary-to-fact situation.

- -

He *may have gone* to the store.   UNCERTAINTY ABOUT
He *might have gone* to the movies.   SOMETHING IN THE
He *could have gone* to see his friend.   PAST
He *must have gone* to see Harry.

I *would have helped* you, if you had asked me.   CONTRARY-TO-
I *could have helped* you, but you didn't call me.   FACT SITUATION
You *should have called* me.   IN THE PAST

- -

Possibility and Certainty

- -

Situation: Tom is a good friend of yours and you know his habits fairly well. He usually goes to the library at night. Sometimes he goes to see his friends. Once in a while he goes to a movie. He almost never goes shopping at night. One night, when you go to his room, he is not there. You try to guess where he might be.

He *might have gone* shopping.   a slight chance
He *may have gone* to the movie.   a small chance
He *could have gone* to see his friends.   a good chance
He *must have gone* to the library.   almost a certainty

Situation: Tom has never been late to class. He always gets up early and wakes up easily. He almost never forgets his books. Sometimes he has trouble finding a parking place for his car. Yesterday he had some car trouble. Today, Tom is late for class. You try to guess why he is late.

He *might have overslept.*	a slight chance
He *may have forgotten* some of his books, so he had to go back to his room.	a small chance
He *could have had* trouble finding a parking space.	a good chance
He *must have had* some more car trouble.	almost a certainty

Might have ... may have .., could have .., and *must have ...* all express uncertainty about something in the past, but they express different degrees of uncertainty, with *might have ...* being the least certain and *must have* on the other end of the scale expressing almost complete certainty.

Exercise 19   Make up sentences for the following situations.

1. Situation: Your instructor is always on time for his classes. Today he came in late. Try to guess why your instructor is late.

   He might have _____ .

   He may have _____ .

   He could have _____ .

   He must have _____ .

2. Situation: Your parents always write you a letter every two weeks. You have not received a letter in three weeks. You know that they were going on a short vacation. Try to guess why you have not received a letter yet.

   The letter might have _____ .

   The letter may have _____ .

   My parents could have _____ .

   My parents must have _____ .

3. Situation: An airplane has disappeared. No one knows where it is. Its course took it over an ocean, across the North Pole, and over some mountains; moreover, several passengers on the plane were terrorists.

   The plane might have _____ .

   The plane may have _____ .

   The plane could have _____ .

   The plane must have _____ .

The same modals, *might, may,* and *could,* without *have,* may express possibility in the present or future with the same differences in degree of certainty. *Must* expresses strong possibility in the present, but since nothing can be certain about the future, *must* is not used to express certainty in the future. (In this case, *should* is used to express expectation.)

- -

Situation: Mary is always a cheerful girl. Today she is very quiet. We know that she has received a telephone call from her parents. We also know that she went to bed late last night because she had a lot of work to do. Moreover, she had just received a test paper back with an *F.* Why is she so quiet today?

She *might* be thinking about her parents.	a slight chance
She *may* be fed up with all her work.	a small chance
She *could* be very tired.	a good chance
She *must* be upset about her low grade.	almost a certainty

She *might, may, could* or *should* feel better tomorrow.

- -

Exercise 20   Make up sentences for the following situations.

1. Situation: Your car usually works well. Today it won't start.

    _____ might _____ .

    _____ may _____ .

    _____ could _____ .

    _____ must _____ .

2. Situation: Your roommate is always in a good mood, but today he is in a very bad mood.

    _____ might _____ .

    _____ may _____ .

    _____ could _____ .

    _____ must _____ .

3. Situation: Registration at your school is always well-organized. Today there is total confusion. Something went wrong.

    _____ might _____ .

    _____ may _____ .

    _____ could _____ .

    _____ must _____ .

Exercise 21 The following article states that lead poisoning *may have contributed* to the fall of the Roman Empire. There are many things about the past that we can prove, but some things we cannot know with certainty. Change the verbs in parentheses into appropriate verb phrases. There are phrases in the present and past tense. Those that are italicized need modals or modals + *have*. Some need the passive voice.

The Wine and Fall

(1) Two-thirds of the emperors of ancient Rome (*be*) mentally unhinged by lead in their wine and food, and that (*contribute*) to the fall of the Roman Empire. Dr. Jerome O. Nriagu of the National Water Research Institute in Burlington, Ontario, (calculate) that Roman aristocrats (*consume*) six times as much lead as modern standards (allow). We now know that lead (*contribute*) to personality changes and mental retardation.

(2) Nriagu (count) twenty rulers between A.D. 30 and 220 who either (be) gluttonous consumers of lead-tainted food or (have) erratic behavior that (*cause*) by lead poisoning.

(3) Nriagu (think) that wine alone (*account for*) half the lead in the Roman diet. Romans often (flavor) their wine with a grape syrup that (simmer) in lead pots or lead-lined copper kettles. According to Nriagu, one teaspoon of such syrup (be) more than enough to cause chronic lead poisoning. The syrup (be) an ingredient of one-fifth of the recipes in a cookbook that (be) still in existence today.

Contrary-to-Fact Situations

- -

	MEANING
If you *had asked* me, I *would have helped* you.	I was willing to help you, but you did not ask me, so I didn't help you.
If you *had asked* me, I *could have helped*.	I was able to help you, but you did not ask me, so I didn't help you.
You *should have asked* me to help you.	It was advisable to ask me for help; but you didn't.
I *would have studied* more if I had not been too tired.	I did not study more because I was so tired.

I *could have received* a higher grade if I had studied more.

I *should not have spent* so much money!

The train *should have arrived* five minutes ago.

John *should have been* here already.

I was not able to receive a higher grade because I didn't study more.

It was not advisable to spend so much money, but I did it anyway.

The train was expected to arrive five minutes ago, but it did not.

I had expected him to arrive before now, but he is not here yet.

- -

Would have . . . , could have . . . , and *should have . . .* all express past contrary-to-fact situations, but they differ in meaning. *Would have . . .* just expresses the meaning that something did not happen in the past. *Could have* expresses the meaning that a possibility or ability in the past was not fulfilled, and *should have* expresses the meaning that something that was advisable or expected in the past did not happen.

Exercise 22   Complete the following sentences in your own words.

1. If you had invited me to your party, I _____

_____ .

2. If you had locked the door, the burglars _____

_____ .

3. If we had known the time of your arrival, we _____

_____ .

4. You _____ called us!

5. If he had not broken his arm, he _____

_____ .

6. He _____ been more careful!

7. If Mary had paid more attention to the teacher, she _____

_____ .

8. She _____ paid more attention!

9. Instead of having painted your house hot pink, you _____

_____ .

10. Instead of having spent all his money on a sports car, he _____

_____ .

11. John drove very fast and had an accident. He _____

_____ .

12. I don't know where John is. He should _____

     _____ .

13. The train is late as usual. It should _____

     _____ .

14. I waited all day long for a call from my parents. They _____

     _____ .

As you saw earlier in this chapter, *would* and *could* may also express a present contrary-to-fact situation. However, sometimes they simply show that something will happen under certain conditions. They may also simply express a polite request.

- -

If I *were* not so busy, I *would* help you.	contrary-to-fact
If I *were* not so busy, I *could* help you.	contrary-to-fact
If you asked me, I *would* help you.	willing under a certain condition
If you asked me, I *could* help you.	able under a certain condition
Would you please help me?	polite request
Could you come over at five?	polite request

- -

Expectation

- -

The train *should* arrive in 10 minutes.	expectation
John *should* be here soon.	expectation
The modal test *should* be difficult.	expectation
I *will* call you tomorrow.	promise
People *will* always fight.	inclination
We *will* be happy to help you.	willingness
Computers *will* be able to think one day.	prediction

- -

Both *should* and *will* are used to show that the speaker expects something to happen in the future. *Should* indicates that the speaker is not entirely sure. *Will,* on the other hand, expresses a lesser degree of doubt or a greater degree of determination.

Exercise 23   Pretend that an airplane has just taken off. Write a paragraph of about seventy-five words in which you predict what the pilot will do within the next thirty minutes.

Advisability and Moral Obligation

I really *should* help you.
I really *ought to* help you.
I *had better* help you.

You *shouldn't* be late for class.   friendly admonition
You *had better* not be late for class.
You *ought* not be late for class.   formal admonition
You *mustn't* be late for class.   strong admonition
You *will* be on time!   demand

Should, ought to, and *had better* may indicate that something is advisable or morally just. And, as you saw earlier, *mustn't* means almost the same as *shouldn't,* but it is slightly stronger in content. *Will* may express a demand on the part of the speaker.

Exercise 24   Your best friends are getting married. You have a lot of advice for them because you want them to have a happy marriage. What are some things that they should or should not do?

    1. *He should share the housework.*

    2. They had better _____ .

    3. She ought to _____ .

    4. He shouldn't _____ .

    5. They mustn't _____ .

    6. She had better not _____ .

    7. They should _____ .

    8. He mustn't _____ .

Past Habit

When I was in high school, I *would* ride my bike to school occasionally.
I *would* have a lot of homework every night.
I *studied* on the weekends.
I *used to* eat lunch at school.

The modal *would,* a simple past tense, and the semi-modal *used to* may express something that was a habit in the past, but *used to* places greater emphasis on the regular custom or habit. Note that a time word such as *occasionally* or *every night* is not needed in the *used to* sentence.

Challenge and Need

- -

He dared to go.	Dare you go?
He needed to help me.	You needn't help me.

- -

Dare means *have the courage to* and *need* expresses a need (not a necessity). They may be followed by either a plain infinitive or a *to*-infinitive. (These auxiliaries used to be modal auxiliaries like *will* or *could,* but, especially in American English, they have become more like semi-modals, such as *have to* and *to be able to.*)

- -

Modal Chart

	PAST	PRESENT	FUTURE
PERMISSION		can	can
		may	may
	to be permitted to	to be permitted to	to be permitted to
	to be allowed to	to be allowed to	to be allowed to
ABILITY natural/learned	could	can	
	to be able to	to be able to	
opportunity		can	can
	to be able to	to be able to	to be able to
NECESSITY		must	must
	to have to	to have to	to have to
	to need to	to need to	to need to
(negative)	didn't have to	don't have to	will not have to
UNCERTAINTY	might have	might	might
	may have	may	may
	could have	could	could
(certainty)	must have	must	(should)
CONTRARY-TO-FACT	would have	would	
(ability/opportunity)	could have	could	
(advisability/expectation)	should have	should	

(Chart continues)

	PAST	PRESENT	FUTURE
EXPECTATION		should	should will
ADVISABILITY/ MORAL OBLIGATION		should ought to had better (mustn't)	should ought to had better (mustn't)
CHALLENGE NEED	to dare to to need to	dare (to) need (to)	dare (to) need (to)
HABIT	would used to (go)	to be used to (going)	

- -

Note: For the following summary exercises refer to the modal chart above and on the preceding page.

Exercise 25 Fill in the blanks with an appropriate modal: *can, could, will, would, shall, should, may, might,* and *must.* You should use each one once.

1. I _____ not study very well last night because the dormitory was very noisy.

2. He asked me if I _____ be able to help him.

3. In order to stay healthy, you _____ exercise and eat healthy foods.

4. _____ we go now?

5. I don't know what I am going to do after finals. I _____ just sleep for a couple of days.

6. He is not in his room. He _____ be at the library.

7. You look very tired. You _____ rest a little bit.

8. I _____ speak very well.

9. By four o'clock this afternoon, I _____ have finished my English homework.

Exercise 26 Match the following clauses. Use the blanks on page 281.

1. He must have studied very hard because
2. He didn't have to come to class because

A. the teacher gave him permission to miss class.
B. he wasn't in class.

3. He was able to study very hard yesterday, so

C. he got an A on the test.

4. He must have gone to the doctor yesterday because

D. he went to see a movie.

5. He had to go to the doctor yesterday; therefore

E. he did very well on his test.

6. He mustn't be absent today because

F. he made only a C– on the test.

7. He should have studied more last night because

G. he couldn't come to class.

8. He could have studied more, but

H. we might have a pop quiz.

1. _____   3. _____   5. _____   7. _____

2. _____   4. _____   6. _____   8. _____

Exercise 27   Fill in each blank with an appropriate modal or semi-modal.

1. I _____ go to the movies last night.
   (permission)

2. Because I _____ study a lot, I received a good grade.
   (opportunity)

3. I don't know where John is. He _____ gone to the library.
   (possibility)

4. This is a very important meeting. You _____n't be late.
   (advisability)

5. He wanted to know whether he _____ hand in his paper
   (necessity)
   yesterday.

6. What is keeping him? He _____ here an
   (contrary-to-fact expectation)
   hour ago.

7. They have never answered my letter. They _____ not _____
   (strong possibility)
   received it.

8. He is smoking a cigarette. He _____ not know that Mary is
   (possibility)
   allergic to smoke.

Exercise 28   Fill in the blanks with an appropriate verb phrase.

1. We _____ to the airport by nine; otherwise, we
   will miss our plane.

2. I _____ my library book yesterday. Now I _____ a late fee.

3. No one _____ without food.

4. My friend asked if he _____ my car to do some shopping.

5. Who broke the window? John, Peter, and Paul were playing baseball. Anyone of them _____ it.

6. He _____ thankful instead of mad.

7. This cake is delicious. You _____ try it.

8. He _____ less if he wants to lose weight.

9. I _____ you at once; I have important news for you.

10. All the students got good grades. They _____ hard.

Solving Problems

Faulty Use of Tense in Contrary-to-Fact Statements

In a contrary-to-fact statement, a past tense and *would* phrase refer to a present situation; a past perfect tense and *would have* phrase to a past situation. *Be* has a separate subjunctive form.

INCORRECT: He acts as if he is the president.
CORRECT: He acts as if he were the president.

INCORRECT: If I was you, I would study hard.
CORRECT: If I were you, I would study hard.

INCORRECT: If you had called me I would come to help you.
CORRECT: If you had called me, I would have come to help you.

Faulty Use of Verb Tense in Real Conditions, or Inconsistent Use of Mood

If the statement expresses not a contrary-to-fact condition but a real condition or possibility, the indicative mood is used. The use of the indicative or subjunctive should be consistent. The contrary-to-fact subjunctive is used after *wish,* the indicative after *hope.*

INCORRECT: I will be finished soon if you helped me.
CORRECT: I will be finished soon if you help me.
CORRECT: I would be finished soon if you helped me.

INCORRECT: I would have finished my work if you helped me.
CORRECT: I would have finished my work if you had helped me.

INCORRECT: I wish I studied harder in high school.
CORRECT: I wish I had studied harder in high school.

INCORRECT: I wish he is here today.
CORRECT: I hope that he is here today.

Faulty Use of *Will* or *Would* in *If*-Clauses

The main clause contains a *will, would,* or *would have* phrase. The *if*-clause has a present, past, or past perfect tense. In addition, a noun clause after *wish* does not have *would* or *would have.* The *if*-clause can contain *will* only if it expresses a willingness on the part of the subject.

INCORRECT: I would help you if you would ask me.
CORRECT: I would help you if you asked me.

INCORRECT: I wish he would have been here yesterday.
CORRECT: I wish he had been here yesterday.
CORRECT: I will wash the dishes if you will dry them.
CORRECT: I will wash the dishes if you dry them.

No Wish-and-Demand Subjunctive in *That*-Clauses after Certain Verbs, Adjectives, and Nouns

In *that*-clauses after verbs like *demand, suggest,* and *desire,* after nouns like *demand, suggestion* and *desire,* and after adjectives that express a necessity, such as *necessary, important,* and *imperative,* the wish-and-demand subjunctive is required.

INCORRECT: He demanded that the class members handed in their work on time.
CORRECT: He demanded that the class members hand in their work on time.

INCORRECT: His demand that the work was handed in on time was reasonable.
CORRECT: His demand that the work be handed in on time was reasonable.

INCORRECT: It is imperative that he takes his medicine.
CORRECT: It is imperative that he take his medicine.

Faulty Use of Modals to Express Past Permission, Opportunity, or Necessity

The modals *may, can,* and *must* can express permission, opportunity, or necessity only in present situations. For past situations the semi-modals must be used.

INCORRECT: I may have gone to a movie yesterday.
(not permission)
CORRECT: I was allowed to go to a movie yesterday.

INCORRECT: I had some extra time yesterday, so I could help him.
CORRECT: I had some extra time yesterday, so I was able to help him.
CORRECT: I couldn't help you with your math because I didn't understand the problems.
(could — past ability)

INCORRECT: I must do my work yesterday.
INCORRECT: I must have done my work yesterday.
(not necessity)
CORRECT: I had to do my work yesterday.

Faulty Use of Modal + *Have*

When a modal is followed by *have* it can express only uncertainty about a past event or a past contrary-to-fact condition, not past permission, ability, or necessity.

The following diagram summarizes the trouble spots.

MODAL/SEMI MODAL	MEANING
He *was allowed to* leave.	He had permission to leave.
He *may have left* already.	It is possible that he has left already.
He *was able to leave* early.	He had the opportunity to leave early.
He *could leave* early.	My suggestion is that he leave early.
He *could have left* early.	It is possible that he left early.
He *could have left* earlier.	He had the opportunity to leave earlier, but he didn't.
He *had to go* to work early.	It was necessary for him to go to work early.
He *must have gone* to work early.	It is almost certain that he has gone to work early.
He *doesn't have to* go to work today.	It is not necessary for him to go to work today.
He *mustn't* be late.	He shouldn't be late.
Would you please *help* me?	Help me, please!
If I *were* you, I *would go.*	I am not you, but I suggest your going.

He *would leave* early.   He usually left early.
He *would have left* already if   Although he wanted to, he didn't leave
  he *had* not *had* a phone call.   early because he had a phone call.

- -

Exercise 29   The following passage contains errors mentioned in the section above. Identify the errors and rewrite the passage correctly.

If we thought that the slight education of a pioneer in the colonial days to be enough for us today, we would have been wrong. In those days, most people lived on farms or in small towns and villages. Nearly all work must be done the hard way — by hand. The men had to build their own homes and hunt their own food. Children might not play a lot. Their parents demanded that they worked long hours — from dawn until sunset — to help make a living. Travel was also slow, and it took months of traveling if a person had gone from New England to Pennsylvania or Virginia. People did not have to be well-educated. If a person would be able to read and write or do some arithmetic, he would have been considered well-educated.

Today this has all changed. Most people live in big cities or other urban settlements. Many people mustn't work by hand because heavy work can now be performed with great ease by means of electrical and mechanical machines. If a person wants to go from San Francisco to New York City, he would need only a few hours to fly. If he wanted to send a message from one of these cities to the other, it takes even less time to call by phone, to send a telegram, or to broadcast a radio message. We no longer lead the simple but laborious life of the pioneer; it is therefore imperative that a person today is educated.

Assignment for Writing

Group Discussion

"The Perilous Adventures of Wiz Walker" is a comic strip taken from an American business magazine. It advises American business people about

The PERILOUS ADVENTURES of
WIZ WALKER
YOUNG EXECUTIVE

STORY BY JAMES MARKLAND
ILLUSTRATED BY BOB LAUGHLIN

● The Business Lunch

It may be polite to ask your guest to select the restaurant, but it is better to choose one you know after calling his secretary to ask about his likes and dislikes. Be careful when selecting ethnic restaurants.

Cultivate a close relationship with the better restaurants in your area that cater to businesspeople. This will ensure preferential seating, impress your guest, and be conducive to a productive luncheon.

Always make reservations, an obvious point, but worth stressing. Even a restaurant you know can't provide appropriate seating if it is not prepared for your visit. And the right seating is important.

Avoid unpleasant surprises. Don't select a restaurant you have never been to or that has not been recommended. The food could be unsatisfactory, spoiling an otherwise good business luncheon.

Know what you are ordering. Certain dishes are difficult to eat and likely to create an embarrassing mess. Don't order a dish implicitly critical of your guest's choice. If he orders a steak, don't order a diet salad.

Recognize the limitation of the luncheon environment. Avoid bringing too many papers which can't be handled comfortably. Don't discuss important business when you know the waiter will interrupt.

The business lunch is no place to demonstrate your drinking prowess. Your executive image will not be enhanced by ordering a fancy mixed drink. Rule of thumb: it is better not to have more than one drink.

If it's your check—never let a guest pay. You can arrange to have the check presented to you or billed to you at your office. By making prior arrangements you can avoid a hassle over who pays the bill.

Have the proper credit cards to pay the bill. (Carry at least two credit cards—just in case.) A 15% to 20% gratuity is appropriate. Always be polite to the staff. It's important to maintain cordial relations.

Last, but not least, don't ask for a doggie bag. If service was poor, don't make a scene. Speak quietly to the maitre'd after the meal. Avoid making the same blunders as Wiz Walker, young executive.

what to do and what not to do when they take guests out for lunch. First, take a look at each picture separately and answer the questions that go with that picture. Wiz Walker is the young executive who takes his guest out to eat. Mr. Cosgrove is his guest.

1. What could Wiz Walker have done instead of asking Mr. Cosgrove what kind of food he likes? Why should he have done that?
2. Why should a businessman be familiar with the better restaurants in the area?
3. Why should Wiz Walker have made reservations?
4. Mr. Cosgrove must have been annoyed when he was watching the cook prepare the food. Why?
5. Why would it be implicitly critical of a guest's choice to order a diet salad when the guest orders a steak?
6. What could Wiz Walker have done instead of bringing all these papers to the restaurant?
7. How must Wiz Walker have felt when his nose landed in the ice cream? How do you think Mr. Cosgrove felt?
8. What would you have done if you had been Wiz Walker when it was time to pay the bill?
9. What mustn't a host do when he is ready to pay?
10. What was the blunder in the last picture?

Writing

You are a journalist, and you have been asked to write an article for a business magazine in America. In this article you will advise your American readers what to do or not to do when a business relation in your own country takes them out to eat. You may use information from the comic strip that you have just read, but you must also incorporate features that are especially particular to your own culture.

Suggestions for Writing

Go over each picture again and discuss the customs in your country. What would a business man or woman in your culture have done in each situation? What would be acceptable in your culture? What would be considered very impolite? Jot your answers down.

1. How do people in your country greet each other? Do they shake hands? Do they bow? Can a woman shake a man's hand?
2. Do business associates often take each other out for lunch? Or is the evening meal preferred?
3. To what kind of restaurant would a business person in your country take a foreign guest? Who orders the food? What kind of food would be served? What kind of drink would be served? Are the food and drinks very unusual for Americans? How should the food be eaten — with fork and knife, with chopsticks, or by hand?

4. Do business people actually discuss business during the meal, or would that be considered impolite?
5. Who pays for the meal? Should the guest offer to help pay? What should he say or do to express his appreciation to his host?

Organization

Organize your paragraphs in logical units. Your introduction should tell your reader what the purpose of the article is. In the first developmental paragraph you may discuss what your reader should do before he or she actually gets to the restaurant. The next paragraph could deal with ordering the meal. Then a paragraph could deal with discussing business during the meal, and the last developmental paragraph with paying for the bill. In your conclusion you might want to summarize your main points of advice.

Proofreading

After you have finished writing your first drafts and are satisfied with the contents and organization, check the grammar.

1. Is each sentence a sentence? Are there any fragments? Fused sentences? Double conjunctions? Subject? Verb phrase? Object? Adverbials?
2. Is each clause a clause? Conjunction? Subject? Finite Verb?
3. Have you been consistent in your use of tense?
4. Have you been consistent in your use of pronouns?
5. Have you used appropriate modals? Check the chart with each modal you have used.
6. Could you have combined any more sentences? Could you have reduced any clauses?
7. Have you used enough transitions?
8. Check on spelling, prepositions, and articles.

Noun Clauses and Reduced Noun Clauses

Review/Preview

Earlier in this text, you studied adverbial clauses and adjective clauses. This chapter will examine the last type of clause, the noun clause. But before going on, we will briefly review the materials that are pertinent to the formation of noun clauses.

In Chapter 1, you saw that nominals may have one of four basic forms: single words, phrases, clauses, and reduced clauses. As you can see in the following diagram, these forms may have one of four basic functions in a sentence: subject, object, complement, and after a preposition to form an adverbial or adjective phrase.

- -

Noun forms	
single word	*John* is my neighbor.
	It is necessary.
noun phrase	I like *the book.*
	I like *the book about Paris.*
noun clause	It is certain *that he will visit us.*
reduced noun clause	It is necessary *to go home now.*
	Seeing is *believing.*
	I don't know *what to do.*

Noun functions	
subject	*The boy sitting there* is my neighbor.
object	I know *what he said.*
complement	My teacher is *the man standing there.*
after a preposition	He was mad because of *what you said.*

You can see in the diagram above that noun clauses and reduced noun clauses may occur after a preposition; however, not all types of nominals can. As you can see below, *that* clauses and *to*-infinitives cannot be used after a preposition.

CORRECT:	I am unhappy because of *what you said.*
INCORRECT:	I am unhappy because of that you said something unfriendly.
CORRECT:	He talked about *working at the university.*
CORRECT:	He talked about *work at the university.*
INCORRECT:	He talked about to work at the university.

In Chapter 2, however, you learned that these two structures, *that* clauses and *to*-infinitive phrases, are often replaced by temporary *it,* especially when they are used as subjects. Remember, though, that gerunds cannot be replaced by *it.*

	It is a fact *that John drives a car.*
	It is necessary *to go.*
INCORRECT:	It is necessary going.

Because the subject has to agree with the finite verb, it is important to know what form the subject has. A noun clause or a reduced noun clause subject is always singular. On the other hand, a noun phrase, which may contain one or more adjective clauses or phrases, is singular or plural depending on the head noun.

The student who came in late	was	reprimanded by the teacher.	noun phrase with singular head noun
The students who came in late	were	reprimanded by the teacher.	noun phrase with plural head noun
Whoever came in late	was	reprimanded by the teacher.	noun clause
Getting to class late	is	inexcusable.	reduced noun clause

Exercise 1   In the following passage identify the forms of the nominals in italics as: (a) single word, (b) phrase (circle the head noun) (c) clause, or (d) reduced clause.

> *The absence of all heat* is *absolute zero.* Of course, *everyone* is familiar with *"zero weather"* and knows *that it is very cold,* but there is still *a great deal of heat in the air.* Otherwise, *it* could not become even colder and fall "below zero." *Absolute zero* is *the stage at which it could not become any colder.* On *the Fahrenheit thermometer,* this would be more than 459 degrees below zero! On *the Celcius thermometer, more often used in science,* it is more than 273 degrees below zero.
>
> As long as there is *any heat at all,* there is *some motion of the tiny molecules that make up all matter.* Absolute zero is *the point at which all motion ceases. Such coldness* can only be imagined; it could never be proved, because *the presence of someone near enough to observe it* would provide *enough heat to raise the temperature.*

There is one other rule, which was discussed earlier in this text, that applies to noun clauses.

In Chapter 4, you learned that the sequence-of-tense rule requires that a verb in a noun clause change tense if the verb in the main clause is a past-tense verb.

Direct Speech	Indirect Speech
"We are leaving tomorrow."	They *said* that they *were leaving* tomorrow (the next day).
"He is not feeling well."	It *seemed* that he *was* not *feeling* well.
"He came to class yesterday."	*We thought* that he *had come* to class the day before.

Exercise 2   Complete the following sentences with information based on the passage in Exercise 1. Make sure your sentences are true and grammatically correct.

1. It is called absolute zero when _____

    _____ .

2. Of course, most people _____ familiar with what we _____

    _____ .

3. It is known that _____ .

4. However, "zero weather" is not the same as _____ because _____ .

5. The stage at which it could not become any colder _____

_____ .

6. "Absolute zero" _____ on the Fahrenheit thermometer.

7. "Absolute zero" _____ on the Celcius thermometer.

8. The Celcius thermometer _____ in science.

9. Some motion of the tiny molecules that make up all matter

_____ as long as there is any heat at all.

10. We _____ such coldness.

11. We cannot _____ it.

12. If someone is _____ enough heat

_____ to raise the temperature.

Grammar and Meaning

Punctuation Rules for Nominals

The punctuation rules for nominals are easy to remember: A nominal is not set off by commas from the rest of the sentence. Sometimes, however, an adjectival following a noun phrase is set off by commas, but subjects, objects, and complements are not.

Exercise 3   Punctuate and capitalize correctly.

dolphins which are often called porpoises are small whales they are mammals not fish and must put their heads above the water to breathe the most wonderful thing about these beautiful creatures is that they are very intelligent and playful their ability to learn tricks very quickly and their willingness to show off make them popular aquarium animals talking to each other in grunts and squeaks dolphins travel together in friendly groups and often follow ships riding on the waves and leaping into the air what is also interesting is that female dolphins help each other look after the baby dolphins

Formation of Noun Clauses

How is a noun clause formed? When you look at the following diagram, you can see that like an adverbial or adjective clause, a noun clause is basically a connecting word plus a sentence. However, unlike them, a noun clause can be made from different types of sentences: declarative, interrogative, and exclamatory sentences. The connecting word depends on the type of sentence from which the clause is derived. What kind of clause requires the connecting word *if?*

Type of sentence		Connecting word	
declarative	He is a good student.	that	It is a fact *that he is a good student.*
declarative	We are leaving soon.		He doesn't know *that we are leaving soon.*
interrogative	Is he a good student?	if/whether	I wonder *if he is a good student.*
interrogative	When are they leaving?	wh-word	I have no idea *when they are leaving.*
exclamatory	What a good student he is!	what	We were amazed at *what a good student he was.*
exclamatory	How soon we must leave!	how	It surprised us to find out *how soon we had to leave.*

This chapter will now discuss the formation of each type of noun clause.

Noun Clauses Made from Declarative Sentences

subject clause	It is a well-known fact *that Mozart was a musician.*
complement clause	The fact is *that he learned to play when he was very young.*
INFORMAL:	It is a well-known fact Mozart was a musician.
direct object clause	Did you know *that Mozart was a famous musician?*
	Did you know *Mozart was a famous musician?*
	I heard *that he learned to play at the age of three.*
	I heard *he learned to play at the age of three.*

When a noun clause is made from a declarative sentence, the conjunction *that* is simply put before the sentence. The word order does not change. As you can see from the last four examples, the conjunction *that* can be deleted if the clause functions as direct object of the sentence. In informal English, *that* is also deleted from subject and complement clauses.

Exercise 4   Read several times through the ad about exploding hospital costs, until you have a general idea about its content. Then complete the following sentences with a noun clause based on information in the ad.

1. That _____ is a well-known fact.

2. Did you know that _____ ?

3. That _____ surprised me.

4. It was unexpected that _____ .

5. It is not logical that _____ .

6. That _____ is obvious.

7. It doesn't matter that _____ .

8. That _____ bothers me.

9. It is hard to believe that _____ .

10. That _____ annoys insurance companies.

Exercise 5   Complete each of the following sentences with a main clause. (The main clauses given in Exercise 4 may be of help to you.)

1. That hospital costs have been rising three times as fast as the cost of living _____ .

2. But _____ that there is a way to contain this explosive inflation.

3. It _____ that the government doesn't pay the full cost of services for Medicare and Medicaid patients.

4. That hospitals can't collect from the government _____

   _____ .

5. It _____ that shifting costs is related to a lack of incentive to contain costs.

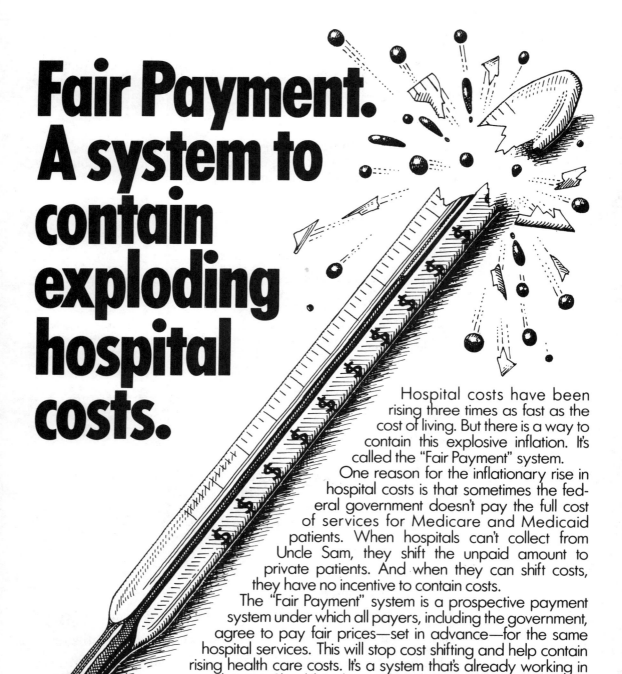

Fair Payment. A system to contain exploding hospital costs.

Hospital costs have been rising three times as fast as the cost of living. But there is a way to contain this explosive inflation. It's called the "Fair Payment" system.

One reason for the inflationary rise in hospital costs is that sometimes the federal government doesn't pay the full cost of services for Medicare and Medicaid patients. When hospitals can't collect from Uncle Sam, they shift the unpaid amount to private patients. And when they can shift costs, they have no incentive to contain costs.

The "Fair Payment" system is a prospective payment system under which all payers, including the government, agree to pay fair prices—set in advance—for the same hospital services. This will stop cost shifting and help contain rising health care costs. It's a system that's already working in several states. Shouldn't it be working in your state?

WRITE FOR MORE
INFORMATION

HEALTH INSURANCE ASSOCIATION OF AMERICA

1850 K Street NW, Washington, DC 20006

6. _____ that a prospective payment system under which all payers, including the government, agree to pay fair prices — set in advance — for the same hospital services is a good idea.

7. _____ that this system will stop cost-shifting and help contain rising health care costs.

8. _____ that this system is already working in several states.

Noun Clauses Made from Imperative Sentences

- -

Go home!	He told me that *I should* go home.
Study hard!	He told us that *we should* study hard.
PREFERRED:	He told us to go home.
PREFERRED:	He told us to study hard.

- -

As you learned in Chapter 8, an imperative sentence is a command, and the subject *you* is implied. When a noun clause is made from an imperative sentence, it has to have a modal, usually *should*. This type of clause is usually reduced to a *to*-infinitive construction.

Noun Clauses with Wish-and-Demand Subjunctives

- -

We demanded *that he leave immediately.*
Her suggestion was *that we try again next week.*
It is imperative *that he tell her the truth.*

- -

You also learned in Chapter 8 that the wish-and-demand subjunctive is required in noun clauses after verbs and nouns that express a demand, suggestion, or desire and after adjectives that express a necessity.

Exercise 6   Complete the following sentences in your own words using information from the ad about hospital costs.

1. It is imperative _____ .

2. The Health Insurance Association of America asks that _____

_____ .

3. It suggests that _____ .

4. The "Fair Payment" plan would require that _____

_____ .

5. The demand that _____ is _____

_____ .

Noun Clauses Made from Interrogative Sentences

- -

Are you going to the movies?

He asked me if I was going to the movies.

When do you want to leave?

He asked me when I wanted to leave.
Did he ask when I wanted to leave?

- -

You can see in the examples that there are several important differences between a noun clause made from an interrogative sentence and the question itself.

First of all, a noun clause does not have a question mark after it unless the whole sentence is a question.

Second, a noun clause does not have question word-order. In other words, in a noun clause the subject comes before the finite verb.

And, since the clause does not have question word-order, the auxiliary *do* is not used in the noun clause.

Examine the following diagram. Why is the helping verb *did* used in the question? In the clause, which part of the sentence comes after *when*?

- -

		wh-word	finite verb	subject	remainder of verb
Question		When	did	he	leave?
		wh-word		subject	verb phrase
Clause	I want to know	when		he	left.

- -

There are two types of interrogative sentences: *yes/no* questions, which start with a finite verb (*Are you leaving now?*) and *wh*-questions, which start with a question word (*Why are you leaving now?*). Both of these types of questions may become noun clauses.

Noun Clauses Made from *Yes/No* Questions

- -

Are you going to the movies?   He asked *if I was going to the movies.*
He asked *whether I was going to the movies.*

Does he go to the movies often?   *Whether or not he goes to the movies often*
                                    is none of your business.

            INCORRECT: He asked was I going to the movies.

- -

When the noun clause is made from a *yes/no* question, the conjunctions *if, whether,* or *whether or not* are used. It is incorrect to leave them out; however, in informal spoken English they are often left out.

Exercise 7

On a separate piece of paper, change the following *yes/no* questions to noun clauses. Don't forget (1) the conjunction, (2) the change in word-order and the leaving out of *do,* (3) the change in tense where necessary, and (4) the change in pronoun where necessary.

1. He asked (Are you from Japan?).
2. We wondered (Is John sick today?).
3. I wanted to know (Do we have to study Chapter 5?).
4. She didn't know (Is she going to leave today?).
5. We don't know (Do we want to stay here?).
6. He asked (Have you ever been to New York?).
7. She inquired (Is the plane going to arrive on time?).
8. I don't know (Do you live far from here?).

Exercise 8

(Quick Oral Drill) Student A asks Student B an original *yes/no* question about the items given. Student B restates the question in reported speech. Then Student B asks Student C a question, and so on.

EXAMPLE:

computers
Student A: Are computers useful?
Student B: *She/he asked me if computers were useful.*

1. weather	11. checking account	21. dance
2. homework	12. course	22. Olympic Games
3. time	13. dog	23. soccer
4. apartment	14. food	24. hospital
5. letter	15. rocket	25. taxes
6. book	16. moon	26. grocery store
7. job	17. New Year	27. university
8. Coca Cola	18. airplane	28. major
9. money	19. car	29. country
10. bank	20. New York	30. teacher

Noun Clauses Made from *Wh*-Questions

- -

How long did he live here?   I wanted to know *how long he had lived here.*

What time is it?	She asked *what time it was.*
	Did she ask *what time it was?*
Where should I go?	I wondered *where I should go.*
	I wondered *where to go.*

- -

A noun clause derived from a *wh*-question is similar to a noun clause derived from a *yes/no* question. The main difference is that when a noun clause is made from a *wh*-question, the *wh*-word or *wh*-phrase becomes the conjunction. The word-order changes: The subject comes after the *wh*-word or phrase and is followed by the finite verb. So the word-order is almost the same as in a statement, except for the fact that the *wh*-word or phrase comes first.

As you can see from the last example in the diagram, this type of clause may be reduced to a *to*-infinitive phrase after the question word if the noun clause contains a modal auxiliary and the subject of the noun clause is the same as the subject of the sentence.

Exercise 9

On a separate piece of paper, change the following *wh*-questions to noun clauses. Provide an appropriate main clause. (Examples: *He wanted to know..., I wondered..., I am not sure..., ...is an important question.*)

1. What is your name?
2. What time is it?
3. Where do you live?
4. What is your favorite color?
5. How much does this car cost?
6. Where is the post office?
7. Which typewriter is yours?
8. Whom does this book belong to?
9. Where should I go?
10. When did you arrive?

Exercise 10

(Quick Oral Drill) Student A asks Student B a *wh*-question with the question word and verb given. Student B restates the question: "She/he wanted to know..." Then Student B asks Student C a question, and so on.

EXAMPLE:

where/live
Student A: Where do you live?
Student B: *She/he wanted to know where I lived.*

1. where/go	5. when/study
2. which/buy	6. how/pronounce
3. what/see	7. which/tape
4. who/call	8. when/watch a movie

9. where/go shopping
10. how/do
11. what/say
12. which/borrow
13. why/wait
14. how long/live
15. how many/send
16. how often/go home
17. how far/walk
18. which/take
19. when/talk
20. who/meet
21. what/like
22. where/study
23. how/play
24. why/leave
25. when/attend
26. where/find
27. which/see
28. how often/go
29. how many/have
30. what/speak

Noun Clauses Made from Exclamations

What an intelligent child he is!   We were amazed at *what an intelligent child he was.*
How intelligent the child is!   We were amazed at *how intelligent the child was.*
   I couldn't believe *how rich he was.*
   I was impressed with *what a good person he was.*

The last type of noun clause is derived from an exclamatory sentence, a statement of surprise that is derived from a sentence. Example: *John is lazy. How lazy John is!* or *John is a lazy student. What a lazy student John is. How* precedes an adjective phrase, and *what* precedes a noun phrase. The *how* or *what* phrase is moved to the beginning of the sentence, but the word order in the remainder of the sentence does not change. Such a statement of surprise can be used as a noun clause. Of course, this type of clause is used only in sentences that express surprise or amazement.

Now that you have learned how the different types of noun clauses are formed, see if you can complete the following passage.

Exercise 11   In the following passage, change the questions in parentheses to noun clauses. Make sure that you add conjunctions, apply the sequence-of-tense rule, and change the word order where necessary. The pronouns have already been changed for you.

Heredity and You

When you were born, your parents had no idea (Who will you look like?) or (What will you grow up to be?). From the first they have probably studied you to find out exactly (Whom in your family do you look like?) and (What abilities may you have inherited?).

Think about yourself for a moment, and ask yourself (Are you light-haired like your father when he was young? Is your hair curly like your mother's? Do you have a talent for music or mathematics? Are you strong and well-coordinated? Are you good in sports? Do you learn things easily?), or (Are you good in some subjects, but not so good in others? Do you like to read books, or would you rather be outside exploring the world around you?).

All of these traits, and many, many more, are partly the result of your *heredity*.

You inherited many physical traits from your parents and grandparents. (What talent do you have?) is also due in part to your heredity.

But what about the world around you? How do you think it has affected you? Ask yourself (What kind of world do you live in?) and (Do you live in a city, in the country, or in a suburb of a large city?). (Where do you live?) and (Who do you live with?) are part of your *environment*. So are your friends, your school, your place of worship, the country you live in, the books you read, the movies you see, and the shows you watch on television. All of these things have an influence on (Who are you?)

Exercise 12   Read over the passage "Heredity and You" again. Then, in a short passage, describe the traits that you might have inherited from your parents or grandparents. Describe how you were also influenced by the world around you.

Reduction of Noun Clauses

Like adverbial clauses and adjective clauses, noun clauses may be reduced. There are three basic structures that may take the place of a noun clause: a *to*-infinitive phrase, a gerund phrase, and an abstract noun phrase.

- -

| that-clause | *That we transport the goods* is necessary.
It is necessary *that we transport the goods.* |
| to-infinitive phrase | *For us to transport the goods* is necessary.
It is necessary *for us to transport the goods.* |

gerund phrase	*Our transporting the goods* is necessary.
	The transporting of the goods (by us) is necessary.
abstract noun phrase	*Transportation of the goods* (by us) is necessary.
	Our transportation of the goods is necessary.

- -

As you can see from the examples above, there are two main differences between a noun clause and a phrase.

First, the verb in the noun clause changes to an infinitive, gerund, or abstract noun. Second, the other words in the original clause may change their forms to modify the infinitive, gerund, or abstract noun.

The second step, determining the form of the modifiers, is probably the one that even the most advanced students may have trouble with. Therefore, the main purpose of the remainder of this unit is to explain what forms the modifiers should have in the three types of reduced noun clauses discussed.

To be able to understand the following discussion, you should understand the following fact:

Verbs and nouns have their own kinds of modifiers. A verb in a sentence has a subject and often an object, which is not preceded by a preposition. On the other hand, nouns are modified by adjectivals (articles, adjectives, adjective phrases, and adjective clauses). Adjective phrases are often preceded by prepositions.

Examine the diagram below. Can you identify the differences between the verb and noun modifiers?

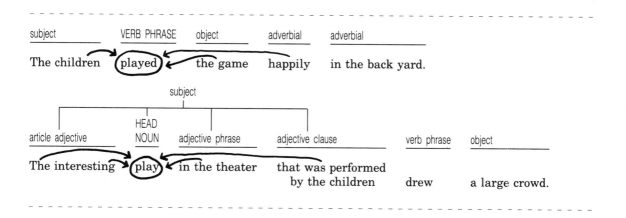

Examine the diagram below. It shows that infinitives, gerunds, and abstract nouns have different kinds of modifiers. Which ones are followed by prepositional phrases?

Noun clause			verb	object		
	That	the soldiers	transport	the goods		is necessary.
Infinitive phrase	*(For-phrase)*		infinitive	object		
			To transport	the goods		is necessary.
		For the soldiers	to transport	the goods		is necessary.
Gerund phrase			gerund	object		
			Transporting	the goods		is necessary.
	adjective		gerund	adjective		
		The soldiers'	transporting	of the goods		is necessary.
Abstract noun phrase			abstract noun	adjective	adjective	
			Transportation	of the goods	by the soldiers	is necessary.

When a clause is made into an infinitive phrase, the modifiers remain basically the same. When it is made into an abstract noun phrase, the modifiers change to adjectivals. However, a gerund phrase may have either verb modifiers or adjectives as long as they are used consistently. (They have to be either all verb modifiers or all noun modifiers).

In the following sections you will learn about each kind of phrase separately.

To-*Infinitive Phrases*

Although a *to*-infinitive phrase is often used as a noun, it is still felt to be more verb than noun; in fact, just like a finite verb phrase, it can show the progressive aspect (*to be writing*), the perfect aspect (*to have written*), or the passive voice (*to be written*).

That	you	attend class regularly	is required.
(For you)	*to attend*	class regularly	is necessary.
		It	is necessary (for you) *to attend* class regularly.

That	you	have been reprimanded	was unpleasant.
(For you)	*to have been reprimanded*		was unpleasant.

That	you	are studying now	is necessary.
(For you)	*to be studying* now		is necessary.

That	you	must get up early	is unpleasant.
That	you	have to get up early	is unpleasant.
(For you)	*to have to get up* early		is unpleasant.

Actually, the formation of a *to*-infinitive phrase is very simple: the finite verb (unless it is a modal) changes to a *to*-infinitive and the other verb forms and modifiers that follow (objects and adverbials) remain unchanged.

However, an infinitive is not a finite verb, so it cannot have a subject in the subject form. For example, it would be incorrect to say, "He to go is necessary." Therefore, the subject is changed to an adverbial form by putting *for* in front of it. Of course, after the preposition the form of some pronouns has to be changed. The correct form is not *for he* but *for him;* the pronouns *I, he, she, we,* and *they* have to be changed to their respective object forms.

Note: The subject is not mentioned if it is the same as the subject of the sentence or if it is understood from the context.

Exercise 13   On a separate piece of paper, change each sentence in parentheses to a *to*-infinitive phrase and insert it into the sentence given.

1. (The student gets up early in the morning.) is difficult.
2. We decided (We will go to the movies tonight.)
3. We cannot afford (We buy a new television set.)
4. (The baby has not awakened during the night.) pleases the parents.
5. (People celebrate Chinese New Year.) is a tradition in many countries.
6. (He is smoking in class.) is unacceptable.
7. (She will be a famous actress.) is Mary's ambition.
8. (The report contains inconsistencies.) is a serious matter.

Exercise 14   Complete the sentences with information from the following situation.

Situation: Mary is an irresponsible student. She is living in an apartment. She parties a lot. She smokes a lot. She drinks a lot of wine. She doesn't sleep much. Her grades are bad. And so on.

1. For Mary _____ worries her parents.

2. For Mary _____ angers them.

3. _____ didn't please them.

4. _____ shocked the instructor.

5. _____ discouraged her friends.

6. It annoys them to _____ .

7. It distresses them _____ .

8. It is necessary for them _____ .

9. It is foolish of Mary to _____ .

10. It will take a whole semester for _____

_____ .

Gerund Phrases

The formation of a gerund phrase can be somewhat confusing because a gerund may have two different types of modifiers: verb modifiers or noun modifiers, which may not be mixed.

When the gerund is felt to be a noun, it cannot show differences in tense, aspect, and mood. In other words, noun modifiers can occur only with a simple gerund form (verb plus *ing;* for example, *transporting*).

On the other hand, when the gerund is felt to be a verb, it can show differences in tense, aspect, and mood (for example, *having been transported*), and it is modified by verb modifiers. Why is the last example incorrect?

Reading	*the book* is necessary.	gerund + object
The reading of the book is necessary.		article + gerund + adjective phrase
Having read	*the book* was necessary.	perfect gerund + object
INCORRECT: The having read of the book was necessary.		perfect gerund with noun modifiers

---

In general, we may say that the gerund with noun modifiers is more old-fashioned and formal than the gerund with verb modifiers. Especially in spoken English, the gerund with verb modifiers is preferred. However, it is important that you understand both so that you will not confuse their structures.

Gerund Phrases with Noun Modifiers

When a noun clause is reduced to a gerund phrase with noun modifiers, all the original sentence parts, (1) the subject, (2) the object, and (3) the adverb(s), must be changed.

Subject

(The soldiers transported the goods rapidly.)

The soldiers' transporting....	possessive form
Their transporting....	possessive form
The transporting *by the soldiers*	by-phrase after a transitive verb

(The birds sang.)

The birds' singing....	possessive form
Their singing....	possessive form
The singing *of the birds* ...	of-phrase after an intransitive verb

---

The subject of the verb is changed to a possessive form. If the gerund is derived from a transitive verb, the subject may be a *by*-phrase. Sometimes, if the gerund is derived from an intransitive verb, the subject may be an *of*-phrase after the gerund.

- -

Object

(The soldiers transported the goods rapidly.)
The soldiers' transporting *of the goods* ....   of-phrase

INCORRECT: The transporting the goods....

- -

The object of a verb phrase becomes an *of*-phrase after the gerund.
Note: If the gerund is preceded by an article, the original object must be changed to the prepositional form.

- -

Adverbs

(The soldiers transported the goods rapidly.)

The *rapid* transporting of the goods....

- -

The adverbs in a sentence are changed to their respective adjective forms.

Exercise 15   On a separate piece of paper, change each sentence in parentheses to a gerund phrase with noun modifiers.

1. (The storm abated suddenly.) was unexpected.
2. (Congress approved the budget.) surprised the president.
3. (The band played the national anthem.) brought tears to his eyes.
4. (He fulfills the requirement.) is necessary.
5. (The moon shone brightly.) helped the burglar.
6. (The library closed early.) made me angry.
7. I hate (The dog barks loudly.).
8. I enjoy (People sing.).
9. He complained about (Mary smoked frequently.).
10. He could not understand (The teacher talked fast.).
11. I am disappointed in (John lied to Mary.).
12. We were surprised at (John won the bingo game.).

The Gerund with Verb Modifiers

When the gerund is felt to be more verb than noun, its formation is very similar to the formation of the *to*-infinitive phrase; the original direct object and adverbials remain unchanged, but the subject often changes.

Subject of the Gerund

(The soldiers	transported	the goods rapidly.)	
The soldiers'	transporting the goods rapidly was necessary.		
Their	transporting the goods rapidly was necessary.		

FORMAL:	*Their*	transporting the goods rapidly was necessary.	subject/gerund phrase
INFORMAL:	*Them*	transporting the goods rapidly was necessary.	

FORMAL:	We appreciated *their*	transporting the goods.	object/gerund phrase
INFORMAL:	We appreciated *them*	transporting the goods.	

CORRECT:	The goods being transported is necessary.	the goods = inanimate
INCORRECT:	The goods' being transported is necessary.	

The subject of a gerund phrase can be changed to a noun or pronoun in the possessive form or in the object form; however, in formal writing the possessive form is usually preferred for an animate subject, especially if the gerund phrase is the subject of a sentence. In spoken English, on the other hand, the object form of the noun or pronoun is more common, and when the subject of the gerund is a thing rather than a person, the object form is preferred.

Aspect and Voice in the Gerund Phrase

		Tense from which the gerund is derived
FORMAL:	I agree with the mother's *punishing*	punishes/punished
INFORMAL:	I agree with the mother *punishing* the child.	is/was punishing
FORMAL:	I agree with the mother's *having been punishing* the child.	has/had been punishing
INFORMAL:	I agree with the mother *having been punishing* the child.	
FORMAL:	I agree with the child's *being punished.*	is/was punished
INFORMAL:	I agree with the child *being punished.*	
FORMAL:	I agree with the child's *having been punished.*	has/had been punished
INFORMAL:	I agree with the child *having been punished.*	

Gerund phrases may be derived from almost any kind of verb phrase and may have progressive, perfect, or passive forms. Only the finite form in the sentence changes to the *-ing* form, and the other verb forms remain unchanged. Therefore a gerund cannot show differences in present or past tense.

Gerund + Verb Modifiers

CORRECT:	Your	missing	of many classes was unacceptable.
CORRECT:	You(r)	missing	many classes was unacceptable.

CORRECT:	You(r)	having missed	many classes	was unacceptable.	*perfect gerund*
INCORRECT:	You(r)	having missed	*of* many classes	was unacceptable.	
CORRECT:	His	not attending	classes	annoys his teacher.	*not + gerund*
INCORRECT:	His	not attending	*of* classes	annoys his teacher.	
CORRECT:	His	wanting	to sing a song is funny.		*gerund + infinitive*
INCORRECT:	*The*	wanting	to sing a song is funny.		

- -

The gerund is definitely felt to be more verb than noun when it has a passive or perfect form, when it is followed by a *to*-infinitive, or when it is preceded by *not*. Therefore, only verb modifiers are used with these types of gerunds, and an article or an *of*-object are not acceptable.

Exercise 16 On a separate piece of paper, change the sentences in parentheses to gerund phrases with verb modifiers and insert them into the main clause given.

1. (Cigarettes are bad for you.) is a well-known fact.
2. (People exercise regularly.) is healthy.
3. (You don't stay up late every night.) is good for you.
4. (The window vibrates because the heater is on.) annoys me.
5. (The baby has cried all night.) kept the parents awake.
6. (The noise was made by the students in the dorm.) kept me from studying.
7. (I did not hand in my work on time.) was a mistake.
8. (My father has to pay my telephone bill.) bothers me.
9. (I had lost my wallet.) left me without any money.
10. (John has admitted the error.) is hard to believe.

Exercise 17 Complete each of the following sentences with a meaningful gerund phrase based on the following situation.

Situation: John is a very diligent and intelligent student, but he has some annoying habits. He answers every question in class. He speaks before it is his turn. He never listens to what other students say. He never gives them a chance to finish a sentence. He has never raised his hand. He wants to show off his knowledge.

1. His _____ bothers me.

2. John's _____ surprises no one.

3. _____ pleases him.

4. He avoids _____ .

5. The students dread _____ .

6. They do not appreciate his _____ .

7. I cannot understand his _____ .

8. The teacher mentioned his _____ .

9. I am looking forward to his _____ .

10. I am amazed at _____ .

Abstract Noun Phrases

An abstract noun, like an infinitive or a gerund, can be derived from a verb (for example, *transportation* from *transport; articulation* from *articulate*). But, unlike them, it can also be derived from a predicate adjective (for example, *ability* from *able*). *Note:* In this sense *abstract* means *derived from,* not *unreal.*

The abstract noun is felt to be a complete noun, so it is modified by noun modifiers: adjectives, adjective phrases, and adjective clauses. Therefore, all modifiers of the verb are changed to noun modifiers.

Subjects of Abstract Nouns

- -

John surprised his friends.
John's surprise for his friends was a great success.   possessive noun

She lost all her money.
Her loss of all her money saddened her.
The loss of all her money saddened her.   understood subject

The diamonds disappeared.
The disappearance *of the diamonds* puzzled us.   *of*-phrase subject (intransitive verb)

The head of the department refused to admit him.
The refusal to admit him *by the head of the department* angered him.   *by*-phrase (long subject—transitive verb)

The child was punished.
The punishment *of the child* was necessary.   *of*-phrase (passive verb)

- -

Subjects are changed to possessive pronouns or nouns. Subjects of intransitive verbs may also occur as *of*-phrases after the noun, and subjects of transitive verbs as *by*-phrases, which usually come after other modifiers.

Objects of Abstract Nouns

- -

People prevent forest fires.   verb + object
The prevention *of forest fires* is necessary.   noun + *of*-phrase
The sound system is studied.
The study *of the sound system* is interesting.

His *preference for* Chinese food is evident.   *to-* and *for*-phrases (idiomatic)
His *answer to* his mother was impolite.
His *resemblance to* his father is amazing.
I envy his *respect for* his father.
His *demand for* money is understandable.
His *obedience to* the sergeant is necessary.

His *trust in* me is touching.

They *struggle for* survival.   verb+preposition
They did not give up their *struggle for* survival.   noun+preposition
He is *amazed at* my ability to sing.   verb+preposition
His *amazement at* my ability to sing is funny.   noun+preposition

He is *able to memorize.*   adjective+*to*-infinitive
He does well on tests due to his *ability to memorize.* noun+*to*-infinitive

He *decided to go.* verb+*to*-infinitive
His *decision to go* surprised me. noun+*to*-infinitive

I *advised him to stay.* verb+pronoun+*to*-infinitive
My advice to him to stay was not followed. noun+*to*+pronoun+*to*-infinitive

He refused *them* the request. verb+indirect object
His refusal *of their* request infuriated them.   noun+of+pronoun

I gave her a new book.   verb+indirect object
My gift *to her* of a new book was appreciated. noun+*to*-phrase
They requested him to come early.
Their request *to him* to come early was granted.

She *enjoys watching* children play.   verb + gerund
Her *enjoyment of watching* them play helped her to be a good babysitter. noun + of + gerund
I *observed him teaching.*
Because of my *observation of him teaching,* I conclude that he . . . .

- -

Objects of abstract nouns are often *of*-phrases, but some abstract nouns are followed by other prepositions.

As you can see from the examples, abstract nouns can also be followed by *to*-infinitive objects. If a verb is followed by an indirect object and a *to*-infinitive, what happens to the indirect object?

When the original transitive verb is followed by an indirect object, the indirect object may have one of three forms. Which ones are they?

What happens to a gerund object?

Other Modifiers in Abstract Noun Phrases

- -

It was very silent in the street.
The *great* silence in the street surprised me.

The boy is very much afraid of the dark.
The boy's *great* fear of the dark amazes me.

- -

Adverbs usually change to adjectives. (Example: *very* is changed to *great*). Prepositional phrases do not change in form.

Exercise 18   On a separate piece of paper, change the sentences in parentheses into abstract noun phrases and insert them into the main clauses given.

1. (The town developed quickly.) surprised everyone.
2. (He applied for an assistantship.) was rejected.
3. (He resembled his father.) was remarkable.
4. (They interrupted his speech.) was impolite.
5. (This problem is solved.) is not easy.
6. (He pronounces English.) is very good.
7. (The children obey their parents.) is necessary.
8. (He resigned from the university.) was unexpected.
9. (Water is scarce.) is bad for agriculture.
10. (He is loyal to the king.) is surprising.

Exercise 19   Change each of the following verbs and predicate adjectives to the corresponding abstract noun. Check a dictionary if you are not sure.

1. arrive _____	16. strong _____
2. generous _____	17. long _____
3. increase _____	18. sane _____
4. curious _____	19. omit _____
5. recover _____	20. expect _____
6. succeed _____	21. aware _____
7. certain _____	22. encourage _____
8. amaze _____	23. avoid _____
9. conspire _____	24. separate _____
10. resolve _____	25. possess _____
11. familiar _____	26. wide _____
12. reject _____	27. pure _____
13. decide _____	28. resist _____
14. foolish _____	29. repeat _____
15. retire _____	30. interfere _____

Exercise 20   In the following sentences, abstract nouns have been replaced by short sentences. Change each short sentence in parentheses back to an abstract noun phrase that fits into the long sentence. Use only the words in italics.

1. Flying a national flag upside down at sea is a signal of (Someone is *distressed*).

2. Fifteen million corncobs are utilized annually in the United States in (People *manufacture corncob pipes*).

3. Toads, in (They are *distinguished from frogs*), have no teeth.

4. Thomas A. Edison once spent two million dollars on (He *invented* something *that proved of little value*).

5. Penicillin does not kill germs; it merely stops (*They grow*) and prevents (*They reproduce*).

6. James H. Doolittle made the first all-instrument (He *flew*) in aviation.

7. The first cheese factory in the United States began (It *operated*) in 1851 in Rome, New York.

8. The most prevalent (It *infects*) in the world today is malaria.

Solving Problems

The first trouble spots reviewed here are found in the formation of noun clauses, the other ones in the formation of reduced noun clauses.

Problems in the Use of Tense and Mood

Remember that the sequence-of-tense rule must be applied when the main clause contains a past tense verb and the wish-and-demand subjunctive must be used after such verbs as *demand, request,* and *desire.*

INCORRECT: He said that he is going home tomorrow.
CORRECT: He said that he was going home tomorrow.

INCORRECT: He requested that he was given a make-up test.
CORRECT: He requested that he be given a make-up test.

Faulty Word Order in Dependent Questions

INCORRECT: He asked what time was it.
CORRECT: He asked what time it was.

INCORRECT: He wanted to know where was the train station.
CORRECT: He wanted to know where the train station was.

Faulty Use or Omission of Conjunction

The conjunction *that* may be deleted if it introduces a direct object clause, but not if it introduces a subject clause. Other conjunctions are not deleted.

INCORRECT: He is rich is a well-known fact.
CORRECT: That he is rich is a well-known fact.

INCORRECT: You will see is very exciting.
CORRECT: What you will see is very exciting.

INCORRECT: It is a well-known fact he is rich.
CORRECT: It is a well-known fact that he is rich.

INCORRECT: He asked could he help.
CORRECT: He asked if he could help.

Fragment (No Main Clause)

INCORRECT: What he said that he was sick.
CORRECT: What he said was that he was sick.

Double Object

When a noun clause is made from a question, the *wh*-word has a function in the sentence. It can be a subject, object, adjective or adverb. Make sure that the clause does not have two objects.

INCORRECT: What I like it is ice cream.
CORRECT: What I like is ice cream.

Mixed Construction

A noun clause functions as a noun (subject, object, or complement), but an adverbial clause does not. It is therefore incorrect to use an adverbial clause as subject, object or complement.

INCORRECT: The reason it seems so cold is because it is very humid.
CORRECT: The reason it seems so cold is that it is very humid.

INCORRECT:	When he won the match was when he was happy.
CORRECT:	When he won the match, he was happy.
CORRECT:	That he won the match made him happy.

The reduced noun clauses are confusing because there are so many details to think about: word forms, articles, and prepositions. A few of the most obvious errors are discussed below.

Faulty Use of Articles and Prepositions in Abstract Noun and Gerund Phrases

If a gerund or an abstract noun is preceded by an article, it is followed by a prepositional phrase.

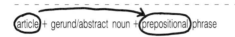

article + gerund/abstract noun + prepositional phrase

INCORRECT:	The reading a book is fun.
CORRECT:	Reading a book is fun.
CORRECT:	The reading of a book is fun.

INCORRECT:	The pronunciation English is difficult.
CORRECT:	The pronunciation of English is difficult.
CORRECT:	English pronunciation is difficult.
CORRECT:	Pronouncing English is difficult.

Faulty Modifiers in Abstract Noun or Gerund Phrases

An abstract noun cannot be followed by a verb modifier, so its object is always a prepositional phrase. Abstract nouns are modified by adjectives, not adverbs.

INCORRECT:	He has a large collection stamps.
CORRECT:	He has a large collection of stamps.

INCORRECT:	I have considerably respect for him.
CORRECT:	I have considerable respect for him.

Abstract nouns are usually non-count nouns and cannot be used in the plural or with the article *a(n)*.

INCORRECT:	I have an information for you.
CORRECT:	I have a piece of information for you.

INCORRECT:	I have informations for you.
CORRECT:	I have some information for you.

Abstract nouns that are not followed by modifiers and that are used in a general sense (not referring to a specific instance) usually do not take an article.

INCORRECT: The speech is a form of communicating.
CORRECT: Speech is a form of communicating.

Many prepositions are idiomatic.

INCORRECT: Mercury is usually found in combination to sulfur.
CORRECT: Mercury is usually found in combination with sulfur.

Faulty Word Forms

Adjective and abstract noun forms are sometimes confused.

INCORRECT: The exchange of heat and moist requires a great amount of energy.
CORRECT: The exchange of heat and moisture requires a great amount of energy.

When a noun is used as an adjective before a gerund or an abstract noun, it does not take an -s; however, if it is used after the gerund or abstract noun, it may take an -s ending.

INCORRECT: He enjoys stamps collecting.
CORRECT: He enjoys stamp collecting.
CORRECT: He enjoys collecting stamps.

INCORRECT: He has a large stamps collection.
CORRECT: He has a large stamp collection.

Exercise 21   Each sentence in the following passage contains one of the errors mentioned above. Identify the errors and correct them.

The Speech Chain

A convenient way of examining what happens during speech is to take the simple situation two people talking to each other. One of them, the speaker, transmits informations to the other, the listener.

What has the speaker to do first is to arrange his thoughts and decide what he wants to say. He then puts what he wants to say into linguistics form.

The message is put into linguistic form by the selecting the right words and phrases to express its meaning and by placing these words in the correct order required by the grammatical rules of the language.

Process of selection and decision is associated with activity in the speaker's brain. And it is in the brain appropriate instructions in the form of impulses along the motor nerves are sent to the muscles. The muscles movements, in turn, produce minute pressure changes in the surrounding air. These pressure changes are what we call them sound waves.

The movements of the vocal organs cause the generate of a speech sound wave that travels through the air between a speaker and a listener.

Pressures changes at the ear activate the hearing mechanism of the listener and produce nerve impulses that travel along the acoustic nerve to the listener's brain.

In the listener's brain, a considerably amount of nerve activity is already taking place, and this activity is modified by the nerve impulses arriving from the ear.

This modify of brain activity in ways we do not fully understand, brings about recognition of the speaker's message.

We see, therefore, that speech communication requires that a chain of events links the speaker's brain with the listener's brain.

Exercise 22   The following exercise tests your ability to manipulate some of the structures you have studied in this chapter. Read the following passage. Then complete the blanks below. Make sure you use appropriate word forms.

By tracing the ancestors of plant and animal life, Charles Darwin became convinced that life on earth progressed through evolution. No two plants or animals were exactly alike. Most of a species' traits were passed on. But sometimes an entirely new trait would appear, thus creating a new species.

What was true for all plant and animal life was also true for humans. They, too, had evolved over a long period of time from primitive beginnings. What shocked many people was the evolutionary fact that humans were related to other animal life, in particular to mammals such as the apes, or to apelike humans discovered in the fossil remains of many thousands of years ago.

Many of the people who opposed Darwin's ideas on evolution thought he did not believe in God. But Darwin was very religious. He believed in God as the creator of things. But he believed he had proof that all things created by God were subject to change and that this was part of God's "Divine Plan."

The most important concept in Darwin's theory of evolution is called *natural selection*. Natural selection is basically nature's way of determining how plant and animal species change over long periods of time. One aspect of this theory is the idea of the survival of the fittest. Each year hundreds of thousands of different animals and plants are born. Many are killed by enemies, disease, or harsh weather conditions. But a certain number usually survive and continue to produce offspring.

By tracing the ancestors of plant and animal life, Charles Darwin came to the _____ that life on earth progressed because life _____ . There were _____ were exactly alike. Most of a species' traits were passed on. But sometimes the _____ of an entirely new trait would _____ a new species.

What was true for all plant and animal life was also true for humans, whose _____ over a long period of time had brought them from primitive beginnings. It shocked many people that there was a _____ between humans and other animal life, in particular to mammals such as the apes, or to apelike humans whose _____ in fossil remains of many thousands of years ago was an evolutionary fact.

What many of the people who opposed Darwin's ideas on evolution thought was _____ he did not believe in God. But Darwin was very religious. He believed that God _____ _____ . But he believed he could _____ that all things created by God might _____ and that this was part of God's "Divine Plan."

The most important concept in Darwin's theory of evolution is called *natural selection*. Natural selection is basically the way that nature _____ how the _____ in plant and animal species over long periods of time occur. One aspect of this theory is the idea that the fittest _____ . Each year hundreds of thousands of different animals and plants are born. Many are killed by enemies, disease, or harsh weather conditions. But a certain number usually survive and continue to produce offspring.

Assignment for Writing

Look at the picture in the ad about American business. What is the man doing? How would you describe the expression on his face? Hamburgers are often called a "fast food." Why?

Read through the ad several times until you have a general idea of its content. Then proceed to the following questions.

Vocabulary

1. How does the dictionary define *gratification?*
2. What earlier words did *gratification* come from?
3. What does the author mean by *instant gratification?*
4. What does the author mean when he or she speaks of a "diet of instant gratification?"
5. There are many abstract nouns in the ad. Several are listed below. Give the verb or adjective from which they have been derived, and explain their meaning.

   a. gratification = to gratify
   b. production
   c. report
   d. figures
   e. investors
   f. earnings
   g. growth
   h. results

   i. profits
   j. solutions
   k. investments
   l. equipment
   m. development
   n. interests
   o. security
   p. decision

6. In the picture you see a man eating. There are many words and expressions in the headline, the first five paragraphs, and the last paragraph, all of which are related to food or eating. For example: *spew out* and *eat up.* Can you find the others?
7. Find fifteen words in this ad that are typical business terms. (for example, *production reports, sales figures.*)

Group Discussion

1. What is W. R. Grace and Co.?
2. What do the first five paragraphs describe? Summarize its content in one or two sentences.

Can American business survive on a diet of instant gratification?

Computers spew out production reports and sales figures hourly. And managers eat them up.

Investors hunger for bigger dividends and faster earnings growth.

The nightly news feeds us today's hot economic story complete with all the freshest buzzwords.

No matter what the economy, much of American business continues to feast on short-term results. Expecting profits to be served up like fast-food burgers. And economic solutions dished out like instant pudding.

To satisfy this appetite for short-term rewards, managers find it tempting to reduce investments for the future. Investments in new plant and equipment; in research and development.

We're W.R.Grace & Co. We've been doing business in all parts of the world, in all kinds of economies for 130 years. Short-term thinking has never been our way of doing business.

In the last 40 years, we've followed a strategy that has allowed us to diversify into growth industries. It's been a transition that has taken Grace from being primarily a Latin American trading and shipping concern to a company with worldwide interests in chemicals, natural resources and specialized consumer services. A company with more than $6 billion in sales.

All that didn't just happen. It was planned that way—by people dedicated to the long-term point of view.

We've always believed in giving the future its fair share of today's resources. Last year at Grace, investment in new plant and equipment was almost 5 times what it was 10 years ago. Research and development expenditures were nearly 3 times what they were a decade ago.

Right now we believe all of us must work to correct a fundamental flaw in the way American business is operating. Short-term results cannot be allowed to become our only criterion for success. Investors must be willing to relax some of the pressure on managers to produce immediate results. Managers must be given more security to make long-term investment decisions.

In turn, those in management must be prepared to make long-term commitments to invest in innovation—in new products and new technologies. And at the same time, to make long-range plans to restore our older industries to full strength.

American business cannot allow itself to overindulge in short-term rewards. Long-lasting results will take time to develop. But that's what makes them so gratifying.

GRACE

One step ahead of a changing world.

W.R. Grace & Co., 1114 Avenue of the Americas, New York, N.Y. 10036

3. What is the purpose of paragraph 6?
4. What is Grace's apparent philosophy? State it in one sentence.
5. What does Grace believe to be the fundamental flaw in the way American business is currently operating? Do you agree with Grace? Can you give specific examples?
6. What does Grace mean by *more security* in the following sentence? "Managers must be given more security to make long-term investment decisions."
7. Why, in your opinion, did Grace place this ad in major business magazines?
8. Do you think that the way of doing business has to change in America? Do you think that it will change? Why, or why not?
9. Are there any major differences between the way businesses in your country operate and the way businesses operate in America? Can you give a few specific examples?
10. Can you think of some situations (other than in business) in which "instant gratification" may be disadvantageous? (for example, studying only the night before a test)
11. Can you think of some situations (other than in business) in which "long-term investments" have paid off?

Writing

Change the headline of this ad to apply to a field in which you are interested and use it as your opening statement. "Can _____ survive on a diet of instant gratification?" (For example, Can *a student, a bank, a parent, a scientist, an engineer* survive on a diet of instant gratification?) Compare your field with a diet, just as has been done in the first five and the last paragraph of this ad. Just as has been done in paragraphs 6–11, you should explain the way you believe investments in the future should be made.

Your composition should explain why your field can or cannot survive on a diet of instant gratification. Support your arguments with specific facts, details, and examples.

Proofreading

When you have finished writing and you are satisfied with the content, organization, and supporting details, facts, and examples, it is time to proofread for grammar errors.

1. Read each paragraph separately. Is it coherent? Can the reader easily understand what you want to say? Do you need more transitions? (conjunctions, conjunctive adverbs, reduced clauses, passive verb phrases?)
2. Look at each sentence separately. Is it a complete sentence? (fused sentence, double conjunction, or fragment?)

3. Look at each clause separately. Is it complete? (conjunctions, finite verb?)
4. Look at each verb phrase separately. (subject-verb agreement, tense, voice, mood? Have you been consistent in your use of tense?)
5. Look at each modifier in the sentence. Have you used adjectives, articles, and adverbs appropriately?
6. Look at each word separately. Check on spelling, capitalization, and the use of each article and preposition.

10

Direct Object Patterns and Related Structures

Review/Preview

In Chapter 1 you saw that there were three types of primary verbs: transitive, intransitive, and linking. Of these three types, transitive verbs are not only the most commonly used verbs but also the most difficult ones because the direct object may have many different forms: nouns, pronouns, noun phrases, noun clauses, infinitives, gerunds, and abstract nouns. Only certain types of verbs may take certain kinds of objects, and especially *to*-infinitives and gerunds are often confused.

This unit will briefly describe all the different object forms that are possible. However, the main purpose is to show you when to use a *to*-infinitive or a gerund. The long lists of examples with each pattern, which are not necessarily to be memorized, should give you a feeling for the types of verbs that take certain objects.

Grammar and Meaning

Verb — Noun or Noun Phrase Object

Not every verb can be followed by a noun clause, a *to*-infinitive, or a gerund, but almost every transitive verb can be used with a noun, pronoun, or noun phrase as object. Some transitive verbs consist of two parts: verb plus particle. Some of these particles precede the object; others follow the object.

Note: A particle is a part of speech that has the form of a preposition or an adverb, but it belongs to a verb. The verb and particle together form a specific meaning. Example: I *called* him *up.* (I telephoned him.) I *called* *on* him. (I visited him.)

Some transitive verbs are followed by objects and a prepositional phrase.

In other words there are four sub-patterns, all of which may be used in passive constructions:

- -

Verb—object.	I *saw* him. I *saw* the man.
Verb—particle—object	I *called on* him. (visit)
Verb—object—particle	I *looked* him *up.* (visit)
Verb—object—prepositional phrase	I *blame* the accident *on* him.

- -

Many of the verb-plus-particle expressions are idiomatic in use. See if you know what they mean in the following exercises.

Exercise 1   Discuss the meanings of the following verb-particle combinations. Then use them in meaningful sentences based on the following situations. *Note:* s.o. = someone; s.th. = something.

Situation: John likes Mary. He wants to invite her to a movie. He telephones her. Mary doesn't want to go out with him. She gives him an excuse. John is very disappointed. He goes to his friend, Peter, who says something to make John happy again.

1. ask s.o. out	6. make up s.th.
2. take s.o. out	7. look s.o. up
3. call s.o. up	8. get along with s.o.
4. think s.th. over	9. cheer s.o. up
5. get out of s.th.	10. get over s.th.

Situation: You saw John in the grocery store. You noticed that he acts just like his older brother. He tries to accomplish the same things his brother does. Their father raised them.

1. run into s.o.	3. keep up with s.o.
2. take after s.o.	4. bring s.o. up

Situation: You are in a math class. You have many problems to solve. You make many mistakes when you have to solve them. You postpone doing your homework. You don't do any more problems. Your instructor tells you that you might fail. You go to your advisor. You want to find out if you can drop the course. You have to complete a form. You have to take the form somewhere.

1. figure s.th. out	6. check into s.th.
2. cross s.th. out	7. look into s.th.
3. put s.th. off	8. drop s.th. off
4. keep s.th. up	9. fill out s.th.
5. point s.th. out	

Situation: What does John do between the time that he wakes up and goes to class?

1. shut s.th. off	7. put away s.th.
2. turn out s.th.	8. hang s.th. up
3. have s.th. on	9. bring s.th. about
4. get on s.th.	10. pick s.th. out
5. put out s.th.	11. look out for s.th.
6. put on s.th.	12. put s.th. up

Situation: John and his brother fight a lot. John thinks his brother took some of his money. He throws something at his brother. Their mother tries to stop their fighting. She asks her friend what to do. Her friend gives her good advice.

1. to accuse s.o. of s.th.	8. to inform s.o. of s.th.
2. to aim s.th. at s.th. or s.o.	9. to advise s.o. of s.th.
3. to ask s.th. of s.o.	10. to prevent s.o. from doing s.th.
4. to ask s.o. for s.th.	
5. to blame s.th. on s.o.	11. to provide s.o. with s.th.
6. to blame s.o. or s.th. for s.th.	12. to punish s.o. for s.th.
	13. to relieve s.o. of s.th.
7. to consult s.o. on s.th.	

Verb — Indirect Object — Direct Object

A small group of verbs is followed by two objects, a direct object and an indirect object. The direct object usually refers to a thing, and the indirect object to a person. Even though this is only a small group of verbs, there are five subpatterns in this group of verbs.

- -

Indirect object with or without *to*	I gave *Mary* the book. I gave the book *to Mary*.
Indirect object with *to* only	I explained the lesson *to Mary*.
Indirect object without a preposition only	I asked *Mary* a question.
Indirect object with or without *for*	I bought *Mary* a book. I bought a book *for Mary*.
Indirect object with *for* only	I opened the door *for Mary*.

- -

The direct object in all of these patterns may become the subject of a passive sentence, but only the indirect object of patterns 1 and 3 may become subjects of passive sentences. (Example: *Mary was given a book. Mary was asked a question.*)

Indirect Object With or Without To

	Active	Passive
give sell send pass bring take	John gave *Mary* a book. John gave a book *to Mary*. John gave it *to Mary*.	*Mary* was given a book. A book was given *to Mary*.
INCORRECT: INCORRECT:	John gave to Mary a book. John gave Mary it.	
write read show teach	He told *me* that he was sick. He wrote (*me*) that he was sick. He showed *me* what to do. He taught *me* how to pronounce that word.	*I* was told that he was sick.
tell	He told *me* to leave. He showed *me* that he was right.	*I* was told to leave.

If the indirect object comes after the verb, it is not preceded by *to*. What happens if the indirect object comes after the direct object? When the direct object is a pronoun, does it have to come before or after the indirect object?

Note: Verbs that denote human expression (*write, read, show, teach,* and *tell*) may be followed by a noun clause or a *to*-infinitive construction. The indirect object is also used before the *that*-clause.

Exercise 2
Create good English sentences with the following verbs with information from the following situations.

Situation: You went to a refugee camp. Many people were starving. They needed food, water, clothes, medicine, and shelter. Besides, they needed to learn how to cultivate the land and to grow their own food. You helped them. You also asked the government for more help.

1. give
2. write
3. read
4. show
5. teach
6. tell
7. sell
8. send
9. lend
10. bring
11. take
12. pass

Indirect Object with To Only

announce   explain   He explained the lesson to *me*.
describe   repeat   He introduced John *to me*.
introduce   say   He explained the lesson.
mention   suggest   He explained that he had to leave.
prove   report   He explained *to me* that he had to leave.

INCORRECT: He explained me the lesson.
INCORRECT: He introduced me John.

Verbs like *explain* express a mode of speaking and may be used with a *that*-clause. They can be used only with a *to* indirect object, which is optional.

Indirect Object Without a Preposition

Active	Passive
He asked *me* a favor.	I was asked a favor.
INCORRECT: He asked a question to me.	A question was asked *of me*.
	I was asked to leave.

The verb *ask* is the only verb with this pattern. If *ask* is followed by an indirect object, the only pattern possible is ask — indirect object — direct object. The indirect object may become the subject of a passive sentence. What happens to the indirect object if the direct object becomes the subject of a passive sentence?

Exercise 3   Create good English sentences with the following verbs (with information from the situation described below).

Situation: You are a grammar teacher. You teach your class about the formation of noun clauses made from sentences, questions, and exclamations. You teach the sequence-of-tense rule, and so on. You will give a test in two days.

1. explain
2. announce
3. describe
4. introduce
5. mention
6. prove
7. repeat
8. say
9. suggest
10. report
11. ask

Indirect Object With or Without *For*

- -

buy   He bought the book (*for me.*)
get   He bought *me* a book.
make   He made a table (*for me.*)
find   He made *me* a table.
do   He found *me* an apartment.

- -

The five verbs that can be used with or without a *for* indirect object denote *doing something for someone.*

Exercise 4   Create meaningful English sentences with the following verbs with information from the following situation.

Situation: You are going home. You buy presents for your family.

1. buy   4. find
2. get   5. do
3. make

Indirect Object with *For Only*

- -

open   He opened the door *for me.*
answer   pronounce   He answered the question *for her.*
close   prescribe   He cashed the check *for the customer.*
cash   Please, pronounce that word *for me.*
change   He changed the money *for me.*

- -

Exercise 5   Create English sentences with the following verbs with information from the following situations.

Situation: You went to the bank. The service at the bank was excellent.

1. answer   3. cash
2. open   4. change

Exercise 6   Create meaningful English sentences containing an indirect object with the following sentence parts.

1. give/present   5. send/a package
2. prescribe/a cough medicine 6. buy/a new car
3. show/new clothes   7. open/the window
4. pronounce/the word   8. pass/the salt
   "beverages"   9. explain/the passive voice

10. do/something nice
11. introduce/my new friend
12. find/a good apartment

13. say/something funny
14. ask/a favor

Verb — Noun Clause

There are many verbs in the English language that may be followed by a *that*-clause. Some of these *that*-clauses may be reduced to *to*-infinitive or gerund phrases, but others cannot be reduced at all.

However, almost all of these verbs have one thing in common: They express actions that require *mental* activity such as *thinking, speaking, forming an opinion,* or *influencing another person;* in other words, the subjects of these verbs are almost always humans.

The exact meaning of the verb and the content of the clause determine whether and how the clause may be reduced. Examine the sentences in the following diagram. Which verbs may be followed by a *that*-clause? Which verbs may be followed by a *to*-infinitive? Which verbs may be followed by a gerund?

The instructor announced that he would give us a test next week.

Announce means to give a notice.

The instructor decided that he would give us a test next week.
The instructor decided *to give* us a test next week.

Decide means to make up your mind to do something.

We thought that the test was very difficult.
We found the test *to be* very difficult.

Think means believe, have the opinion.

I remember that we took a test last week.
I remember *taking* a test last week.

Remember refers to something in the past.

I admit that I have not studied.
I admit not *having* studied.

Admit usually refers to something that isn't good.

I hate *studying* for tests.

Hate shows how you feel about something.

The meaning of the verb determines the form of the object. Try to answer the following questions and examine the sentences again. Can you draw some conclusions before you go on to the next sections?

When a person announces something, does that mean that he wants to do something? When a person decides to do something, does he usually want to do what he decides? When a person thinks that a test is difficult, is it a fact or an opinion? When a person remembers taking a test, what happened first, taking the test or remembering? When a person admits doing something, is he proud or not proud of it? Does the verb *hate* express an opinion or an attitude?

You will find the answers to the questions above in the next sections, in which each type of verb will be discussed separately. *Note:* As was mentioned earlier, the purpose of this chapter is not to make you memorize the lists of verbs, but to help you develop a feeling for the language.

Verb — That-*Clause*

- -

He *announced* that we would have a test.　　He *reported* that the weather was bad.
He *declared* that the test would be difficult.　　He *said* that he was sick.
He *hinted* that the test would be long.　　He *indicated* that he wanted to leave.
He *remarked* that the food was good.　　He *complained* that the food was terrible.
He *notified* me that he had been accepted　　He *argued* that it was too late to leave.
He *assured* me that he would come.　　He *informed* me that he had received my letter.

- -

Verbs like *report,* which simply describe a mode of speaking, can be followed by *that*-clauses. These cannot be reduced. They report what somebody said or what happened as facts. The subject or the speaker of the sentence does not imply that he is unsure about the fact, that he wants to do something, or that he is giving his opinion.

Verb — Wh-*Clause*

- -

He *announced* to us what we would have to do.
He *announced* to us what to do.
He *told* us where we needed to go.
I don't *know* when the party starts.
I *wonder* who our next president will be.

- -

Verbs that express a mode of speaking or thinking can often be followed by a *wh*-clause. The *wh*-clause is usually preceded by an indirect object. If the *wh*-clause contains a modal, it is usually reduced to a *to*-infinitive construction.

Exercise 7　　Astronaut Navy Captain Bruce McCandless II spoke the following words during the first untethered space walk, February 7, 1984. Report what he said during the first few seconds of his spacewalk with the following verbs followed by a *that*-clause or a *wh*-clause. *Note:* Make sure that you apply the sequence-of-tense rule.

"Well, that may have been one small step for Neil, but it's a heck of a step for me. . . . Just for the record, I don't see any stars out here. . . . I'm trying to see what sort of landmass that is we're coming up on. It looks like Florida. It is Florida . . . . It's nice, the sun just came into my eyes; that's a little bright but not a big deal . . . . I show myself about eighty feet out, something like that. I could go faster, but why rush it?... Are you going to want the windows washed or something while I'm up here?... The view you get is like the difference between the view you get flying in a heavy aircraft looking out the little window and flying in a helicopter.... Is this Africa I'm coming over? Boy, it's beautiful down there."

1. announce	7. report
2. explain	8. say
3. hint	9. indicate
4. observe	10. complain
5. notify	11. learn
6. assure someone	12. see

Exercise 8   Pretend that you are an astronaut. In a short passage describe the feelings that you might have when you see the world from space. In your first sentence, use a descriptive adjective like *overwhelming* and support this adjective with the other sentences in your paragraph.

Uses of the *To*-Infinitive

Many verbs may be followed by *that*-clauses and/or *to*-infinitive objects. What verbs may be followed with a *to*-infinitive? Do these verbs have any special meaning? Why do we say: *I want to go* but *I enjoy going*?

When you look back over all the preceding chapters, you will see that very often a clause with a modal auxiliary verb, a wish-and-demand subjunctive, or an imperative can be substituted by an infinitive construction.

Look at the following examples:

Clause with Modal	To-Infinitive Construction
He went to the store so that he *might* buy some rice.	He went to the store *to buy some rice.*
He is so tired that he *cannot* study.	He is too tired *to study.*
He is so sleepy that he *can* go to sleep immediately.	He is sleepy enough *to go to sleep immediately.*
Mr. Johnson is the man whom you *should* see.	Mr. Johnson is the man *to see.*
I asked what I *should* do.	I asked what *to do.*
I advised that he *go.*	I advised him *to go.*
He commanded that the soldiers *attack.*	He commanded the soldiers *to attack.*
He said, "*Go* home!"	He said for me *to go home.*

The *to*-infinitive is used wherever in the past a subjunctive verb form or a modal auxiliary was required. Nowadays, a wish-and-demand subjunctive verb or a modal auxiliary sounds awkward and old-fashioned, so the *to*-infinitive is usually preferred. Therefore, by examining exactly when the subjunctive mood and the modal auxiliaries are required, we might better understand when the *to*-infinitive is used.

The following quotation, which describes the general use of the subjunctive, is taken from a book written by George O. Curme, a well-known grammarian.

> The function of the English subjunctive is to represent something, not as an actual reality, but only as desire, plan, demand, requirement, eventuality, conception, thought; sometimes with more or less hope of realization, or in the case of a statement with more or less belief; sometimes with little or no hope or faith. The subjunctive is also often used of actual facts, but it represents them as conceptions of the mind, general principles rather than as facts.... Thus though the subjunctive has a number of distinct functions, they are all united in a higher unity — they all represent the action or state as a conception of the mind rather than as a reality.

The last sentence is the key sentence: the subjunctive represents the action or state as *a conception of the mind* — as an idea, a plan, or an opinion.

For example, all the modal auxiliaries express ideas and opinions rather than facts. In the sentences *I may go, I must go, I should go,* or *I can go,* it is not a fact that I will go, only a possibility. Likewise, in the sentence *I want to go,* it is not a fact that I will go, only an idea.

In general, we can say that verbs that express conceptions of the mind, which in the past were followed with subjunctive clauses or clauses with modal auxiliaries (to express fulfillable wishes, demands, contrary-to-fact situations, permission, ability, necessity, uncertainty, expectation, advisability, moral obligation, daring, need, and so on), can be followed by *to*-infinitives. We will divide these verbs into two main groups:

1. verbs that express an idea or plan, and
2. verbs that express an opinion.

To Express a Plan or Idea

The verbs in this group express meanings similar to the meanings of the modal auxiliaries. Most of the following verbs express the notion that an idea or a plan has been formed in the mind. Usually, the subject wants something to happen in the future. These verbs express a degree of willingness (or unwillingness) on the part of the subject. In fact, many verbs in this general group could be replaced with *want.* Example: *I decided that I would go. First I thought about it, and then I wanted to go.*

Verbs like *Decide*

	That-Clause with Modal	To-Infinitive Construction
A fulfillable wish	I *hope* that I will be there on time. I *pray* that I will see you again.	I *hope to be* on time. I *pray to see* you again. (old-fashioned)
Intention	I *intend* that I will help you. I *planned* that I would go to the party. I *decided* that I would go. I *decided* that you would go. I *resolved* that I would help you. I *determined* that you should go. I *meant* that you should leave. I *arranged* that we would have a party. I *forgot* that I would mail the letter.	I *intend to help* you. I *planned to go* to the party. I *decided to go.* I *decided for you to go.* I *resolved to help* you. I *determined for you to go.* I *meant for you to leave.* I *arranged for us to have* a party. I *forgot to mail* the letter.
Expectation	I *expect* that I will arrive at ten.	I *expect to arrive* at ten.

Verbs like *decide* may be followed by a *that*-clause containing a modal, such as *will* or *shall,* or a *to*-infinitive construction. If the subject of the sentence and the infinitive are the same, the subject is not expressed. If the subjects of the two are not the same, the subject is expressed in a *for* phrase.

Exercise 9 Create meaningful English sentences with the following verbs with information from the following situation.

Situation: You were going on a picnic. What were your plans? What kinds of food and drinks were you going to bring? Who else was going?

1. hoped 5. meant
2. expected 6. forgot
3. intended 7. resolved
4. decided 8. arranged

Verbs like *Agree*

	To-Infinitive	For + To-Infinitive
Consent	I *agreed* to go. I *consented* to go.	I agreed for you to go.
Desire	I *seek* to succeed. I *want* to go. I *wish* to go.	I want (for) him to go. I wish for him to leave.

I *strive* to succeed.
I *struggle* to survive.

I *choose* to go.

I *prefer* to go.

I *deserve* to go.

I chose for him to go.

I prefer for you to go.

I deserve for him to help me.

Unfulfilled desire

I *failed* to help you.
I *neglected* to help you.
I cannot *afford* to buy a new car.

I cannot afford for you to buy a new car.

Refusal

I *decline* to accept the invitation.
I *refuse* to see him.

I *hesitate* to leave.

I *managed* to leave early.

I refuse for him to see me.

I hesitate for him to leave.

I managed for them to go.

Verbs like *agree,* which are usually followed by a *to*-infinitive phrase and not a *that*-clause, are similar in meaning to the *decide* group.

If the subject of the sentence and the infinitive are the same, the subject is not expressed, but if they are not, the subject of the infinitive is expressed in a *for*-phrase. (Those verbs that can be used with the *for*-pattern are given in the examples.)

Exercise 10 Create meaningful English sentences with the following verbs from information in the following situation.

Situation: You went shopping. You were trying to find a new car. You tried to get the most value for your money. You wanted power steering, automatic transmission, AM-FM radio, cruise control, tinted glass, air conditioning, and so on. To what agreement did you and the salesman come?

1. agree	5. hesitate
2. consent	6. manage
3. deserve	7. fail
4. decline	8. neglect

Verbs like *Beg*

Subjunctive *That*-Clause	To-Infinitive	Passive Construction
I demand that I be released.	I *demand* to be released.	
I command (him) that he leave now.	I *command* him to leave now.	He was commanded to leave.
I order (him) that he be on time.	I *order* him to be on time.	He was ordered to be on time.
I instruct (him) that he attend class.	I *instruct* him to attend class.	He was instructed to attend class.

I tell him that he should attend class.	I *tell* him to attend class.	He was told to attend class.
I forbid (him) that he watch that movie.	I *forbid* him to watch that movie.	He was forbidden to watch that movie.
I ask (you) that you stay.	I *ask* (for) you to stay.	You were asked to stay.
I ask you that I may stay.	I ask to stay.	
I beg (you) that you let him go.	I *beg* you to let him go.	You were begged to let him go.
I implore (him) that he help me.	I *implore* him to help me.	He was implored to help me.
I entreat (him) that he help me.	I *entreat* him to help me.	He was entreated to help me.
I required *of her* that she help me.	I *required* her to help me.	She was required to help me.
	I required for her to help me.	
I desire *of him* that he is polite.	I *desire* him to be polite.	
	I desire for him to be polite.	
I prefer (*of him*) that he leave now.	I *prefer* him to leave now.	
	I prefer for him to leave now.	
I ask *of you* that you stay.	I *ask* you to stay.	
	I ask for you to stay.	

Verbs like *beg,* which are the verbs requiring a subjunctive mood in a verb following a *that*-clause, also express a kind of willingness—they express what the subject wants another person to do. (See Chapters 4, 6, and 9)

Verbs that express a mode of *telling* someone something may take an indirect object, which becomes the subject of the infinitive, which, in turn, may become the subject of a passive sentence.

Verbs that express a request (favor) of a person can be followed by an *of*-indirect object. With these verbs, there are two possible constructions. Can you explain the difference between the two structures?

Verbs like *Teach*

	To-Infinitive	Passive Construction
Enablement	He *taught* me to speak English.	I was taught to speak English.
	He *enabled* me to succeed in my studies.	I was enabled to succeed in my studies.
	He *reminded* me to mail the letter.	I was reminded to mail the letter.
Request	He *wanted* me to be on time.	I was wanted (to be) on time.
	He *needed* me to help him.	I was needed to help him.
	He *invited* me to go to his house.	I was invited to go to his house.
Permission	He *allowed* me to go with him.	I was allowed to go with him.
	He *permitted* me to help him.	I was permitted to help him.
	He *forbade* me to go there.	I was forbidden to go there.

Encouragement	He *encouraged* me to study.	I was encouraged to study.
	He *inspired* me to study.	I was inspired to study.
Persuasion	He *convinced* me to enter the contest.	I was convinced to enter the contest.
	He *persuaded* me to take another course.	I was persuaded to take another course.
	He *induced* me to drink too much.	I was induced to drink too much.
	He *tempted* me to eat too much.	I was tempted to eat too much.
	He *challenged* me to drive fast.	I was challenged to drive fast.
	He *dared* me to drive fast.	I was dared to drive fast.
	He *provoked* me to hit him.	I was provoked to hit him.
	He *coerced* me to rob the bank.	I was coerced to rob a bank.
	He *got* me to sing a song.	
	He *caused* me to drop my book.	I was caused to drop my book.
	The weather *forced* me to leave.	I was forced to leave.

- -

Verbs like *teach* are similar to the verbs like *beg,* but they can be followed only by a *to*-infinitive and not by a subjunctive clause.

All these verbs express the notion that the subject of the verb has influence, authority, or power over another person (the indirect object of the verb, which may become subject of a passive sentence) and that the subject wants or is willing for the other person to do something. Note that the examples are ordered to the degree of influence that the subject of the sentence has over the other person.

Exercise 11   Create meaningful English sentences with the verbs in the sentences below by using information from the following passage.

Robinson Crusoe was modeled after a real person, sailor Alexander Selkirk. His ship was anchored to make repairs in September 1704 at a deserted island called Mas a Tierra, 400 miles off the coast of Chile. Selkirk quarreled with his captian just as the ship was about to leave. In his anger he demanded to be put ashore. His request was granted.

Selkirk was marooned on the island. He was able to survive by eating fish and turtles. Later he hunted goats. He made pets of the wild cats that roamed free, and used them to help control a booming rat population. He made clothing from goatskins and read his Bible to keep his mind alert. For more than four years, Alexander Selkirk lived entirely alone. In 1709 a passing ship saw Selkirk's signal fire and rescued him.

1. After his fight with the captain, Selkirk wanted to be _____

   _____ .

2. During his exile, he was challenged to _____

   _____ .

3. Selkirk taught himself to _____ .

4. The fish and turtles enabled him to _____

_____ .

5. Because he did not have any clothes he was forced to _____

_____ .

6. The wild cats roaming around free allowed him to _____

_____ .

7. Reading his Bible every day forbade his mind to _____

_____ .

8. The booming rat population provoked him to _____

_____ .

9. Selkirk's signal fire caused a passing ship to _____

_____ .

10. Probably after his rescue, Selkirk was motivated to _____

_____ .

11. He probably did not again persuade a captian to _____

_____ .

12. After his four-year exile, he was probably not again inspired to

_____ .

Exercise 12   Complete the sentences below with *to*-infinitive phrases. Your sentences should be true according to the information in the passage and grammatically correct.

(a) Leonardo da Vinci created two of the world's most famous paintings, *The Last Supper* and *The Mona Lisa*. (b) But the great Italian artist was so busy learning that he completed very few paintings in his lifetime.

(c) Leonardo studied the way that light and shadow blend so that his paintings would be more lifelike. (d) He studied the muscle and bone structure of humans and animals and made careful, detailed drawings of what he saw.

(e) But more astonishing is the wide variety of the inventions he dreamed of. (f) Leonardo's notebooks contain the earliest known diagrams for a parachute, a helicopter, a paddlewheel boat, a self-propelled car, and many other advanced ideas.

(g) These ideas were impractical in the late 1400s and early 1500s. (h) Today they are a part of everyday life. (i) Leonardo was a man whose ideas were hundreds of years ahead of his time and technology.

a. Leonardo da Vinci managed _____ .

b. But, instead of painting, Leonardo preferred _____

_____ .

c. In order to make his painting more lifelike, he decided _____

_____ .

d. The study of the muscle and bone structure enabled him _____

_____ .

e. Leonardo wanted _____ .

f. Leonardo hoped _____ .

g. These ideas failed _____ .

h. People today could not manage _____

_____ .

i. I don't hesitate _____ that Leonardo

was a man _____ .

j. Leonardo deserves _____ .

Exercise 13 Write a paragraph describing how you were able to make a difficult decision. Describe what your plans, your expectations, and your hopes were. Also describe how the permission, encouragement, and persuasion of another person affected your decision.

To Express Opinions

There are two types of verbs that express the opinion of either the subject of the sentence or the speaker. There are also some adjectives that may express the opinion of a speaker. These verbs and adjectives may be followed by *that*-clauses and *to*-infinitives.

Note: There is one important difference between the *to*-infinitive expressing a plan or an idea and the one expressing an opinion. The *to*-infinitive expressing a plan or idea usually refers to a future event. Example: *He decided to go.* (First he decided; then he went.) On the other hand, the *to*-infinitive expressing an opinion may refer to something present, future, or past (with a perfect infinitive). Example: *He is believed to be sick (now)* or *He is believed to have been sick (past).*

Verbs like *Believe*

That-Clause with Be-Verb	To-Infinitive	Passive Construction
I *feel* that John is very lazy.	I feel John to be very lazy.	He is felt to be very lazy.
I *imagine* that John is considerate.	I imagine him to be considerate.	He is imagined to be considerate.
I *fancied* that John was rich.	I fancied him to be rich.	He was fancied to be rich.
I *believe* that he is sick.	I believe him to be sick.	He was believed to be sick.
I *suppose* that he is resting.	I suppose him to be resting.	He was supposed to be resting.
I *presume* that he is a hard worker.	I presume him to be a hard worker.	He was presumed to be a hard worker.
I *thought* that he was a good worker.	I thought him to be a good worker.	He was thought to be a good worker.
I *judged* that he was guilty.	I judged him to be guilty.	He was judged (to be) guilty.
I *hold* that he was responsible.	I hold him (to be) responsible.	He was held responsible.
I *understand* that he is a good worker.	I understand him to be a good worker.	He is understood to be a good worker.
I *trust* that he is helpful.	I trust him to be helpful.	
I *calculated* that it was costly.	I calculated it to be costly.	It was calculated to be costly.
I *considered* that he was a weak leader.	I considered him to be a weak leader.	He was considered (to be) a weak leader.
I *revealed* that he was guilty.	I revealed him to be guilty.	He was revealed to be guilty. He was revealed (to be) guilty.
I *proved* that he was guilty.	I proved him to be guilty.	He was proven to be guilty. He proved (to be) guilty.

The verbs in the examples, which are all basically synonyms of *believe,* express an opinion, not a fact. (Example: the sentence *I believe that he went to the store* expresses not a fact but a degree of uncertainty.) The examples are ordered according to the degree of uncertainty expressed by the verb, beginning with the greatest degree of doubt and ending with just a slight degree of doubt. Some verbs have more than one meaning. In this list they are all used as near synonyms of *believe.*

Note the possible grammatical reductions: When the noun clause contains the linking verb *be,* it may be reduced to a *to be*-phrase, which in turn may occur in passive constructions. Example: *I believe him to be rich. He is believed to be rich.* And, in very formal written English, the infinitive *to be* is sometimes deleted. This construction may also occur in the passive voice. Example: *I believed him to be rich* becomes *I believed him rich. (He was believed [to be] rich).*

The passive forms of *reveal* and *prove* can, in turn, be changed to active forms, so that they may function as linking verbs when *to be* is deleted.

Exercise 14   With the verbs listed below, create meaningful English sentences based on information from the following situation. You may use *that*-clauses or *to*-infinitive constructions.

Situation: There is a student in your class. His father is very rich; he has an oil well. The student has a sports car. He wears new, expensive clothes. Make some educated guesses about this person. (Where do you think he is from? Does he have to worry about money? How much allowance does he get every month? And so on.

1. doubt   5. think
2. imagine   6. understand
3. guess   7. consider
4. suppose   8. prove

Verbs like *Pretend*

That-Clause	To-Infinitive
He *pretended* that he had a lot of money.	He pretended to have a lot of money.
He *claims* that he plays tennis well.	He claims to play tennis well.
He *proclaims* that he is innocent.	He proclaims to be innocent.
He *professed* that he was my friend.	He professed to be my friend.

Verbs like *pretend* are very similar to the *believe* group in meaning and structure. *To pretend something* means *to make another person believe.* Example: *He pretended that he was leaving* means that he tried to make people believe that he was leaving. In other words, the clause expresses a contrary-to-fact statement. The speaker of the sentence does not believe he was leaving.

A clause after a verb like *pretend* can be reduced to an infinitive form even if it does not contain the verb *be.* A passive construction is possible if the subject of the sentence and the subject of the *that*-clause are not the same. Example: *He proclaims that we are rich* becomes *He proclaims to be rich* (no passive). But: *He proclaims that they are innocent* becomes *They are proclaimed (to be) innocent.*

Exercise 15   With the verbs listed below, create meaningful English sentences based on information from the following situation.

Situation: You are in a courtroom. The defendant acts as if he were not guilty. He says that he was not on the scene at the time of the murder. He says he has an alibi. He says he went to the movie at the time the murder was committed. He says he did not know the victim. You don't believe this person at all because you saw him commit the murder.

1. pretend   4. proclaim
2. claim   5. profess
3. maintain

Verbs like *Seem*

That-Clause	*To-Infinitive*		*Adjective*
It *seems* that he is sick.	He seems to be sick.		He seems sick.
It *seems* that he is a doctor.	He seems to be a doctor.	NOT:	He seems a doctor.
It *appears* that he is happy.	He appears to be happy.		He appears happy.
It *appears* that he is a student.	He appears to be a student.	NOT:	He appears a student.
It *happened* that he was there.	He happened to be there.		

Seem and *appear,* which also express the opinion of the speaker, can be used in constructions with *to be,* which may be deleted when an adjective follows. The verb *happen* when it expresses a chance occurrence is used with a similar type of *to*-infinitive construction.

Exercise 16
With the verbs listed below, create good English sentences based on information from the following situation.

Situation: A bank is being robbed. What do the robbers demand? What do the bank employees say? What do the customers in the bank say? How do the robbers, bank employees, and customers act?

1. demand   6. seem
2. command   7. appear
3. order   8. happen
4. instruct   9. pretend
5. implore   10. claim

Exercise 17
Rewrite the following information using verbs of opinion and *to*-infinitive constructions. (See the list of verbs on p. 339)

EXAMPLE:

The Babylonians imagined the world to be an island.

The Babylonians thought that the universe was as follows: The earth is an island. It rises from the middle of a great sea. If a man could travel far enough beyond the horizon, to the end of the sea, he would come to a range of mountains that disappear in the clouds. Those mountains encircle the sea and hold up the solid dome of the sky. The heavenly dome is the ceiling of the world. The mountains are the walls. And the island earth with its surrounding sea is the floor.

After Adjectives Expressing an Opinion

An adjective can also express a speaker's opinion about an action or his judgement on the behavior of a person. Example: John completed a course. He thought that was difficult. He might say: *It was difficult to complete the course.* Another example: John interrupted his teacher several times. You might say: *It was very rude of John to interrupt the teacher.*

- -

It is necessary that they help us.
It is necessary for them to help us.

- -

Adjectives expressing an opinion may occur with *that*-clauses or *to*-infinitive constructions, both of which usually occur with a temporary *it*. Some infinitives have a *for*-subject and some an *of*-subject.

- -

It is important *for you* to come on time.	*What* is important? (Not *Who* is important.)
It is foolish *for you* to be late.	*What* is foolish? For you to be late is foolish.
It is foolish *of you* to come late.	*Who* is foolish? You are foolish.
It is generous *of you* to help.	*Who* is generous? (Not *What* is generous.)

- -

The choice between a *for-* or an *of*-subject depends on whether the adjective describes the quality of an action or the quality of a person.

The following lists of adjectives are divided into four groups: those that describe an action, those that describe a person, those that may describe both, and those that describe an emotion. Near-synonyms or opposites are given with each one.

- -

Adjectives Followed by *For*-Phrase + Infinitive

It was *useful* (for him) to review the grammar.	useful; worthwhile; useless
It is *important* (for a student) to be prepared.	important; necessary; essential; pertinent; relevant
It is *delightful* (for her) to watch her baby.	delightful; pleasant
It is *difficult* (for you) to speak English?	difficult; easy; hard
Is it *possible* (for us) to stay there?	possible; impossible
It is *fatal* for them to inhale the gas.	fatal; hopeless
It is *beneficial* (for me) to study in the library.	beneficial; (dis)advantageous
	advisable; good; preferable

Adjectives Followed by *For-* or *Of*-Phrase + Infinitive

It was *discourteous* of you (or: for you) to interrupt.	(dis)courteous; impertinent; (im)polite; (im)proper; rude
It was *foolish* of you (or: for you) to jump in the water.	foolish; rash; stupid; (un)wise
It was *noble* of you (or: for you) to help the poor.	noble; wicked; loyal; malicious

It was *right* of you (or: for you) to say that.   right; wrong
It was *strange* of him (for him) to be so quiet.   strange; (un)natural

Adjectives Followed by *Of*-Phrase + Infinitive

It was *generous* of you to help me.   generous; good; worthy; nice; magnificent; intelligent

Emotive Adjectives

It is *alarming* to see so many dead birds.   alarming; startling; disturbing; troubling; terrifying; shocking
It is *amazing* to see him jump so high.   amazing; surprising; astonishing; astounding; puzzling
It is *pleasing* to watch the children play.   pleasing; interesting; entertaining; amusing; exhilarating; fascinating; intriguing
It is *annoying* to have to do so much work.   annoying; irritating; disappointing; embarrassing; disgusting; distressing

---

Exercise 18   Read the following passage. Then reword the information given to fit the unfinished sentences below.

A 14-year-old gymnast from Romania made world headlines at the 1976 Montreal Olympics. Nadia Comaneci had done what once seemed impossible. She had made a perfect score of 10 out of 10 points in an Olympic gymnastic event. Even the scoreboard computers couldn't keep up with her excellence. They were set to go only as high as 9.9.

Nadia kept on giving flawless performances during the Olympic competition. She scored three more 10s on the uneven bars and then three on the balance beam, winning the gold medal in each event. Her record-breaking overall score gave Nadia a third gold medal: as best all-around woman gymnast!

1. It was exhilarating _____ world headlines at the 1976 Montreal Olympics.

2. Before Nadia Comaneci, people thought it was impossible _____ _____ in an Olympic gymnastic event.

3. Even for the scoreboard computers it was difficult _____ _____ .

4. It was possible for them only _____ .

5. It was astonishing that _____ .

6. It was not easy for her _____ .

7. It seemed easy for her _____ in each event.

8. Her record-breaking overall score was high enough _____

_____ as best all-around woman gymnast!

Exercise 19   Read the following passage. It is written in choppy sentences. Use the information given to write a coherent paragraph of your own. Give your opinion about Edison. Try to use at least five *to*-infinitive constructions.

> Thomas Edison was one of the greatest inventors in history. He came up with improvements in the motion picture camera, the storage battery, the telephone, and the light bulb. One of the cleverest inventions was the phonograph.
>
> He came up with the idea in 1877. He sketched plans. An assistant built a working model. The assistant brought him the new instrument. Edison put a piece of tinfoil in it. He lowered a needle onto the foil. He turned a crank. He recited the words "Mary had a little lamb."
>
> Edison moved the needle back to the starting position. He turned the crank again. He and his assistant were thrilled. They heard Edison's voice coming from the machine. Thomas Edison's recital of a nursery rhyme was the world's first phonograph recording.

> EXAMPLE:
>
> *I believe Thomas Edison to have been one of the greatest inventors in history.*

Uses of the Gerund

There are several differences between verbs that are followed by a *to*-infinitive and verbs that are followed by a gerund. First of all, a *to*-infinitive usually refers to something that will happen later, but the gerund may refer to a past event. Example: *I decided to go to the movies.* (First I decided; then I went.) But: *I acknowledged having gone (or going) to the movies.* (I acknowledge now that I went to the movies earlier.) In addition the *to*-infinitive usually expresses a planned event; gerunds, on the other hand, often express an attitude about an event.

To Report Past Events

Not every verb that reports a past event can be followed by a gerund phrase. There are two types of verbs that may be followed by a *that*-clause or a gerund phrase: verbs like *remember* and *admit*.

Verbs like *Remember*

That-Clause	Gerund
I remember that I helped you yesterday.	I *remember* helping you.
I recall that I saw John yesterday.	I *recall* seeing John yesterday.

I recollect that I mailed the letter.	I *recollect* mailing the letter.
I will never forget that I saw this beautiful play.	I will *never forget* seeing this beautiful play.

BUT:

I remembered that I was to bring the book.	I remembered to bring the book.
I forgot that I was to help you.	I forgot to help you.

Verbs like *remember* may be followed by a gerund phrase if the gerund describes an event that took place before the act of remembering.

Note: Remember and *forget* may be followed by either a gerund or a *to*-infinitive phrase depending on whether it expresses an event that was planned for the future or an event that took place before the moment of remembering. Example: What did you do last night? *I remember visiting my friend.* But: Did you forget your homework? *No, I remembered to bring it.*

Recall and *recollect* can be followed only by a gerund phrase, not by a *to*-infinitive phrase, because they express past events only.

Exercise 20   Change each verb in parentheses to a *to*-infinitive or gerund phrase.

Last night I forgot (do) my homework. I remember (sit) in front of the TV and (talk) to my friend. He reminded me (do) the last exercise in Chapter 10, but I had forgotten (bring) my book home from the library. I recalled (go) there and (study) there, but I could not recollect (put) my book back in my bag. I will never forget (be) so careless! Next time I will not forget (put) my books in my bag.

Verbs like *Admit*

That-Clause	Gerund
He *acknowledged* that he was tired.	He acknowledged being tired.
He *admits* that he stole the money.	He admits stealing the money.
He *confessed* that he had robbed the bank.	He confessed having robbed (or robbing) the bank.
He *regretted* that he had hurt her feelings.	He regretted having hurt her feelings.
He *denied* that he had stolen the money.	He denied having stolen (or stealing) the money.

As you saw in the section called "Verb—Noun Clause," several verbs of reporting may be followed by a *that*-clause (Example: *He announced that we would have a test.*) This small group of verbs of reporting may be followed by either a *that*-clause or a gerund phrase, because they do not merely report an event but express the notion that the subject does or did not really want to say or agree with what is being said. In other words, by using one of these verbs, the speaker shows that the subject of the sentence had a negative attitude towards saying something.

Acknowledge, admit, and *confess* all express the meaning that the subject was unwilling or not eager to say that something is true. Of these verbs, *acknowledge* expresses a slight degree of unwillingness and *confess* a great degree of unwillingness. *Deny* expresses the meaning that the subject does not agree with the statement in the *that*-clause.

Exercise 21   With the verbs listed below, create meaningful English sentences based on information from the following situation. Use a gerund when possible.

Situation: You are in the courtroom again. The defendant has finally given up. He said that he was guilty. He had not been to the movie at the time of the murder. He had gotten into a serious fight with the victim. He had gotten very angry. He had pulled his knife and he had killed the victim. He said that the murder was not premeditated.

1. remember   5. confess
2. recollect   6. regret
3. acknowledge   7. deny
4. admit   8. recall

To Express Consideration

The *to*-infinitive often expresses the idea that a person has made up his mind to do something, (Example: *He decided to go to the movies*); the gerund, on the other hand, often expresses the idea that a person is thinking about something before he makes a decision.

Verbs like *Consider*

- -

I *am thinking about* going to the movies.
I *am considering* going for a walk.
I *am contemplating* staying home tonight.

We *were discussing* having a party.
We *were talking about* having a party for the class.

- -

These verbs express the idea not that the subject has made up his mind to do something or that he wants to do something, but that he is merely thinking about the advantages and disadvantages.

Exercise 22   Complete the sentences below with information from the following situation.

Situation: The class is planning an end-of-the-year party. There are several plans that are being considered. The following questions must be answered: When and where is the party going to be? Who will bring food, drinks, napkins, cups, and so on? What kinds of foods will there be?

1. _____ is considering _____
   _____ .

2. _____ is thinking about _____
   _____ .

3. _____ is contemplating _____
   _____ .

4. _____ is discussing _____
   _____ .

5. _____ is talking about _____
   _____ .

Verbs like *Suggest*

That-Clause	To-Infinitive	Gerund
I *suggest* that you work hard.	I suggest for you to work hard.	I suggest working hard.
I *propose* that we change our plan.	I propose for us to change our plan.	I propose changing our plan.
I *recommend* that he seek help.	I recommend for him to seek help.	I recommend seeking help.
I *advise* that he go home.	I advise for him to go home.	I advise going home.
	I *encourage* him to work harder.	I encourage working harder.
I *advocate* that minors do not drive.	I advocate for minors not to drive.	I advocate no driving for minors.
		I *sanction* the punishing of criminals.

Verbs like *suggest* may be followed by gerunds or by *to*-infinitives. There is not a great deal of difference in meaning between the infinitive phrase and the gerund phrase, but there is a slight difference in tone. *I suggest for you to leave* expresses the idea that the subject of the sentence wants something. (I would like for you to leave.) On the other hand, *I suggest leaving* merely puts an idea up for consideration. (I think that leaving is a good idea. It is up to you whether you leave or not.)

To Express an Attitude

Whereas the *to*-infinitive is used to express the notion that someone's mind has been made up, the gerund may express something that is done intuitively, without conscious reasoning or study. Example: *I avoided seeing him.* In addition, verbs followed by gerunds may express a feeling, an attitude about something. They do not indicate that a person wants to do something. Example: *I enjoy swimming.* This sentence describes a positive attitude towards swimming. On the other hand, *I would like to swim* indicates that a person wants to swim. *Note:* Whenever these verbs are used with the hypothetical *would,* the verb must be followed by a *to*-infinitive.

- -

Gerund	To-Infinitive
I *enjoy* swimming.	
I *like* swimming.	BUT: I would like to swim.
I *love* swimming.	BUT: I would love to swim.
I *relish* living in a free country.	
I *don't mind* swimming.	
I *miss* living in my country.	

He *could not help* hitting the car.
   averted
   avoided
   evaded

He *shirked* going to the doctor.
   delayed
   deferred
   postponed
   put off

He *cannot bear* living in a mess.
   cannot stand
   cannot tolerate
   endure
   dislike
   detest
   hate   BUT: I would hate to live in a mess.
   resent
   scorn
   abhor
   disdain
   scorn

He *tried living in an apartment.*   BUT: He tried to leave early.
(He didn't like it.)   (He wanted to, but he couldn't.)

- -

Exercise 23   Read through the ad for Air-India. Then with the following verbs create meaningful English sentences based on the information in the ad or

AIR-INDIA'S NEW EXECUTIVE CABIN TO LONDON AND INDIA.

Extraordinary comfort at a comfortable price.

Air-India's new Executive Cabin. It's forty big, new seats that give you over three feet of leg room (more than anyone else to London, in fact).

It's a newspaper for every passenger, plus sleeping masks, slippers and comfortable muff-type headsets for music and the movie.

It's also free drinks, including champagne and wine, hot hors d'oeuvres, a choice of Continental or Indian food, plus dinner service that doesn't look like it came from an airline—which means crystal glasses, porcelain plates and damask table linens.

Air-India's new Executive Cabin to London and India. It goes a long way to making a long way feel more comfortable. At a price you will be comfortable with, too.

For details and reservations, see your travel agent or Corporate Travel Manager.

Executive Cabin Flights include free N.Y. Helicopter service between Manhattan, LaGuardia, Newark and Kennedy.

ANANDA SHANKAR'S **DANCES OF INDIA.**
An Associate Program of The Festival of India.
Carnegie Hall, Sat., May 26, 8 P.M.
Tickets at box office or call (212) 977-7700

एअर-इंडिया **AIR-INDIA**

THE EXECUTIVE CABIN
400 Park Avenue, New York, NY 10022
Executive Reservation Service
Monday through Friday—9 AM to 5 PM
Continental U.S. 800-223-2250; N.Y. State 800-442-4455; N.Y. City 212-407-1456

concerning other things that you do or do not enjoy when you travel by plane.

1. enjoy	8. hate
2. love	9. resent
3. don't mind	10. scorn
4. avoid	11. dislike
5. shirk	12. try
6. dread	13. can't help
7. cannot bear	14. like

Related Structures

A few groups of verbs, most of which were discussed in Chapter 2, are followed by present participle or plain infinitives. These are verbs of aspect, verbs of perception, verbs like *catch,* and verbs like *have.*

Verbs of Aspect

-ing Form	*To*-Infinitive
He *began* dancing.	He began to dance.
He *commenced* attending classes.	
He *started* singing.	He started to sing.
He *went* dancing.	
He *continued* working.	He continued to work.
He *kept on* writing.	
He *keeps* working.	
He *is busy* working.	
He *spends time* painting.	
He *finished* working.	
He *gave up* working.	
He *ceased* working.	
He *stopped* working.	BUT: He stopped to rest.

Just as the verb *be* is an auxiliary of progressive aspect, verbs like *begin, continue,* and *stop* may be regarded as helping verbs showing that an action is in progress.

Some of these verbs may be followed by only a present participle and some by either a present participle or a *to*-infinitive. However, since *to*-infinitives can only denote futurity, only verbs of beginning and continuing, not those of stopping, are used with *to*-infinitives.

There is very little difference in meaning between a verb followed by a present participle or a *to*-infinitive. However, one could say there is a slight difference in aspect. Example: *He started to go.* (He had not started yet.) *He started going.* (The action of going had already started.)

In addition, the present participle seems to emphasize the continuation of the action. Example: *He continued going to that store.* (He shopped there regularly.) On the other hand, the *to*-infinitive is used more often for a single event. Example: *After he had stopped for a minute, he continued to go to the store.*

The verb *stop* can also be followed by either a present participle or a *to*-infinitive, but in this case there is a great difference in meaning. *Stop* plus the present participle indicates that an action has stopped; a *to*-infinitive after *stop* is a reduced clause of purpose. (See Chapter 5.) Example: *He stopped driving.* (He stopped the action of driving.) But: *He stopped to eat.* (He stopped [an action] in order that he might eat.)

Exercise 24   With the verbs listed below, create meaningful English sentences based on information from the following situation.

Situation: A typical workday for nurses is busy. They make morning rounds, take patients' temperature, check blood pressure, give needed medicine, check and adjust IVs, fill out charts, report to the doctor, and so on.

1. begin
2. start
3. proceed
4. continue
5. quit
6. stop
7. keep on
8. finish

Verbs of Perception and Others

Most of the verbs in the following diagrams were discussed in Chapter 2. They are given here for a quick review.

Verbs of Perception

-ing Form	Plain Infinitive
I *saw* him walking down the street.	I saw him walk down the street.
I *observed* her teaching.	I observed her teach.
I felt a bug biting me.	I felt a bug bite me.
I *heard* the telephone ringing.	I heard the telephone ring.

Have, Let, and *Make*

He *had* them recite the poem.
She *let* them leave early.
We *made* her behave.

Catch, Find, Keep, and *Leave*

We *caught* him stealing the car.
We *found* him sitting in a corner.
They *kept* us waiting for an hour.
We *left* them laughing.

Help

We *helped* him paint the house.
We *helped* him to paint the house.

Verbs like *Necessitate*

The plan will *involve* borrowing money.
This job *entails* working independently.
His behavior *justifies* reprimanding him.
Our job *involves* interviewing people.

- -

Exercise 25   On a separate piece of paper, create meaningful English sentences with the following sentence parts.

1. see/rocket/be launched
2. catch/the dog/eat from the garbage can
3. let/my friend/borrow my car
4. hear/the administrator/complain about enrollment
5. keep/the teacher/stand
6. feel/the water/touch my fingers
7. entail/study hard
8. find/the president/peruse his papers
9. have/the barber/cut my hair
10. help/the instructor/grade papers
11. make/the doctor/explain the problem
12. involve/work hard
13. observe/the printer/set the type
14. justify/spending $100
15. let/the nurse/take blood pressure

Solving Problems

Besides having different meanings and functions, infinitives and gerunds have some simple structural differences between them (see Chapter 1), differences that will be briefly reviewed and discussed here.

Faulty Use of an Infinitive After a Preposition

A preposition can be followed by a gerund, but not by a *to*-infinitive. *Note:* There is a good reason for this. The particle *to* in front of the infinitive used to be a regular preposition like *on* or *in*. But it has lost almost all of its meaning. In the English language prepositions are never used together. It is therefore understandable that a *to*-infinitive is not found after a preposition. Sometimes it is difficult to distinguish the preposition *to* and the particle *to* in front of an infinitive. Usually, if the verb is used in a passive construction, it is followed by a preposition.

CORRECT:	I agreed to help you.
INCORRECT:	I agreed on to help you.
CORRECT:	I agreed on helping you.
CORRECT:	I am accustomed to helping you.
INCORRECT:	I am accustomed to help you.
CORRECT:	I am looking forward to helping you.
INCORRECT:	I am looking forward to help you.

Faulty Use of a Gerund After an Indirect Object

A gerund cannot come after an indirect object. Only a *to*-infinitive can come after an indirect object. However, the small groups of verbs discussed under "Related Structures" are each followed by a noun and a present participle.

INCORRECT:	I ask him going. (him = indirect object)
CORRECT:	I ask him to go.
INCORRECT:	I cause him going.
CORRECT:	I cause him to go.
INCORRECT:	I advise him going.
CORRECT:	I advise him to go.
CORRECT:	I advise going.
CORRECT:	I see him going.
CORRECT:	I caught him stealing an apple.

Faulty Use of a Gerund After an Adjective

An adjective is usually followed by a *to*-infinitive, not a gerund. However, one exception is the adjective *busy,* which is followed by an *-ing* form.

INCORRECT:	I am surprised seeing you.
CORRECT:	I am surprised to see you.
CORRECT:	I am surprised at seeing you.

INCORRECT:	I used to seeing him often.
CORRECT:	I used to see him often. (used to = would)
INCORRECT:	I am used to see him.
CORRECT:	I am used to seeing him. (used to = accustomed to)

INCORRECT:	It is necessary going.
CORRECT:	Going is necessary.
CORRECT:	To go is necessary.
CORRECT:	It is necessary to go.

INCORRECT:	I am afraid going.
CORRECT:	I am afraid to go.
CORRECT:	I am afraid of going.

Faulty Use of an Infinitive with a Past Meaning

The *to*-infinitive after verbs of willingness has a future meaning. The gerund, on the other hand, usually expresses a simultaneous or past event.

CORRECT:	I decided that I would help him.
CORRECT:	I decided to help him.

CORRECT:	I decided that I was too tired to go.
INCORRECT:	I decided to be too tired to go.

CORRECT:	I agreed that I would help him.
CORRECT:	I agreed to help him.

CORRECT:	I agreed that the test had been too difficult.
INCORRECT:	I agreed for the test to have been too difficult.

CORRECT:	I remember that I mailed the letter.
CORRECT:	I remember mailing the letter.

CORRECT:	I admit that I am wrong.
CORRECT:	I admit being wrong.

CORRECT:	I remembered that I would mail the letter.
CORRECT:	I remembered to mail the letter.

Look at the picture of the domed building in Rome called the Pantheon. Read the caption. The following exercise is about the Pantheon.

UP FRONT

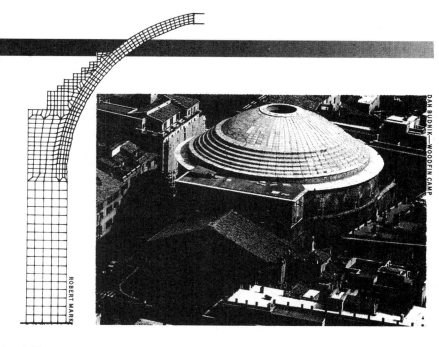

The Romans didn't girdle the dome of the Pantheon with rings just for decoration, but to hold it up—apparently in a novel way. This computer's-eye view of a cross section of the wall and roof of the venerable temple provides a clue to the secret.

ROBERT MARK

DAN BUDNIK—WOODFIN CAMP

Exercise 26   In the following passage, change the verbs in parentheses to finite verbs, gerunds, or *to*-infinitives. Explain your choices. For clues, look at the diagram above.

Since it was built some nineteen centuries ago, at the height of the Roman Empire, the Pantheon has never ceased (awe) visitors to Rome. But researchers have always been interested in (study) what the staying power is of its 142-foot wide dome, the world's largest for a millennium and a half.

Until now, architects have believed its endurance (be related) to the strength of Roman concrete. But a new study at Princeton Universtiy proposes that the real explanation (lie) in the curious step-like rings at the base of the dome.

Traditionally, these rings were presumed (act) like a hoop, keeping the fourteen-story-high dome in compression and preventing it from (collapse) under its weight. But Princeton engineer Robert Mark had his doubts. He said it was important (understand) that even modern concrete, which is stronger than the Romans', has very little tensile strength, or ability to resist (be) torn apart. "No designer would consider (build) a concrete dome without steel reinforcing rods," says Mark. "The concrete codes wouldn't allow it."

So, with the help of architecture historian Slobodan Curcic and student Fred Hutchinson, he decided (devise) a computer model to simulate the stresses acting within the Pantheon. Only when the researchers assumed that the concrete (have) little or no tensile strength was it possible for the model (predict) accurately the pattern of cracks in the building. This enabled him (conclude) that the rings aren't acting as a hoop.

What are they doing then? They are thought (perform) a function similar to the buttresses of a Gothic cathedral, says Mark, who for a long time has been dedicated to (study) these medieval edifices. The extra weight of the rings, he says, helps (stabilize) the lower portion of the dome: "Rather than functioning like a conventional dome, the Pantheon seemed (behave) like a circular array of arches, with the weight of the rings holding each arch in place." If the Roman builders had omitted the rings, would the Pantheon still be standing? Mark admitted not (have) looked at that question in great detail, but he assumed the probability of failure (have) been far greater.

The use of infinitives and participles is also confusing because they can be used in so many parts of the sentence: in the verb phrase and as part of a nominal, adjectival, or adverbial.

The following chart summarizes the uses of the verb forms that have been discussed in this text. After studying this chart, proceed to Exercise 27.

Infinitive		Present participle	Past participle
to-infinitive	plain infinitive		
IN THE VERB PHRASE			
after semi-modals	after modals	after progressive *be*	after perfect *have*
I have to go.	I must go.	I am listening.	I have read the book.

after *do*		after passive *be*
I don't like it.		The book was read by me.

AS NOMINAL

---

after verbs of planning	after *have, let, make*	after verbs like *remember*
I decided to go.	I had him paint the house.	I remember going there.
after verbs of opinion	**after verbs of perception**	**after verbs like *consider***
I believe him to be wrong.	I heard him sing.	I considered going there.
after adjectives of opinion	**after *help***	**after verbs of attitude**
It is necessary to go.	I helped him paint.	I enjoy swimming.
after *begin, start*, etc.		**after *begin, start*, etc.**
He started to talk.		He started talking.
in reduced *wh*-clauses		**after verbs of perception**
I don't know where to go.		I heard him singing.
		after *catch, find*, etc.
		I kept him waiting.

AS ADJECTIVAL

---

in reduced modal clause	in reduced active clause	in reduced passive clause
The man to see is Mr. Smith.	The man sitting there is....	The man seen by him is....
after nouns like *decision*		
His decision to go was wise.		

AS ADVERBIAL

---

to express purpose	to express time/reason	to express time/reason
He went to the store to buy....	Being interested, I read....	Interested in the movie, I....
to express negative result	**to express means/manner**	
He is too tired to study.	He sat in the chair sleeping.	
to express positive result	**in reduced clause with conjunction**	
I am smart enough to pass the test.	When studying, turn off the radio.	

- -

Exercise 27   The following exercise discusses a book written by Joseph Needham, who studied the Chinese culture. It tests your ability to relate structure to meaning. Read the passage below. Then change each verb form in parentheses to an appropriate form. It should be one of the following:

1. a finite form in the present or past tense
2. an infinitive form
3. an *-ing* form
4. a past participle form
5. an abstract noun form (singular or plural)

For more than thirty-five years, Joseph Needham has been (do) what he (call) "reconnaissance" work on twenty-five centuries of Chinese (think) in the fields of science, technology, and medicine. (train) as a biochemist at Cambridge University, Needham was (inspire) in 1937 by the (arrive) of several Chinese researchers (learn) their language, and then to wonder why modern science (have) originated only in Europe. After a posting to China in World War II, he proceeded (pursue) that question, and the result is his (pioneer) series: *Science and Civilization in China.* To date four volumes have been (publish), but at age eighty-one he has (predict) his series (run) to about twenty volumes. Five lectures he (give) in Hong Kong, (publish) as *Science in Traditional China,* give a brief but (detail) look at the work of this remarkable man.

A recent story in *The Sciences* magazine (suggest) just how remarkable he (be). (travel) in China years ago, Needham and some Chinese friends were (approach) by a band of marauders on horseback. Needham walked slowly forward, (bow) solemnly, performed an English folk dance, bowed again and (return) to his group. One of the horsemen then dismounted, did a (dance) of his own and (withdraw). End of threat.

Needham had begun his (study) by (wonder) why the experimental methods (develop) in Galileo's time did not (arise) in China. He soon discovered that for fourteen centuries before Galileo, the Chinese had (learn) much more about the natural world and how (use) it. They were way ahead of the West in the systematic (study) of astronomy, optics, acoustics, and magnetism; they (develop) the world's first decimal system, seismograph, biological pest control, and gunpowder; they (have) a prototype wave theory in physics and such sophisticated ideas and tools that in the eighth century they (conduct) a geodetic survey of a 2,500 kilometer meridian arc.

The origins of modern chemistry have long been (credit) to ancient and medieval alchemy, but it turns out that Chinese alchemists were busily (mix up) elixirs for immortal life about two centuries before the Greeks tried (turn) base metal into gold. Far from (dismiss) alchemy as arrant superstitious nonsense, Needham explains how much the Chinese (learn) about the nature of chemical change, how their (know) was (disseminate) by Persian and Arab merchants, and how the medical (preoccupy) of Chinese alchemists differed from the metallurgical (interest) of the Greeks. Paracelsus, much later, said: "The business of alchemy is not (make) gold, but (prepare) remedies for human ills."

No (discuss) of Chinese science would be complete without a reference to acupuncture, and Needham (offer) several (explain) for the way this mysterious (treat) works as an analgesic: perhaps the needles block the (transmit) of pain signals to the brain—or they may stimulate the body's own morphine analogues, endorphin and enkephalin.

Needham seeks an answer to his original question—why modern science (do) not develop in China after the eighteenth century—in the (differ) between Chinese and Western attitudes toward time and change. In the end he (conclude) that Chinese culture, like European culture, is (dominate) by linear concepts and that the failure spontaneously (develop) modern natural science had nothing to do with Chinese attitude toward time. For him (suspend) judgment and (leave) so large a question not (answer) is not an (admit) of defeat but an act of the greatest intellectual discipline. As Sir Richard Burton (write) in the nineteenth century, "He knows not how (know) who knows not also how (unknown)."

Exercise 28 In a brief paragraph explain what Joseph Needham wanted to find out and what his conclusion was after all his research. Also explain what the last sentence has to do with Needham's conclusion.

Read through the ad about the space station several times and do not look up words until you have a general idea of its content. Then proceed to the following exercises and questions, which are designed to help you understand the meaning of the words and the general contents of the ad.

Exercise 29 Complete the following sentences. Your sentences should be grammatically complete and based on the first part of the ad about the space station.

1. A manned space station will enable (use: *have*) _____

   _____ .

2. It will be possible to _____ beyond the Earth's limitations.

3. Scientists will enjoy (use: *work*) _____ in the space environment because _____ .

4. It also permits scientists (use: *scan*) _____ our planet without _____ .

5. Moreover, a lot of other out-of-this world advantages are _____

   _____ .

6. It makes good business sense (use: *have*) _____

   _____ .

7. Not only can a space station help (use: *revolutionize*) _____

   _____ , but it can also help (use: *create*) _____ .

8. It will be possible _____ with a manned space station.

9. It will be good for the people of the world _____

   _____ .

10. And a manned space station will permit America _____

    _____ .

THE WORLD NEEDS A PLACE LIKE NO PLACE ON EARTH—NASA SPACE STATION.

A manned space station will offer governments, industries and people opportunities that cannot be matched on Earth.

It will make possible technology advances held back by Earth's limitations. The space environment offers a weightless, vibrationless, moistureless, soundless vacuum in and with which to work; an obstruction-free perspective for scanning our planet and a host of other out-of-this-world advantages.

A manned space station makes good business sense. A space station can revolutionize medicine, metallurgy, communications, energy generation, meteorology and dozens of other sciences and technologies—ones that exist now, and

new ones a space station can help create.

A manned space station will help promote understanding. It will offer the people of the world an opportunity to unite in peaceful enterprise.

And a manned space station will help America maintain its momentum in space science and exploration.

Working to make the space station a reality.

For almost three decades, one company has been at work to make a manned space station operational. The name of that company is McDonnell Douglas.

Since 1959, space station studies have continued at McDonnell Douglas Astronautics Company without interruption—some com-

missioned by the government, others as our own investment. The thrust was always to set the pace. We've done analytical tool development. Design and test activities. Metallurgical studies. Wet workshop studies. Space cabin simulator operations. Thermal control development.

McDonnell Douglas' unwavering support for a human role in space is exhibited by its space life sciences department, maintained continuously for two and a half decades. We built the Mercury and Gemini spacecraft for NASA; provided launch stages for Apollo moon missions; and built and flew unmanned launch systems and spacecraft, learning to integrate them

with payloads and systems built by others.

Skylab was a forerunner.

McDonnell Douglas was NASA's contractor for Skylab, the first device that the world could call a space station. It was a gigantic system for its time. In it, American government and industry first explored the technologies and experimental projects that will find fulfillment in a space station of the 1990s.

But we need not dwell on laurels. Management, system integration and technical prowess gained in early programs continue: Payload integration on the space shuttle; shuttle simulation programs, astronaut training, and mission planning for NASA. In aerospace

programs throughout McDonnell Douglas, we draw on the skills of other major companies across America. We are NASA's integration contractor for the multi-nation European Spacelab, and we celebrate ongoing successes with international industry partners on a dozen different space, aviation and missile programs.

An experienced team.

We have teamed with Honeywell, IBM and RCA for a major segment of a NASA contract for definition and preliminary design of the

manned space station. And already we're developing the pharmaceutical technologies and the production factories that will find their full potential in the space station environment.

At McDonnell Douglas, our capabilities are focused on making a space station a reality by the next decade—and we offer exciting opportunities to companies and the men and women in them who want to help.

Because the world needs a place like no place on Earth.

MCDONNELL DOUGLAS

Exercise 30 The following sentence parts are from the second part of the ad, "Working to make the space station a reality." Restate them in your own words.

1. to have been at work to
2. to make something operational
3. without interruption
4. commissioned by
5. the thrust
6. to set the pace
7. metallurgical studies
8. wet workshop studies
9. space cabin simulator operations
10. unwavering support
11. a human role in space
12. space life sciences department
13. launch stages for Apollo moon missions
14. learning to integrate them with payloads and systems built by others.

Exercise 31 Fill in each blank with an appropriate word in the right form. Most of the blanks require only one word, but a few require a *to*-infinitive.

McDonnell Douglas had a _____ with NASA for Skylab, the first device for the world _____ a space station. It proved _____ a gigantic system for its time. In it, the technologies and experimental projects to be _____ in a space station of the 1990s were _____ for the first time.

But _____ on laurels is not necessary.

The ability _____ , the ability _____ systems, and the unprecedented ability to improve _____ that _____ gained in early programs continue. We have continued to _____ payloads on the space shuttle; we have _____ shuttle programs, _____ astronauts, and planned _____ for NASA. In aerospace programs throughout McDonnell Douglas, it has been _____ for us _____ on the skills of other major companies across America. We have a contract with NASA _____ the multination European Spacelab, and we have been _____ in a dozen different space, aviation, and missile programs _____ international industry partners.

Exercise 32 Use the following information to write a coherent paragraph. You may look at the original paragraph for ideas, but your sentences should have structures different from the ones in the ad.

   1. We formed teams with Honeywell, IBM, and RCA.
   2. Together we completed a major segment of a NASA contract.
   3. We defined and designed a manned space station.
   4. We developed pharmaceutical technologies.
   5. We developed production factories.
   6. These will be used in the space station environment.

Exercise 33 In your own words, state what the goals are at McDonnell Douglas.

Assignment for Writing

Group Discussion

   1. Why, in your opinion, did McDonnell Douglas put this ad in a major magazine?
   2. What is the purpose of Part I of this ad?
   3. The first sentence states: A manned space station will offer *governments, industries* and *people* opportunities that cannot be matched on earth.
    a. How will it offer opportunities to industries? Give three examples.
    b. How will it offer opportunities to governments? Give one example.
    c. How will it offer opportunities to people? Give five examples.
   4. How will the space environment help technology?
   5. How will a manned station make good business sense?
   6. How will a manned station help to promote understanding among people?
   7. How will a manned station help America maintain its momentum in space and exploration?

Writing

  Note: For this writing assignment you will have to do some research. Your teacher may want you to provide a bibliography and footnotes.

  Use one of the paragraphs in the first part of this ad (see questions 4, 5, 6, or 7) as your introductory paragraph.

  Support each point made in the paragraph with specific examples and details. You should have at least three paragraphs in the body of the composition and a conclusion.

  For example, in the second paragraph, the point to be proven is that technology will advance more in space because space does not have certain limitations that the Earth has. The paragraph mentions five specific differences between space and the Earth that are advantageous to the development of technology.

A manned space station will make possible technology advances held back by Earth's limitation. The space environment offers a (1) *weightless,* (2) *vibrationless,* (3) *moistureless,* (4) *soundless vacuum* in and with which to work; (5) an *obstruction-free perspective for scanning our planet* and (6) a host of *other out-of-this-world advantages.*

If you choose this paragraph as your introduction, you should show how each of these points make possible technology advances in space that are not possible on Earth.

Proofreading

When you have finished writing, and when you are satisfied with the content, organization, and supporting details, facts, and examples, it is time to proofread for grammar errors.

1. Read each paragraph separately. Is it coherent? Can the reader easily understand what you want to say? Have you used enough transitions? Can you combine more sentences?
2. Look at each sentence separately. Does it have a main clause? Are there any fused sentences, double conjunctions, fragments?
3. Look at each clause separately. Is it complete?
4. Look at each verb phrase separately. Subject-verb agreement, tense, voice, mood? Have you been consistent in your use of tenses?
5. Look at each verb form separately. Is it part of a verb phrase, nominal, adjectival, or adverbial? Does it have the right form? (Check the chart in this chapter.)
6. Look at each word separately. Check on spelling and capitalization. Check your use of articles and prepositions.

Appendix A: Writing Workshop

These are suggestions for group reading and group editing. Your instructor may want you to divide in groups and read and edit other students' papers. These lists will be useful for you not only to identify the strengths and weaknesses in their papers but also to check your own papers before you hand them in.

Reading for Content

Divide in groups of three. Quickly read through each essay; then together discuss each essay. One person reads the essay aloud, stopping after each paragraph to comment on and evaluate these questions:

Excellent Poor

5 4 3 2 1	a. Does the introduction prepare you for what is ahead?
5 4 3 2 1	b. Is the first sentence of the essay compelling? Does it make you want to read the composition?
5 4 3 2 1	c. Is the main idea clear?
5 4 3 2 1	d. Are the body paragraphs unified? Do they discuss only one topic?
5 4 3 2 1	e. Do you easily recognize the topic sentence or main idea in each paragraph?
5 4 3 2 1	f. Are arguments, statements, or generalizations supported with illustrations or examples?
5 4 3 2 1	g. Are transitions between sentences and paragraphs smooth and clear?
5 4 3 2 1	h. Does the conclusion restate the main idea of the essay?
5 4 3 2 1	i. Does the conclusion add an insight?
5 4 3 2 1	j. Is the writing detailed, concrete, and exciting, or is it vague, abstract, and difficult to grasp?

5 4 3 2 1					k. Are sentences varied and interesting or short, choppy, and boring?
5 4 3 2 1					l. Are the beginnings of the sentences varied?
5 4 3 2 1					m. Is the vocabulary varied and interesting or monotonous and boring?
5 4 3 2 1					n. Are words used appropriately or are they misused or overused?
5 4 3 2 1					o. Is the writing concise and to the point, or is it wordy (using more words than needed)?

Group Editing

Each student in the group takes a task (if necessary tasks 3 and 4 can be combined) and looks for only the errors mentioned. If the student is not sure about an error, he or she should consult the other students in the group or the instructor. Once sure about an error, the student underlines it and marks it with the appropriate code — for example, by putting a 1.a. by a suspected fragment.

Student 1. Read each *sentence* separately:
   a. Is it a complete sentence? Or is it a fused sentence, a comma splice, or a fragment?
   b. Is it clear, or is the wording awkward or unidiomatic?
   c. Could the sentence be combined with another sentence?
   d. Is it correctly punctuated?

Student 2. Look at each *verb phrase* in each sentence separately:
   a. Do the subject and verb agree?
   b. Is the tense appropriate?
   c. Has tense been used consistently?
   d. Have the other verb forms in the sentence been used correctly? (*-ing* form; *to*-infinitive; plain infinitive)

Student 3. Look at each *noun and pronoun* separately:
   a. Does each count noun have an article?
   b. Does each noun have the correct form? (singular or plural)
   c. Is each pronoun used correctly? (pronoun reference; pronoun case)

Student 4. Look at each *word* separately:
   a. Is it spelled correctly?
   b. Does it have the right form? (adjective or adverb; noun or verb, and so on)

Appendix B: The Use of Determiners

Every noun in every sentence needs a determiner like *the, a, this, each, some,* or *zero* (meaning no article). Suppose you use a noun and aren't sure whether or not you need a determiner; how can you find out? First, you need to determine which kind of noun it is: proper, count, or non count. This identification is easier said than done, however, because even a dictionary does not give you this information. The only way to really know is to have a feeling for the meaning of the noun and its subtle idiomatic uses, which can be developed only by being exposed to a great deal of the spoken and written language. A few rules, though, can help you develop a feeling for the use of determiners. To help internalize the use of determiners, you may want to expand the lists below with your own examples.

This diagram shows you what proper, count, and non-count nouns are. Then each one is discussed separately.

Proper:
John is my friend.
I like *New York*.
Where are the *Philippine Islands*?

A proper noun is the name of a person, thing, or place. It is generally not preceded by an article unless it is plural or contains a common noun like *republic* or *island*.

Count:
I bought a *book* in the university *bookstore*.
A task *force* has been formed.
It wants to find a serial *killer*.
Serial *killers* are dangerous.

A count noun is a noun that can be counted. It has a singular and a plural form. It has to be preceded by an article when it is used in the singular, but not in the plural.

Non count:
People need *food, water,* and *air*.
The fire created a lot of *smoke*.

A non-count noun does not have a plural form. It can be used with the article *the*, but not *a(n)*.

Proper Nouns

Most proper nouns do not use an article. Proper nouns which are plural or those which have a common noun, however, like *republic, kingdom, river, mountain, party,* or *dynasty* as a part of the name usually take an article.

The left column shows the proper nouns that take an article, and the right column those that don't.

Geographical Names

names of	with article	without article	
planets	the earth the planet Mars the universe	Earth, Mercury, Venus, Mars in space	
continents		Africa, Antarctica, Asia, Australia Europe, North America, South America	
countries	the Soviet Union the United States the Netherlands the Kingdom of Thailand the United Kingdom	Russia France America Taiwan Holland Cyprus Thailand Greece England Japan France Saudi Arabia Malaysia	Plural proper nouns or proper nouns containing a common noun take an article.
islands	the Philippines the Fiji Islands the Bahamas	Madagascar Bali Haiti	Groups of islands are plural and take the article.
cities	The Hague	Bombay Melbourne Tokyo Buenos Aires New York	Names of cities usually do not have an article unless the article is part of the name.
oceans seas gulfs, bays	the Pacific (Ocean) the Indian (Ocean) the Red Sea the Gulf of Mexico the Yellow Sea the Bay of Bengal	 Hudson Bay	With bodies of water the common nouns *ocean, river,* and so on are understood.
lakes	the Great Lakes	Lake Erie Lake Victoria	
rivers	the Mississippi (River) the Niger the Nile		
mountains	the Himalayas the Rocky Mountains the Rockies	Mount Everest Mount Elbert	

Like other proper nouns, names of buildings take an article when a common noun follows (or is understood) after the name, but when the common noun starts the name no article is used.

- -

Manmade Structures

universities colleges schools	the University of North Carolina the Sorbonne	Harvard University Georgia Tucker Elementary School Oxford University Louisiana State University
hotels motels inns	the Holiday Inn the Hilton (Hotel) the Grand Hotel	Hotel Alexander
buildings	the Empire State Building the Civic Center the Natatorium the Museum of Fine Arts the Smithsonian	Carnegie Hall Sandel Library Masur Museum St. Paul's Methodist Church Red Temple

		NOTE: to go to school, college,
		  university, church, town,
		  jail, prison
		to go home, downtown

boulevards avenues streets roads highways parks		Park Boulevard Rochelle Avenue Main Street White's Ferry Road Highway 80 Chenault Park Central Park
bridges towers	the Golden Gate Bridge the Eiffel Tower	

- -
- -

Time Expressions

seasons	in the winter in the summer	in winter in summer
holidays	the Fourth of July	Christmas, New Year, Ramadan Thanksgiving, Easter Chinese New Year
months days	the first of May the last day of the week	January, February, March, and so on Monday, Tuesday, Wednesday, and so on
parts of the day	in the afternoon in the morning during the day	at noon, at night, at midnight

- -

Names of People

the Johnsons	Mr. Johnson	Names of people usually do not
A Mr. Johnson called.	John, Carl	have an article unless they
The Mr. Johnson who lives	Judy, Linda	are plural or used in a
next to you is a teacher.		special sense.

If the noun is not a proper noun, it is either a count noun or a non-count noun. As you can see from the diagram below, both types take the article *the,* but only singular count nouns take the article *a(n).* (- means no article.)

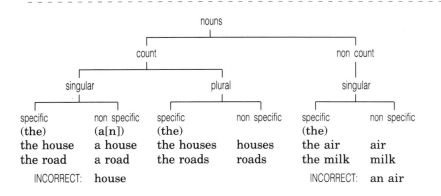

INCORRECT: house

INCORRECT: an air

The, which used to mean *this,* has a strong demonstrative meaning and points out nouns used with a specific sense. On the other hand, *a(n),* which used to mean *one,* has a strong countable meaning and is used to point out singular count nouns with a non-specific sense.

In the diagram below, you can see some other determiners that are used with count and non-count nouns. Some determiners are followed by *of the* phrases and some are not. (The parentheses around the phrase *of the* mean it is optional.) The phrase *of the* usually refers to a specific noun.

Determiners with Count and Non-Count Nouns

singular count	plural count	non count
a road	roads	milk
one road	two/both roads	
a kind of road	kinds of roads	a kind of milk
	several (of the) roads	

the road	the roads	the milk
this road	these roads	this milk
that road	those roads	that milk
our/his road	our/his roads	our/his milk
every road	every one of the roads	
each road	each (one) of the roads	
either road	either of the roads	
any road	any (of the) roads	any (of the) milk
none of the road	none of the roads	none of the milk
	no roads	no milk
all of the road	all (of the) roads	all (of the) milk
half (of) the road	half (of) the roads	half (of) the milk
most of the road	most (of the) roads	most (of the) milk
more (of the) road	more (of the) roads	more (of the) milk
much of the road	many (of the) roads	much (of the) milk
some of the road	some (of the) roads	some (of the) milk
little of the road	few (of the) roads	little (of the) milk
less of the road	fewer (of the) roads	less (of the) milk
a little (of the) road	a few (of the) roads	a little (of the) milk

----

A non-count noun is usually not used with the article *a* or *an*. Many non-count nouns, however, when used in a special sense, take *a* or *an*.

For example, when the word *milk* is used with its general meaning, it does not take an article, but when it refers to a glass of milk, it may take an article. *Example:* I like milk. *But:* I ordered a hamburger and *a* milk (a glass of milk).

The article *a(n)* may also be used with a non-count noun when it means *a kind of. Example:* People need food. *But:* An apple is a food (a kind of food). *Or:* Apples and oranges are fruits (kinds of fruit).

The article *a(n)* before a non-count noun may also give it another meaning. *Example:* A sergeant has authority (command) over soldiers. *But:* He is an authority (an expert) on military affairs. In this last example, the non-count noun has become a count noun and can be used with plural determiners. *Example:* We checked with several authorities on this matter.

This list shows which nouns are usually count and which ones non count, but when you use them in your own sentences, keep in mind the exceptions just mentioned.

----

non count	count (singular or plural)
money, wealth, poverty	a dollar, cent, dime, quarter, riches (pl)
weather, air, rain, snow, wind, darkness	a climate, storm, tornado, hurricane, a heat wave

vocabulary, slang, jargon	a word, a question, a reply
communication, news, information	the media (pl), a piece of news, a piece of information
evidence, proof	a piece of evidence
advice	a piece of advice
mail, postage	a letter, a stamp
transportation, traffic	a car, bus, airplane
machinery, equipment	a machine, a piece of equipment
furniture	a piece of furniture, chair, table, desk
work	a job
music	a piece of music
jewelry	a jewel, a diamond, a pearl
life	a life, a person, people (pl)
honesty, loyalty, liberty	
intelligence, ignorance	
knowledge, significance	
courage, good luck, bad luck	an accident, an opportunity, a chance
patience, peace	
beauty, ugliness	
fun, enjoyment, happiness, sadness	a good time, a bad time
progress, violence, poverty	an act of violence, the poor (pl)
food, water, bread	a meal, a loaf of bread
fruit	an apple, orange, banana, potato, vegetable
milk, butter, cheese, yoghurt	an egg, dairy products
chicken, meat, pork, roast steak	a porkchops, a steak, a roast
pepper, salt, paprika	seasonings
gas, oil, fire, silver, gold, iron smoke	
history, mathematics, English, psychology	
hair	a hair, a moustache, a beard
grass	a blade of grass, a lawn

- -

Appendix C: Irregular Verbs

begin	began	begun
drink	drank	drunk
ring	rang	rung
shrink	shrank	shrunk
sing	sang	sung
sink	sank	sunk
spring	sprang	sprung
stink	stank	stunk
swim	swam	swum
cling	clung	clung
dig	dug	dug
sling	slung	slung
slink	slunk	slunk
spin	spun	spun
awake	awoke	awoken
break	broke	broken
choose	chose	chosen
freeze	froze	frozen
steal	stole	stolen
speak	spoke	spoken
weave	wove	woven
blow	blew	blown
grow	grew	grown
fly	flew	flown
know	knew	known
throw	threw	thrown
draw	drew	drawn
overdraw	overdrew	overdrawn
withdraw	withdrew	withdrawn
bear	bore	born
tear	tore	torn
swear	swore	sworn
wear	wore	worn

arise	arose	arisen
dive	dove	diven (dived — dived)
drive	drove	driven
ride	rode	ridden
rise	rose	risen
stride	strode	stridden
strive	strove	striven (strived — strived)
thrive	throve	thriven (thrived — thrived)
write	wrote	written
beat	beat	beaten
bite	bit	bitten
hide	hid	hidden
forsake	forsook	forsaken
mistake	mistook	mistaken
partake	partook	partaken
shake	shook	shaken
take	took	taken
forbid	forbade	forbidden
forgive	forgave	forgiven
give	gave	given
eat	ate	eaten
fall	fell	fallen
see	saw	seen
forget	forgot	forgotten
get	got	gotten
mow	mowed	mown
sew	sewed	sewn
show	showed	shown (showed — showed)
sow	sowed	sown
strew	strewed	strewn
broadcast	broadcast	broadcast (broadcasted — broadcasted)
cast	cast	cast
sit	sat	sat (intr)
bleed	bled	bled
breed	bred	bred
feed	fed	fed
lead	led	led
speed	sped	sped
hold	held	held
creep	crept	crept
keep	kept	kept
kneel	knelt	knelt (kneeled — kneeled)
leave	left	left
mean	meant	meant
meet	met	met
sleep	slept	slept
sweep	swept	swept
weep	wept	wept

bend	bent	bent
lend	lent	lent
rend	rent	rent
send	sent	sent
shed	shed	shed
spend	spent	spent
bet	bet	bet
let	let	let
set	set	set (trans)
dream	dreamt	dreamt (dreamed — dreamed)
hear	heard	heard
leap	leapt	leapt (leaped — leaped)
read	read	read
spread	spread	spread
bid	bid	bid
build	built	built
hit	hit	hit
knit	knit	knit
rid	rid	rid
slide	slid	slid
slit	slit	slit
spit	spit	spit
split	split	split
cost	cost	cost
lose	lost	lost
shoot	shot	shot
sell	sold	sold
tell	told	told
abide	abode	abode
shine	shone	shone (intr)
stand	stood	stood
understand	understood	understood
win	won	won
burst	burst	burst
cut	cut	cut
hurt	hurt	hurt
put	put	put
shut	shut	shut
thrust	thrust	thrust
beseech	besought	besought
bring	brought	brought
buy	bought	bought
fight	fought	fought
seek	sought	sought
think	thought	thought
catch	caught	caught
teach	taught	taught

bind	bound	bound
find	found	found
grind	ground	ground
wind	wound	wound
come	came	come
become	became	become
overcome	overcame	overcome
run	ran	run
make	made	made
shine	shined	shone (shined — shined)
be	was	been
do	did	done
go	went	gone
lie	lay	lain (intr)
lay	laid	laid (tr)

Acknowledgments (*continued from page iv*)

"Auguste Piccard." From *The Superman Book of Superhuman Achievements*. Copyright © 1981 DC Comics Inc. Used by permission.

"Science Newsfront: Lighter Shuttle." Page 16, *Popular Science,* January 1985. Reprinted from *Popular Science* with permission © 1985, Times Mirror Magazines, Inc.

"Business Survival Kit." Reprinted by permission of International Paper Company.

CHAPTER TWO   "Naomi Uemera." From *The Superman Book of Superhuman Achievements*. Copyright © 1981 DC Comics Inc. Used by permission.

"Almond Tree." Adapted from *Illustrated World Encyclopedia,* Inc. New York. Reprinted by permission of Bobley Publishing Corporation.

"The Alphabet." From *The Superman Book of Superhuman Achievements*. Copyright © 1981 DC Comics Inc. Used by permission.

"Ethan Allen." Adapted from *Illustrated World Encyclopedia,* Inc. New York. Reprinted by permission of Bobley Publishing Corporation.

Exercises 15, 16, and 17. Reprinted from *Salted Peanuts* by E. C. McKenzie by permission of the publisher, Baker Book House. Copyright 1972.

"Konstantin Tsiolskovsky." From *2000 Years of Space Travel* by Russell Freedman. Holiday House Publishers. Copyright 1963 by Russell Freedman. Reprinted by permission of the author.

Excerpts from Ann Landers column on professional note takers. From the *News-Star-World,* Monroe/West Monroe, Louisiana. Reprinted by permission of Ann Landers and News America Syndicate. Copyright News America Syndicate.

"The Rosetta Stone." From *The Superman Book of Superhuman Achievements*. Copyright © 1981 DC Comics Inc. Used by permission.

"The Magic Eye." From *Electronics* by Robert Irving. Copyright © 1961 by Robert Irving. Reprinted by permission of Alfred A. Knopf, Inc. and John K. Payne Literary Agency, Inc.

"The Murder Mystery." From *More Fun with Puzzles* by Joseph Leeming (J. B. Lippincott). Copyright 1947 by Joseph Leeming. Reprinted by permission of Harper & Row, Publishers, Inc., and McIntosh and Otis, Inc.

"Road Test Ad." Reprinted by permission of the American Trucking Association Foundation, Inc.

CHAPTER THREE   "Baboons and Panda." From *Unusual Animals* by Kathleen N. Daly © 1977, 1976 Western Publishing Company, Inc. Used by permission.

"Hummingbird." From *Unusual Animals* by Kathleen N. Daly © 1977, 1976 Western Publishing Company, Inc. Used by permission.

"Current Events Ad." From *The Atlantic*. Reprinted by permission of *The Atlantic*.

Exercise 16. Reprinted from *Salted Peanuts* by E. C. McKenzie by permission of the publisher, Baker Book House. Copyright 1972.

"Alabaster." Adapted from *Illustrated World Encyclopedia,* Inc. New York. Reprinted by permission of Bobley Publishing Corporation.

"Annie Oakley." From *The Superman Book of Superhuman Achievements*. Copyright © 1981 DC Comics Inc. Used by permission.

"Academy Awards." Adapted from *Illustrated World Encyclopedia,* Inc. New York. Reprinted by permission of Bobley Publishing Corporation.

"Charles Lindbergh." From *The Superman Book of Superhuman Achievements.* Copyright © 1981 DC Comics Inc. Used by permission.

"Radar." From *Electronics* by Robert Irving. Copyright © 1961 by Robert Irving. Reprinted by permission of Alfred A. Knopf, Inc. and John K. Payne Literary Agency, Inc.

United Technologies Ad. Reprinted by permission of United Technologies.

CHAPTER FOUR   "Roosevelt." From *Men in History* by L. Dixson and Herbert Fox. Reprinted by permission of Regents Publishing Co., Inc.

"Robert Goddard." From *The Superman Book of Superhuman Achievements.* Copyright © 1981 DC Comics Inc. Used by permission.

"Wordless Workshop." Page 110, August 1982. Reprinted from *Popular Science* with permission © 1982, Times Mirror Magazines, Inc. Reprinted also with permission from Roy Doty.

Exercise 19. Reprinted from *Salted Peanuts* by E. C. McKenzie by permission of the publisher, Baker Book House. Copyright 1972.

"Celebrating Liberty." From Vol. 60, No. 7–8, July/August 1986, *National Parks,* The Magazine of the National Parks and Conservation Association. Reprinted by permission of *National Parks.*

Illustration of Statue of Liberty. Copyright 1986 The Statue of Liberty-Ellis Island Foundation. Reprinted by permission of The Statue of Liberty-Ellis Island Foundation.

"A Place for Birds of Prey." From *Southern Living,* June 1986. Copyright by Southern Living Inc. Reprinted with permission.

"Marriage Ceremony Anecdote" by Ken Langbell. Reprinted with permission from the November 1984 *Reader's Digest.* Copyright © 1984 by The Reader's Digest Assn., Inc.

"This Could Save Your Life. But You Can't Have It." Ad for airbags. Reprinted by permission of the Insurance Information Institute.

CHAPTER FIVE   "Gone with the Wind: 50 Years Later." From *Southern Living,* June 1986. Copyright by Southern Living Inc. Reprinted with permission.

"Down With Cholesterol." Reprinted with permission of Procter & Gamble.

Exercise 13. Reprinted from *Salted Peanuts* by E. C. McKenzie by permission of the publisher, Baker Book House. Copyright 1972.

Exercises 17, 19, and 20. Reprinted from *Salted Peanuts* by E. C. McKenzie by permission of the publisher, Baker Book House. Copyright 1972.

"The City of Baghdad." Pp. 52–53 from *The Wonderful World of Mathematics,* by Lancelot Hogben, copyright 1968 Aldus Books Limited London by permission of copyright owner.

Exercise 39. Reprinted from *Salted Peanuts* by E. C. McKenzie by permission of the publisher, Baker Book House. Copyright 1972.

"Walter Reed." From *Men in History* by L. Dixson and Herbert Fox. Reprinted by permission of Regents Publishing Co., Inc.

"Aberration of Light." Adapted from *Illustrated World Encyclopedia,* Inc. New York. Reprinted by permission of Bobley Publishing Corporation.

"One Way Is Fabulous. The Other Is Free." Queen Elizabeth 2 Ad. Reprinted by permission of Cunard.

CHAPTER SIX   "Phototube." From *Electronics* by Robert Irving. Copyright © 1961 by Robert Irving. Reprinted by permission of Alfred A. Knopf, Inc. and John K. Payne Literary Agency, Inc.

"Phototube Thermometer." From *Electronics* by Robert Irving. Copyright © 1961 by Robert Irving. Reprinted by permission of Alfred A. Knopf, Inc. and John K. Payne Literary Agency, Inc.

"Understanding a Loan Shouldn't Be Harder Than Getting One." GOOD Software Corporation ad. Reprinted with permission of GOOD Software Corporation.

"Health Front: Children's Health News: Noisy Toys May Cause Hearing Loss." By the American Academy of Pediatrics in *Prevention,* June 1986, Vol. 38, #6, page 14. Reprinted by permission of *Prevention* magazine. Copyright 1986, Rodale Press, Inc. All rights reserved.

"From Quill to Computer." *Psychology Today.* February 1985. Reprinted with permission from *Psychology Today* magazine. Copyright © 1985 American Psychological Association.

"Information About Energy America Can Count on Today." Reprinted by permission of the Committee on Energy Awareness.

CHAPTER SEVEN   Exercises 1, 2, 4, 12, and 15. Reprinted from *Salted Peanuts* by E. C. McKenzie by permission of the publisher, Baker Book House. Copyright 1972.

"The Kangaroo." From *Unusual Animals* by Kathleen N. Daly © 1977, 1976 Western Publishing Company, Inc. Used by permission.

"Gravity." Adapted from *Illustrated World Encyclopedia,* Inc. New York. Reprinted by permission of Bobley Publishing Corporation.

"Think of It as a Fortress for Your Food." Gott cooler ad. Reprinted by permission of Gott Corporation, a subsidiary of Rubbermaid Incorporated, and Valentine-Radford Advertising.

"Blondin, Robert Goddard, and Othmar H. Amman." From *The Superman Book of Superhuman Achievements.* Copyright © 1981 DC Comics Inc. Used by permission.

"Visit Georgia's Architectural Puzzle." *Southern Living,* p. 86, March 1984. Copyright by Southern Living, Inc., March 1984. Excerpt adapted. Reprinted with permission.

"Cells: The Building Blocks of Life." From the book *Heredity* by Robert Dunbar. Copyright © 1978. Reprinted with permission of the publisher, Franklin Watts.

"Immortal Shrine to an Emperor's Love" by Trevor Hoskins. Reprinted with permission of the author and *Reader's Digest* from the November 1983 *Reader's Digest,* p. 161.

CHAPTER EIGHT   Exercise 6. Reprinted from *Salted Peanuts* by E. C. McKenzie by permission of the publisher, Baker Book House. Copyright 1972.

Commodore 64, The Manager ad. Reprinted by permission of Commodore Business Machines, Inc.

"Are You Ready for High Performance Photography?" Minolta ad. Reprinted with permission of Minolta Corporation.

"This Year, You've Earned the Grand." Marriott's Grand Hotel ad. Reprinted with permission of Marriott's Grand Hotel, Point Clear, Alabama.

"The Wine and Fall." From "News from the World of Science" in the *Reader's Digest*. Reprinted with permission from the September 1983 *Reader's Digest* and used by permission of the Associated Press.

"The Perilous Adventures of Wiz Walker, Young Executive" from *Business Week's Guide to Careers,* December 1984. Reprinted with permission of the author, James Markland, the illustrator, Bob Laughlin and *Business Week*.

CHAPTER NINE   "Absolute Zero." Adapted from *Illustrated World Encyclopedia,* Inc. New York. Reprinted by permission of Bobley Publishing Corporation.

"Dolphins." From *Unusual Animals* by Kathleen N. Daly © 1977, 1976 Western Publishing Company, Inc. Used by permission.

"Fair Payment. A System to Contain Exploding Hospital Costs." Reprinted with permission of Health Insurance Association of America.

"Heredity and You." From the book *Heredity* by Robert Dunbar. Copyright © 1978. Reprinted with permission of the publisher, Franklin Watts.

Exercise 20. Reprinted from *Salted Peanuts* by E. C. McKenzie by permission of the publisher, Baker Book House. Copyright 1972.

"The Speech Chain." Adapted from pages 3 and 5 of *The Speech Chain,* Bell Telephone Laboratories, Inc. Copyright 1963. Reprinted by permission of Bell Telephone Laboratories, Inc.

"Natural Selection." From the book *Heredity* by Robert Dunbar. Copyright © 1978. Reprinted with permission of the publisher, Franklin Watts.

"Can American Business Survive on a Diet of Instant Gratification?" Grace ad. Reprinted with permission of W. R. Grace & Company.

CHAPTER TEN   "Robinson Crusoe and Leonardo da Vinci." From *The Superman Book of Superhuman Achievements.* Copyright © 1981 DC Comics Inc. Used by permission.

"The Babylonians." From *2000 Years of Space Travel* by Russell Freedman. Holiday House Publishers. Copyright 1963 by Russell Freedman. Reprinted by permission of the author.

"Nadia Comaneci and Thomas Edison." From *The Superman Book of Superhuman Achievements.* Copyright © 1981 DC Comics Inc. Used by permission.

"Air-India's New Executive Cabin to London and India." Air-India ad. Reprinted by permission of Air-India.

"Rings Around the Pantheon." © *Discover* Magazine 3/85, Time Inc. Reprinted by permission.

Photo of the Pantheon. Copyright Dan Budnik/Woodfin Camp. Reprinted by permission of Woodfin Camp.

Book review by Jean Strouse of Joseph Needham's *Science in Traditional China.* Adapted from *Newsweek.* Copyright 1982 by Newsweek, Inc. All Rights Reserved. Reprinted by permission.

NASA ad. Reprinted with permission of McDonnell Douglas Astronautics Company.

Index

noun modifier with, 306–307
structure of, 306
subject of, 308
verb modifier with, 307–309

Habit, modal to express, 278–279
have
as auxiliary verb, 59, 64
functions of, 64–65
infinitive with, 65
past participle with, 64, 124
as semi-modal, 65
as transitive verb, 65
Helping verb. *See* Auxiliary verb
hence, 102

Imperative mood, 255, 256
Imperative sentence, noun clause from, 297
in consequence, 102
in other words, 104
Indicative mood, 255, 256
Indirect object, 13–14, 325–328
for and, 328
infinitive after, 353
in passive construction, 208
without preposition, 327
to and, 326–327
Infinitive, 45
as adjectival, 70
after adjective, 353–354
as adverbial, 69
expressing anticipated result, 179
as complement, 69
confusion with participles, 246
distinguished from gerund, 348
enough and, 183
have with, 65
after indirect object, 353
misuse of, 353, 354
expressing opinion, 338–343
plain, 67–68
expressing plan or idea, 332–336
vs. present participle, 76
reducing noun clause, 297, 300, 304–305
reducing *wh*-clause, 330
reduction of, with *be*, 180
replacing imperative, 331
replacing modal clause, 331, 332
replacing subjunctive, 331, 332
as subject, 69
to form, 69–70
without *to*, 67–68
too and, 181
uses of, 331–342
with *used*, 213, 215
in *wh*-clause, 69

Infinitive phrase, 165, 291
reduced adjective clause and, 242–243
subject of, 305
-ing form. *See* Present participle
Interrogative sentence, 59
noun clause from, 298–300
wh-, 298, 299–300
word order in, 27
yes/no, 298–299
Intransitive verb, 15–16
Inversion
lack of, 107
of subject and finite verb, 26–31
Irregular verb, 50, 51
list, 371–374
it, impersonal, 173
Items in a series, 85

Linking verb, 17
progressive form of, 116

Main clause, 21
missing, 36, 244. (*see also* Compound sentence)
Main idea, 112
Manner
adverbial clause of, 167–168
sentence connector to express, 190
Means
participial phrase to express, 174–175
sentence connector to express, 190
Modal, 57, 266–267
expressing ability or opportunity, 268–269
expressing advisability, 278
expressing certainty, 272–274
expressing challenge, 279
chart of uses, 279–280
expressing contrary-to-fact situation, 275–277
expressing expectation, 277
list of, 279–280
misuse of, 193, 284
expressing moral obligation, 278
expressing necessity, 270
expressing need, 279
with noun clause, 297
expressing past habit, 278–279
expressing permission, 267–268
expressing possibility, 272–274
reduced to infinitive phrase, 242–243
expressing request, 277
Modifier, dangling, 173, 192
Mood, 255
imperative, 255–256, 297
inconsistent use of, 282–283
indicative, 255, 256
misuse of, 313
modals and, 266–280

in passive voice, 203–204
subjunctive, 134, 163, 168, 255, 257–266 passim, 335

Name
geographical, 368
man-made structure, 369
of person, 370
Necessity, modal to express, 270
Need, modal to express, 279
Negative, 59
sentence inversion with, 28–29
Negative condition
conjunctive adverb to denote, 102
sentence connector to express, 189
neither . . . nor, 94
Nominative absolute, 177
Nonrestrictive clause, 226–227
nor, meaning of, 92
not only . . . but also, meaning of, 94
Noun, 290
article with, 370, 371
count, 367, 370–372
determiner with, 371
proper, 367–370
Noun clause, 290
formation of, 294
made from declarative sentence, 294–295
made from exclamations, 301
made from imperative sentence, 297
made from interrogative sentence, 298–300
made from subjunctive, 297
misuse of tense in, 150
as object, 329–330
as object of preposition, 291
reduced (*see* Reduced noun clause)
sequence-of-tense and, 292
subject of, 291
subjunctive with, 258
tense change in, 129–131, 136
Noun phrase
abstract, 310–312, 315–316
as object, 323–324
following preposition, 185

Object
direct, 12–13, 208, 323–326
double, 314
indirect, 13–14, 208, 325–328
present participle as, 71
two-part, 209
Object patterns
verb–indirect object–direct object, 325–328
verb–noun clause, 329–330
verb–noun object, 323–324
verb–*to*-infinitive, 331–333
verb–gerund, 334–349

Obligation, modal to express, 278
of-expression, 233–235
only if, sentence inversion with, 29
Opinion
adjective expressing, 342
infinitive expressing, 338–343
Opportunity, modal to express, 268–269
Organization of writing, 42, 81
otherwise, 102

Paragraph
arrangement of, 289
order of, 42
Parallelism
in compound sentence, 86–87
lack of, 107
Paraphrase, conjunctive adverb to denote, 104
Participial phrase
expressing means, 174–175
expressing reason, 175–177
expressing simultaneous action, 174–175
expressing time, 175–176, 177–178
with reduced adverbial clause, 174–176
Participle
past, 202
past vs. present, 216
Particle, 324
Passive, 199–216
aspect in, 203–204
be and, 63
confused with progressive, 216
constructions (*see* Passive constructions)
defined, 199
formation of, 201–202
mood in, 203–204
past participle in, 72, 202
tense in, 203–204
in *to*-infinitive expressions, 182
use of, 200
Passive constructions, 207–213
indirect object as subject, 208
object of two-part verb as subject, 208
preposition in, 211–213
in reduced adjective clause, 210
that-clause in, 208–209
two-part object in, 209
Past participle, 48–49
as adjectival, 73, 76
confused with present participle, 216
confusion with infinitive and present participle, 246
functions of, 72–73
have with, 64, 124
in passive construction, 72, 202
vs. past tense, 75
and perfect tense, 72